Doing Things with Games

Social Impact Through Play

Doing Things with Games

Social Impact Through Play

Lindsay Grace

Knight Chair of Interactive Media, University of Miami,
School of Communication

CRC Press
Taylor & Francis Group
Boca Raton London New York

CRC Press is an imprint of the
Taylor & Francis Group, an **informa** business

CRC Press
Taylor & Francis Group
6000 Broken Sound Parkway NW, Suite 300
Boca Raton, FL 33487-2742

Printed on acid-free paper

International Standard Book Number-13: 978-1-138-36727-2 (Hardback)
International Standard Book Number-13: 978-1-138-36726-5 (Paperback)

Library of Congress Cataloging-in-Publication Data

Names: Grace, Lindsay D., author.
Title: Doing things with games : social impact through play / Lindsay D. Grace.
Description: First edition. | Boca Raton, FL : CRC Press/Taylor & Francis
Group, 2019. | Includes bibliographical references and index.
Identifiers: LCCN 2019010670| ISBN 9781138367265 (pbk. : acid-free paper) |
ISBN 9781138367272 (hardback : acid-free paper)
Subjects: LCSH: Games--Social aspects.
Classification: LCC GV1201.38 .G72 2019 | DDC 306.4/87--dc23
LC record available at https://lccn.loc.gov/2019010670

Visit the Taylor & Francis Web site at
http://www.taylorandfrancis.com

and the CRC Press Web site at
http://www.crcpress.com

Contents

SECTION II   **Application**

Acknowledgment

There are far too many people to thank than space on this page. Instead, I want to thank every student who took the time to ask the hard questions, every fellow faculty member who saw the potential in such work, and the generation of games researchers that have continued to move game design research forward.

A very special thank you to the people who gave me my first chance. Mitch Hennes, for giving me that first games teaching gig at the Illinois Institute of Art. Peg Faimon and Glenn Platt who created a space at Miami University to foster such research. The American University faculty and staff, who supported the founding of one of the few social impact focused game design curricula and academic game studios in the world. Most recently to the faculty and staff at the University of Miami School of Communication, who continue to create a supportive, collegial environment that fosters such work.

I must acknowledge both Dean Jeffrey Rutenbeck for his unwavering support and vision and Dean Gregory Shephard for his knack for leadership and seeing the long-term potential in such work. This work could not have been completed without the support of the James S. and John L. Knight Foundation and the financial support of C. Michael Armstrong.

A general thanks to the many organizations, clients and collaborators who supported this research as practice in the real world, especially Deloitte, the Smithsonian American Art Museum, ETS and Games for Change. Education Testing Service's Tanner Jackson was instrumental in converting game ideas into empirical research. Peter Jamieson at Miami University has remained a generous and brilliant collaborator for nearly a decade. And to Roger, Mia, and Andy for being great researchers and wonderful friends.

And as always, to my mom, whose perseverance taught me how to keep going in the face of adversity, and my father whose propensities for writing inspired me to finish this project.

Author

Lindsay Grace is the Knight Chair of Interactive Media and an associate professor at the University of Miami School of Communication. He is Vice President for the Higher Education Video Game Alliance.

His work has received awards and recognition from the Games for Change Festival, the Digital Diversity Network, the Association of Computing Machinery's digital arts community, Black Enterprise, and others. He has authored or co-authored more than 50 papers, articles, and book chapters on games since 2009. His creative work has been selected for showcase internationally including in New York, Paris, Sao Paolo, Singapore, Chicago, Vancouver, Istanbul, and others. Lindsay has curated or co-curated Blank Arcade, the Smithsonian American Art Museum's SAAM Arcade, the Games for Change Civic and Social Impact and others.

He has given talks at the Game Developers Conference, SXSW, Games for Change Festival, the Online News Association, the Society for News Design, and many other industry events.

Between 2013 and 2018 he was the founding director of the American University Game Lab and Studio. He served as Vice President and on the board of directors for the Global Game Jam™ non-profit between 2014 and 2019. From 2009 to 2013 he was the Armstrong Professor at Miami University's School of Art. Lindsay also served on the board for the Digital Games Research Association (DiGRA) between 2013 and 2015.

I

Understanding

CHAPTER 1

An Introduction

T HERE ARE MANY DIFFERENT ways to describe social impact games and play. This chapter introduces you to those uses and briefly explains the concepts needed to understand the power of play, the ways in which play is understood, and how designers can employ the design of play for toys, interactives, and games. This chapter serves as a basic orientation.

1.1 WHY USE SOCIAL IMPACT PLAY?

If you've started reading this book, there's a good chance you have an idea or interest in employing play for some purpose. This may be social impact, training, health, empathy, or some other aim. If you need the simplest answer as to why—the answer is engagement. After more than a decade researching impact, play, and audiences, there's a very simple way of explaining the value of games and social impact. Readers read, viewers watch, and players do.

Play is active. Playing a game requires full attention during play. It is not a passive medium. Unlike television, for example, players do not typically leave a game playing itself while they prepare breakfast. They do not fall asleep to a game as white noise. Play demands our attention. Play demands action. How appropriate then, that those looking to demand the attention of an audience employ play through games.

As for reading, it remains one of the most common ways to disseminate information. The irony of writing a book about games, yet championing the value of play, is not lost here. The challenge in a global society is that reading requires literacy. If something is written in a language you don't understand, it requires translation. This is the literacy challenge of the written word. If that something is data-driven or mathematical, it may likewise require a kind of data or numerical literacy. Statistics, for example, are often as widely misunderstood as they are quoted, shared, or littered in conversation. If literacy focuses on a specific domain, it may require additional reading. For some, reading is engaging, for others, it is inaccessible because they don't know the language.

Play, however, can be more universal. Psychologists identify play as essential to development. Play is common to many animals, including the human animal. Play is not limited by language and often does not require it. Play is also part of learning. It is something that pervades cultures globally. Play is practiced by all humans, to varying extents.

Play requires a kind of ludo-literacy or understanding of how to play. The benefit of ludo-literacy is that can require very little instruction. It can serve as a more universal language than the most well-spoken languages in the world. American television personality and minister, Fred Rogers of the famed *Mister Rogers' Neighborhood* show frames it thus, "Play is often talked about as if it were a relief from serious learning. But for children play is serious learning. Play is really the work of childhood" (Moore, 2014).

If play is the work of childhood, then ludo-literacy is perhaps one of humanity's native languages. Play is a way of understanding and a way of explaining. Play and relationship games function as a way for players to understand and designers to explain. We play with ideas to understand and explore them, we play with objects to know their properties, and we role play to examine the complexities of human interaction. There are so many ways we play on a daily basis, that we forget play is present. It might be the joke we shared, the meme we reposted, the crumpled paper we offer as a layup to the trash bin, or the hours we play swiping on mobile phones or saving the world on our home console.

This book aims not to champion games and play as the only way to communicate or initiate social impact. Instead, it champions the opportunities to include play in social impact efforts. It champions the idea that designers can do things with games. The aim is to improve the world, to make something a little more accessible, a little more meaningful, or a little more beautiful.

Until relatively recently in human history, play was discarded as a childish thing that must be left behind when entering adulthood. This is a myopic view of play. It fails to recognize the powers of play demonstrated through research in psychology (Brown, 2009), anthropology (Huizingha, 2014), and art (Melissinos and O'Rourke, 2012). Play is not the activity that bookends the frivolity of childhood and the leisure of retirement. It is not merely building blocks, throw-catch volleyball, bocce, or shuffleboard. It is the way we find flow, alleviate stress, explore new concepts, and understand the world around us.

As Brian Sutton Smith, author of more than ten academic books on play put it—"the opposite of play isn't work, it's depression" (2009). This oft-cited reference reminds us of one important thing—work is necessary, but play is too. If you want to create impact, creating impact through play should be in your toolset. Just as we play with an idea or concept, impact can come from employing play. The serious work of social impact is not in opposition to play, it is a tool to its success.

1.2 INTERACTIVES, TOYS, AND GAMES

It is often useful to understand the difference between interactives, toys, and games. When people first consider a digital solution, it's important to consider how play will be employed toward your goal. As discussed, play is really about offering an engaging way to examine and explore a problem.

An interactive is any designed experience through which a user acts and receives feedback. While much discussion has been had about what it means to be interactive, it's often easiest to start with a simple definition and a set of examples. For our purposes, to be interactive, a designed experience need simply allow someone to act and provide feedback on that action. So, any experience from improvisational comedy shows to desktop calculators could be considered an interactive.

In the past 30 years, interactive experiences have become so commonplace that we sometimes forget that they are interactive. We also forget that in the history of art, for example, it was appropriate to feel and touch the paintings that now hang behind security glass. The same is true of theater. The notion of a non-interactive audience in theater is a relatively new concept for humanity, credited by some as a product of the Industrial Revolution and as a way of asserting power. Even the structures of education, a movement from the interactions of life lessons to the classroom space, have been critiqued as a movement away from interactivity and toward the convenience of large-scale, one-way delivery (Conners, 1983)

Interaction is so common to the human experience that we nearly take it for granted. Conversations and dialogue, for example, are interactive, but we don't always remember them as such. The most common pattern for an interaction is action and reaction. This is also a useful way to frame any design task, by designing both the user or player action and the subsequent reaction.

It's important to recognize the pattern of interaction, action, and reaction, as it serves as the foundation for any standard mode of play. Imagine for a minute how a child learns through play. At first, it is merely about making something happen. Discovering that something pushed moves, and, depending on the properties of that thing, moves in distinct ways. Each interaction with a ball becomes more interesting as the actions and reactions of the ball differ. A light ball requires little action for a big reaction, a big ball the opposite. Children learn these properties not by being told how they work, but instead through action.

That early play with a ball turns to more complex play as the skills are mastered. Pushing a ball becomes passing a ball or catching a ball. It might also become rolling a ball into other objects or discovering what happens when the ball is dropped in the toilet or hits another person in the face. These are all patterns of play. They are also patterns of learning. From the start, humans are wired to learn through play.

As you can likely see, the pattern of playing with a ball changes. The play evolves into some sort of game. Throwing and catching can become a game, where catches are counted, or the winter is the first person not to drop the ball. The game might also involve other forms of play, such as building blocks which once constructed are demolished with a single throw.

This is similar to the evolution of games. The first digital games were a triumph simply in the fact that they worked. The ability to play with or through a computer is a clear triumph in the evolution of human–computer interaction. Prior to games like *Pong* or *Spacewar!* (Kent, 2010), people were users of computers, not players. They could interact with the computer, but they were fairly limited in their play.

Computer-mediated play changed the ways in which we could play. Adding a computer to play opened up a variety of new interactions that were computational and graphical. Computers afforded the ability to play with numbers at an unprecedented apex of speed and scale. But like that first experience with a ball, there was much to be discovered. Before we fully mastered one computer, new ones, with new capabilities and new challenges, were developed.

Regardless, we played with making games, until the medium evolved into more complex goals. We turned to familiar experiences like choose your own adventure books and turned them into interactive fiction like

Zork (Anderson and Galley, 1985). We turned military simulation into *Missile Command* and car simulation into *Pole Position.* Each iteration looked to explore possibility playfully.

This is the foundation of play. Play is about exploration. Play also has no explicit end and no resolution. Play ends simply when we stop playing. The borders of play are wider and more complex than those of a game. Its rules are more opaque and its start and end is less apparent than a game.

Games, on the other hand, are structured play. Games take the ephemeral properties of play and the play state and turn them into something with a distinct start and a distinct end. Games structure interactive play. Games are discrete, with a measurable start and measurable end.

How do games structure play? First, they operate via toys. Toys are the unit of play. A ball is a common toy. The games we play with that toy vary, as in the difference between a tennis ball and a volleyball. Likewise, throw–catch volleyball changes significantly when played with a medicine ball (also known as a Hooverball). The toy helps shape the game and its rules.

Games structure the play, organizing the relationships between players and toys. The idea of a toy extends beyond physical games. Wordplay, for example, employs words or letters as toys. In many games, toys are the units of play. This is why for some toy-focused designs, game designers begin with a toy concept and then divine the rules from that toy (Figure 1.1).

Computers expanded the opportunities for play exceptionally. Computers function not only as toys, but they also provide new opportunities for toys. Toys in the physical world, for example, are limited by the physical properties of nature. Until we are playing volleyball on the moon, the core physical characteristics of tossing and hitting a ball over a net will

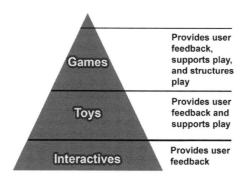

FIGURE 1.1 Interactives, toys, and games, a way of understanding different types of designs.

remain the same here on earth. But, with computers, we are able to simulate a variety of physical scenarios.

Beyond simulation, computers afford the creation of toys that are physically and sometimes mentally impossible. The millions of calculations make for complex models and prognostications. In short, the computer not only changed toys, they changed our concept and expectations of toys. They turned our imagined play experiences into the nuances of virtual pets or the scale of flying a million-dollar Mig-29 (NovaLogic, 1988). Digital play affords for the creation of new toys, resulting in new games. The computer was not just a toy, it offered a completely new possibility space.

1.3 WHAT'S NEXT

These are, of course, simplified definitions to provide orientation. Any explorer will note that in order to know where you are going, you must know where you are. This book is structured to help you understand where interaction, games, and play are, have been, and may go. This book is designed to provide both resource and guidance on the many ways in which play and games are employed to meet social impact agendas. Brian Sutton-Smith writes in *The Study of Games*, "Each person defines games in [their] own way—the anthropologists and folklorists in terms of historical origins; the military men, businessmen, and educators in terms of usages; the social scientists in terms of psychological and social functions. There is overwhelming evidence in all this that the meaning of games is, in part, a function of the ideas of those who think about them" (Avedon and Sutton-Smith, 1971).

Each reader of this book has a goal in reading. Perhaps you are interested in supporting a specific project. Perhaps you were assigned this book by someone who knows the field. Perhaps you are interested in learning about the ways your agendas can be supported by games. Each reader, like each player, has their own journey based on their starting point and their end goal.

In this journey, you'll notice that there are exceptions to rules. You'll also realize that there is far more left to explore than has been explored. It is hoped that you'll also find yourself willing, excited, and eager to employ play in more ways.

1.4 BOOK OVERVIEW

Before you start this journey, you'll want a map. This book is structured in three sections. The first is designed to provide an overview of the core concepts that apply broadly to social impact games and purpose-driven play design. It is a good idea for all readers to read Section I completely.

Section II examines specific types of social impact play. These are large groupings of games aimed at improving education or physical and mental health, for example. This section is designed to be read either in order or as selected chapters in any order. A person who may be interested in creating a political game might want to read the chapter on education (Chapter 4) and then skip to the chapter on persuasive play (Chapter 7). This second section is designed to meet that need. Please choose your chapters appropriately, and feel free to read Section II in its entirety.

Section III is aimed at helping explain project implementation. It answers the who, what, where, and why for readers who will be engaged in making games and play. This includes project managers, independent developers, consultants, students, and those people who want to construct requests for proposals or hire others to create a project for them. This third section is your basic blueprint for understanding the elements common to the production of any social impact play project.

Like any blueprint or travel itinerary, you'll want to adjust it to your needs.

This book is designed to be useful to those who have never done such projects and for those who have. For those who have, this book should help focus, formalize, and inform your process. For those who haven't, consider this book a jumpstart to your journey. Whether your project is 2 weeks or 2 years, learning from the experience of others should make the project much smoother.

At the end of most chapters, there are some activities that should help you practice the topics outlined in the chapter. These are typically framed as a task and the kinds of questions a designer might ask when trying to accomplish the task. They're the kind of questions a reader can answer with a lot of experience or with no experience, because they are the kinds of questions that people who practice design ask.

Please keep in mind that the observations, framings, and recommendations from this book are informed by years of practicing game design. It's important to remember that design, any design, is a practice. It is practice in the same way that amateur and professional musicians practice an instrument. Such practice focuses on mastering skills and creative exploration. It's also practicing in the way that a medical professional practices medicine. There are many lessons learned, skills required, and standard ways to address challenges, but each case is a new one with new ways to practice helping people.

REFERENCES

Anderson, Tim, and Stu Galley. "The history of *Zork.*" *The New York Times* 4, no. 1–3 (1985): 6–7.

Avedon, Elliott M., and Brian Sutton-Smith. *The Study of Games.* New York: Wiley, 1971.

Brown, Stuart L. *Play: How It Shapes the Brain, Opens the Imagination, and Invigorates the Soul.* New York: Penguin, 2009.

Conners, Dennis A. "The school environment: A link to understanding stress." *Theory into Practice* 22, no. 1 (1983): 15–20.

Huizinga, Johan. *Homo Ludens.* London: Routledge, 2014.

Kent, Steven L. *The Ultimate History of Video Games: From Pong to Pokemon and Beyond: The Story Behind the Craze that Touched Our Lives and Changed the World.* New York: Three Rivers Press, 2010.

Melissinos, Chris, and Patrick O'Rourke. *The Art of Video Games: From Pac-Man to Mass Effect.* New York: Welcome Books, 2012.

Moore, Heidi. "Why Play is the Work of Childhood." Fred Rogers Center for Early Learning and Children's Media at Saint Vincent College. Fred Rogers Center, 23 Sept. 2014.

NovaLogic. *MiG-29 Fulcrum.* THQ Nordic, 1988.

Sutton-Smith, Brian. *The Ambiguity of Play.* Cambridge, MA: Harvard University Press, 2009.

CHAPTER 2

An Overview of Designing for Social Impact

I T MAY NOT BE a surprise to you that games have always had a purpose. According to sociologists and cultural anthropologists, games serve to support the community, to communicate and maintain culture, to practice social skills, retain stories, and a myriad of other benefits (Sutton-Smith, 2009). As early as 1949, Huizinga observed in his seminal work that some even speculated that play "must have some kind of biological purpose" (2014 reprint). According to psychologists, games are both developmentally essential and functionally important. Psychologists and biologists often state the games and play serve core needs in the human as an animal (Smith, 1982). These are often identified as evolutionary benefits. At the same time, education scholars continue to identify play as valuable to education and development (Van Horn et al., 2014). These core values are best summarized as play being a natural way to practice and experiment.

When we witness animals playing, the contemporary understanding is that they are practicing some real-world skill. For some animals, play mimics hunting, such as a young tiger who follows the predatory behavior of their adult parents when wrestling with other young tigers. Scientists have readily identified a whole host of innate animal play behaviors that serve a biological and psychological function for the animals that play them.

It is then no surprise that the same can be said of the human animal. The games that we play have always served a function. Tag serves a need to practice playing hunting and hunted. Simon Says is widely used as a tool to help children practice impulse control. Hide and seek is likewise an opportunity to practice evasion and detection. These games persist across the globe, although admittedly under different names.

The truth is that play is an excellent teacher. Play helps the player experiment in a safe environment. It offers the opportunity to learn without the threat of major consequence. Playing hunted and hunter, or tag, offers many of the benefits of learning to hunt or to avoid being prey, without the risks. No one dies and no one needs to die.

More interestingly, such play offers the variability of human behavior. Beyond the obvious mechanics of practicing specific survival skills, these age-old games afford the practice of human dynamics. Recall playing tag, and you'll notice it was not merely about evasion. There were strategies. Running toward a slower player might distract the chaser. Lying about your hiding place when playing hide and go seek, might bate the seeker to search for you there. Changing your tone when playing Simon Says might change the outcome.

These games have a basic set of goals and interactions, but they quickly change when played. As players get better, they adapt, change, and refine the experience. As players, they do what a teacher does, they change the assignment to increase the challenge, to make the experience more interesting. They turn that initial play into a game, adding rules and structure. Tag becomes freeze tag, hide and seek gets its variants, and the tricks in Simon Says become cleverer.

Games then are merely the structure we apply to that play. A good game designer structures play in a way that engages players. There are many ways to understand engagement, but at the start you can begin with a core mantra—a good game improves play. How a designer improves play is as vast as the universe. You can think of play as all the possible notes available to the world of music. The designer is the composer of those notes. As new notes, or more aptly, ways of arranging those notes, become available, the opportunities for new compositions increases. Jazz introduced new ways of composing music, as did rock, and later, rap. Each of these has some basic characteristics about their arrangement, but plenty of opportunity for fusion too.

If you're not a music fan, the analogy holds true for visual art too. The game designer is the person responsible for organizing the elements of play in such a way that they work. What they do when they work is entirely up to the person or people behind the project. If they aim to sell the merits of a healthy diet, emphasize the importance of a news item, or change the way people think about a situation—the core of their work remains arranging play elements.

While it is true that play has existed well beyond recorded history, it is also true that in the last 100 years, the kinds of play have also greatly expanded. Humanity spent centuries rolling dice and moving pieces on boards before it ever ventured into playing cards. Playing cards were a new technology, one that required a certain numerical literacy and interpretation of symbolic language. As the graphic design historian Philip Meggs claims, "playing cards were the first printed pieces to move into an illiterate culture, making them the earliest European manifestation of printing's democratizing ability: the game of kings could now become the games of peasants and craftsmen" (2011). Well before games were outwardly identified as having a social impact, of being capable of changing lives, and of precipitating social or technical change, they were doing so.

One of the greatest technological innovations of the last two centuries is the growth in computing. Computing history begins well before the modern computer, to include devices from Ancient China and Greece. Yet while the version of the ancient Chinese abacus may be present in toy chests around the world, the profound change to the way we play comes from the modern digital computer.

In the 20th century, the ability to play with computers not only defined a new way to play, it aided an interest in learning the language of computing. In the early 1980s, as the first wave of video game mania hit its peak, it was common for at home hobbyists to make and sell their games. In the 1990s, PC gamers had to configure their games, learning the functions of batch (bat) files, adjusting interrupt request channels (IRQ), allocating random access memory in initialization files (ini), and installing sound cards to make games work. This work was the technological analog to buying the perfect hockey stick, calculating and memorizing runs batted in (RBIs), or combing a doll's hair or optimizing Barbie outfits. It was the work that prefaced and enabled play.

Even more importantly, computer-based play emerged out of an apex of technical and sociological realities that birthed all-new potentials for the way we play. It offered the potential to change the scale of action, affording millions of calculations in minutes. It improved the ability to simulate in play and later offered the ability to play across continents in real time. It also offered the opportunity to play in virtual environments and to augment our existing world.

In the first two decades of the 21st century, it's evident that the scale of play, as demonstrated in esports, and the pervasiveness of games, as demonstrated by the number of gamers and the number of games played on mobile devices, is greatly changed. Likewise, the return of virtual reality (first introduced on computers in the 20th century), hints at new potentials for play.

If a game designer structures play, a purpose-driven game designer structures the play to meet strategic goals. It is then essential that effective game designers understand play, games, and the ways in which they affect players. Much like a good composer, a game designer must be familiar with each of the elements from which they are to compose.

2.1 WHAT IS PLAY?

Definitions of play range from the highly philosophical to the highly pragmatic. Some academics and designers typically start with the philosophical definitions of play offered by Callois (2001). Roger Callois defines play as free, separate, uncertain, rule-bound, and make-believe. He admits early in his book that "there is also no doubt that play must be defined as a free and voluntary activity" (2001). While he offers a formal categorization of games and play, in the *Structure and Classifications of Games* (1955), his is not the only definition worth considering. Others prefer to begin with Johan Huizinga's definition, which relies heavily on play as being opposite to "ordinary life" (2014). A more contemporary view includes Prensky, who emphasizes the notion that "Play is something one chooses to do, play is intensely and utterly absorbing, play promotes the formation of social groupings" (2001).

One of the simplest ways to frame play is simply to start by defining it as a state. This state is outside of the ordinary operations of the everyday world and voluntarily engaged. Its start is the moment the play state has been started and acknowledged. Its end is when that play state has been withdrawn.

For designing playful experiences, this loose definition affords a very wide set of opportunities. Beyond conventional games, which typically have a very clear start and end, such a definition affords for:

- Playful banter among friends

- Play in public space, such as dancing and flash mobs

- Playful sport and competition

- Many, many others

Sutton-Smith provides a long list of the many ways in which play is engaged from the subjective elements of mind play (e.g., playing with words or daydreaming) to the playful performances of parades and the risky play of extreme sports (2009). For each of these, the same concept governs their encapsulation. They are each encapsulated in the play state, a mental framing that places the activity outside of the ordinary world and one which the player engages freely. Admittedly, it's important to note that because play is influenced by sociological factors, its beginning and end are sometimes hard to identify.

One of the more interesting challenges with purpose-driven play is that designers often want the experience of the design to carry beyond the playful experience. So, purposeful play often wants to make an effect that carries beyond the playful experience into the ordinary world. It is this effort to cross the transom of play and non-play that makes such design interesting.

Unfortunately, purpose-driven play is in itself an odd way to describe play, if you understand why humans play. From multiple perspectives, all play transcends the play state and benefits the non-play world. All play, in theory, serves a purpose outside of the play state. At the least, it alleviates stress, but more likely, it serves as practice and experiment. But, the notion of purpose-driven play is a way for framing even more specifically play designed to meet a specific aim. It is a way of emphasizing distinction and value, in much the way that people differentiate between healthy food and junk food. Arguably, all food offers some nutrients, but some food offers more benefit than others.

2.2 WHAT IS A GAME? GOAL, OBSTRUCTION, AND MEANS

It should be clear now that a game is essentially structured play. However, the structure of that play varies. Across the vast majority of games, it's safe to say the foundation of the structure is simply three things: *goal, obstruction*, and *means*. Players are given a goal to achieve, the designer incorporates an obstruction to the goal, and the designer provides a means to achieving that goal. Nearly every game can be framed as goal, obstruction, and means to achieving the goal.

Blackjack, or 21, the simple card game where players are aiming to come as close to 21 without going over 21 fits this structure nicely. The player's goal is to show cards that aggregate to a value of 21, without going over. The player's obstructions are centered on imperfect knowledge. They include not knowing what cards are shuffled in the deck, not knowing what cards will be drawn by other players and dealer, and so on. The means to achieving their goal is initially either choosing to draw a card from the deck or not. However, like most good games, the simple structure of the game allows for a changing dynamic between goal, obstruction, and means.

In blackjack, each card drawn changes the obstruction, as players now know what cards are available. They can make better informed decisions. Each card drawn also indicates the player's distance from their goal. A low early card means high variability, a high card increases potential risk. While goal, obstruction, and means seem to stay the same, the structure of the game's design actually affords for iterative adjustment of each. If the person with the highest card values wins, the goal for some players changes from reaching 21 to merely beating others at the table. If a player can keep track of a deck, they can calculate their probability of getting a specific card, thus adding to their means. If a player draws a card that another player needs, the obstruction has been adjusted as part of play (Figure 2.1).

This card game is clearly not the quintessential game, but it's an easy to understand example of how goal, obstruction, and means work. In digital games, I often use the example of *Super Mario Bros.* (Nintendo Creative Department, 1985). The global goal of the game is to save the princess. That goal is met by meeting smaller level completion goals. The princess is reportedly at the end of the gauntlet of challenges the player

FIGURE 2.1 The game blackjack, or 21, is an example for understanding goal, obstructions, and means. (Courtesy of pxhere [https://pxhere.com/en/photo/542997] through the public domain.)

helps the player character (PC), Mario, handle. Each one of those challenges is an obstruction to the player's goal. Each chasm, step, and non-player character (NPC) that gets in the player's way is an obstruction. The player's means, exercised through the Mario PC, are largely movements in space: running, jumping, and when available, shooting. These three basic dynamics, between goal, obstruction, and means, are organized in such a way that they define the platformer game type and launch a specific type of play into the milieu of play experiences (Figure 2.2).

You'll also notice that unlike blackjack, the goal in *Super Mario Bros.* remains pretty much the same throughout the game. As we'll discover

FIGURE 2.2   Games, like this example platformer, are often a collection of problems and solutions created and provided by the designer.

later in this book, having a static goal that doesn't change makes a game easy to understand, but it doesn't necessarily make it boring.

To further the analogy of musical composition, think of a game designer as having a few standard notations that help to communicate the composition. Designers vary in the ways they compose and how they document it, but there are a few essential elements that nearly all games have. I call these the five essentials of every game design. If, as a designer, you leave one undefined, it's very hard to make a successful game. You can make something playful, a toy, but games tend to require some version of each of these.

In concept, every game requires these five elements. In practice, there may be ways to design engaging experiences without adhering to this list. However, this framework is flexible enough to apply to just about every game that has been imagined. If you employ this framework in the evaluation of game designs, you will not only be able to understand the game quickly, you will be able to identify improvements in design. The five essentials of every game are competition, implements, territory, inventory, and rules.

2.2.1 Competition

Competition is our goal in the game. It is often set and evaluated by a marker that demonstrates progress. Competition is often evaluated by the player's distance from that marker.

Competition often involves a goal and a natural obstruction to the goal. In a race, players compete to be the first to reach the destination (aka a marker). In golf, the player's competition is focused on their distance from par. In more traditional contests, like boxing, wrestling, trivia, or football, the competition is adversarial, based on comparative performance to others.

2.2.2 Implements

Implements are what we use to eliminate the obstruction to our goal. In non-digital gameplay, implements are the balls, bats, game pieces, cards, and so on that we use to accomplish our goals. In blackjack, our implements are the standard set of 52 playing cards.

In digital gameplay, implements refer to the simulated items used to accomplish the goal. For our *Super Mario* example, the implements are the characters (aka Mario and Luigi) we pilot to meet our in-game goals. In a first-person shooter (FPS), the avatar's gun is the implement, not the mouse we use to communicate the action. In this case, the mouse is more of a technique, in the way a pitcher might use their left or right arm to throw a ball. FPS games are controlled by a variety of hardware, but the play experience on screen is the focus of the play's implement.

2.2.3 Territory

Territory is the physical or theoretical parameters of the game. It defines the boundaries of the game and helps determine where play ends and the rest of life begins. Conventional territories include a playing field, the board of a board game, or the virtual space of a third-person shooter. It's useful to remember that even for games for which there isn't an obvious play space, such as name-calling games like playing the nines (i.e., your momma jokes) there remains a territory. In such games, play ends when someone says something too personal or crosses an emotional, personal, or other psychological boundary.

Territory is also easily identified in the rules of games designed to protect players. It is why play stops to allow an injured player to move off the field or why, when a child injures themselves at recess the game is typically halted. Our animal brain often recognizes the implicit end or edge of play, even without a designer's explicit description of it.

2.2.4 Inventory

Inventory refers to the items players accumulate during play. In digital games, inventory elements often include points, mana, and currency. Inventory is anything the player accumulates as an indication of success or failure in the game environment. In Microsoft's *Project Gotham Racing* (Bizarre Creations, 2001) franchise, the inventory is Kudos, which the player acquires when they drift or skid the car well. In any game, inventory can be miles driven, boars killed, rounds completed, tiles placed, and so on.

It's common for seasoned people to think of inventory as implements. They often think of inventory as the collection of items available to them as they play (as is common to role-playing games). To differentiate this, think of inventory as the marker of progress. In digital games, unlocking that next great weapon is often the result of accumulating enough inventory (e.g., experience with the game). Implements act on the game world, inventory is the result of play in the game world.

2.2.5 Rules

Rules dictate how the other four elements will be used. Rules establish the relationships between competition, implements, territory, and inventory. Rules are what distinguish baseball from cricket or dodgeball from soccer.

Leaving one or more essential out often results in something that may be playful, but it may not be a game.

2.3 UNDERSTANDING GAMES, RHETORIC, AND MECHANICS

Designing a game can be immensely complex or as simple as you'd like to make it. But designing a game with specific meaning adds another level to the complexity of the design task. Anyone familiar with media will understand that median can convey meaning. We accept this of books, whether fiction or non-fiction, and we understand this of music, film, and more recently, of games.

Like other products of creativity, it's also clear that meaning can be interpreted. However, the aim of an effective designer is to mitigate interpretation. A game that aims to teach people about the dangers of smoking, but instead encourages them to smoke, exemplifies the risk of not mitigating interpretation. If your players misinterpret your intention, you could be causing more harm than good.

It's important to note that we often learn more from our mistakes than we do our success. As such, it's important to note not only the games that really succeeded, but also the ones that absolutely failed. This section contains some examples of success and failure. It is not intended to deride the people who helped create these games, but instead to acknowledge what can be learned from those experiences. I place my own work in this category to admit very readily that I have made these mistakes myself.

There are a variety of ways to mitigate the risk of misinterpretation, but for simplicity, we will start with the most basic. If your game goal, obstruction, and means are analogous to the focus of your purpose-driven game, then it is likely a clear, although not necessarily entertaining, way to manage the message of your game. This is how many of the first-generation games with a message worked. They framed a process, aligned the goals, obstruction, and means to the real world and then asked players to play.

In my first journey as an educational game designer, this was the first mistake I made (Figure 2.3).

The reality is that such games often weren't really very playful. If you've been reading carefully, you'll already know why. A game that seems an awful lot like the real world doesn't offer much space for play. Play is outside the ordinary. This is why games about doing your chores, adhering to mundane daily activities, or doing normal stuff are very hard to make fun. It can be done, but in gamer terms, starting by trying to make the

FIGURE 2.3 The *Health-E* game, which I made as a student, contained many of the mistakes I try to prevent students from making now.

mundane interesting is like starting a game on expert mode. It's not a good place to begin for a beginner.

Starting your first game design by breaking ground in a new genre or attempting to do far more than anyone has ever done before is not an easy way to start. Every professional starts with practice. Each design is simply practice for creating something better. The art of game design is a practiced art. One that requires the skill developed from experience.

The second common approach is to try to adapt existing popular games using the framing of our purpose-driven goals. This is the approach that attempts to turn platformers like *Super Mario Bros.* into educational games. One example is the game *Captain Novolin* (Sculptured Systems, 1992). *Captain Novolin* was a side scrolling game in which the PC must deal with evil aliens and rescue the diabetic mayor of Pineville held captive by the aliens. The aliens appear in the form of junk food, which the player must avoid. Avoiding the aliens and collecting healthy food items helps the PC, Captain Novolin, manage his blood glucose levels. If the PC's glucose levels go too high or too low, the PC dies. Players also earned bonus points by correctly answering questions related to diabetes.

When the game was evaluated formally, it received strong reviews from the relatively limited audience with which it was tested (Brown, 1993). By several accounts "the Captain Novolin Video game was evaluated in a study with 23 parent-child pairs … the majority of children said that it would be easy to play the games with their friends" (Street et al., 2013). It was so well-received in that test that "all parents approved of the game and appreciated its potential to help them discuss diabetes with their children"

(Street et al., 2013). The game's package even notes that it was endorsed by the Juvenile Diabetes Foundation.

Such a game sounds promising, but by other accounts, it is just the opposite. If you reread that game and the experience it may not sound compelling at all. A game littered with trivia questions about diabetes may not sound appealing. Likewise, you may have noticed that 23 participants is not a very large group for a formal study. Or you may have noticed, if you were being critical, that the name of the game is the same as an insulin brand. The game was, of course, sponsored by an insulin manufacturer.

By some accounts, the game was not successful. An *Electronic Gaming Monthly* review of the "20 worst games of all time" placed *Captain Novolin* at number four (Seanbaby, 2009). It exists in some designer's notebooks as the quintessential example of what not to do with such game designs. But, in the defense of its designers, it was an early design whose successes and mistakes helped further the practice of design.

Being an early example is never easy. There are many more examples of early purpose-driven games that are held as examples, but at times do not hold up to the rigor of analysis. Part of the challenge of developing such play and games is the changing landscape in which such work is evaluated. It's also true that such game design and its potential effects are not trivial to analyze. This example stands to impart the opportunities and challenges of designing such games.

2.4 GAMES AND RHETORIC

Fast forward many years and many games later. What we later learned, with the help of masterful game academic Ian Bogost and others, is that games have rhetoric. Their meaning comes not only from the representation on screen or on a board, but in the dynamics between play implements, the rules, the ways in which inventory is acquired, and in the explicit competition. In short, the five essentials of games inform the game's meaning.

One of the easiest ways to understand this is to consider obstruction in a game design. When we provide players with goals, they are typically aimed at an achievable and familiar agenda (explicitly or implicitly). There are goals like collecting all of the items, gaining wealth, or going farther. This is a shorthand trick to make a game easily understood. Players know these goals, so the logic goes, so they will understand how to play the game quickly.

Our goal is immediately countered by an obstruction. Gain as much wealth as you can, but every player is seeking to take money from you.

Collect as much as you can, but you only have two minutes to do it. The obstruction informs the player about the problem. In short, a designer can articulate the obstruction by framing it as a problem.

For every goal, the game offers a challenge—the obstruction. So, if you are making a game about anything, the designer is setting the stage for the problem and what's causing it. If your goal is wealth, but other players keep taking it from you, then the problem, as designed, is the other players. That has a clear meaning. That meaning can be further emphasized by aligning each player with a country, a concept, or an organization. A political game might pit players, representing specific interests, against each other for a limited amount of the federal budget. In that game, the goal is to get as much as the player can, the obstruction is competing interests, and the means—well we haven't designed the means yet.

The designer must also specify the solution to the problem, via the means. The means in our fictitious political game might be bartering with other players, it might be rallying more support from voters, it might be individual conversations with decision makers. As you can see, each means frames the solution to the problem differently. Goal and obstruction frame the problem, the means frames the solution. That's worth reiterating—goal and obstruction frame the problem, the means frames the solution.

This is one of many ways that games promote a sense of meaning. They give us problems and tell us what our options are for solving those problems. If there are enemies, shoot them. If you need a car, take it from someone else. Such are the common solutions in FPS games or games like *Grand Theft Auto V.* Their solutions focus the problem in one of many possible ways. Other ways of offering means could include: if there are enemies, negotiate with them, if you need a car, ask for a ride. These are two different ways of solving the same problems, with a clearly different meaning.

You may notice that many common goals are actually informed by cultural standards. Bigger is better is not a universal human truth. More wealth is better isn't a universal truth either. Much of the meaning is already baked into our framing of problems and goals before we even play. It is present the first moment you start to design your own game. They are part of our assumptions as designers.

Recognizing these, either by taking stock of them or by practicing a critical view of them, can make your design practice more productive and creative. Every new genre, whether, music, film, literary, or otherwise, is often born from a departure from the norm. The first notes of electronic music or the first murder mystery began with a step away from what most people were creating. This is not to say that affirming standards are a problem, as standards are a great shortcut to helping players understand something new. It is, however, important, especially when seeking meaning, to be critically aware of the meaning that comes with some of those standards.

All good designers, whether games, graphics, interior, or cake, are able to ask critical questions about their assumptions. Although it's a bit philosophical and perhaps Zen, it's important to ask questions about your own assumptions as a designer or as a person working with a designer. What do you assume to be true and are those assumptions accurate? Keep in mind, for example, that beyond the experiences in your own background, you are part of a variety of communities. While the word community is often applied to regional locations or cultures, there are also communities of players. Those communities of players have specific assumptions about what's rewarding gameplay and what's not. They have a localized language for their play activities, using terms that are specifically meaningful in the community they play. As a designer, it's important to recognize that language and those assumptions as they can limit your design. They can also help you empower your design by understanding what's working and why. This is why formal decomposition of designs and design assumptions is so useful. If a doctor just practiced medicine by doing the same things and never asking questions, they wouldn't be practicing for long. As you embark on the design process, try to ask critical questions about your own cultural assumption. Ask yourself how your own cultural assumptions may prevent you from meeting your goals in engaging a community with which you may not be a part. Often when doing things with games, the games are being designed for people other than the designer.

2.5 CONCEPT STATEMENTS AND GAME DESIGN DOCUMENTS

At this point you may be thinking—this is a lot to consider. It can be, but it doesn't have to be. The simplest way to think about a game is to think small. A game concept statement, or premise, is a short, direct description of the situation of a game. It describes the player's goal, the obstruction to that goal, and the means through which that goal will be accomplished. Concept statements serve as a kind of mission statement for the game design. They help to frame the challenge of the game and they help to focus the aims of the player.

A short concept statement might read as follows.

In *Trick or Treat*, the player characters have been trapped in the labyrinth of an ancient haunted house. They must escape by destroying adversarial monsters, avoiding traps, and solving the maze. *Trick or Treat* is a third-person perspective action game.

The goal of a concept statement is to give the reader a sense for the game. At a minimum, it should answer two basic questions:

1. What is the goal of the game?

2. How is the goal of the game accomplished?

Concept statements are often three sentences because they often follow the format of goal, obstruction, and means.

Concept statements are not designed to pitch the game to other people, as they focus on the design. They serve as a kind of pin on a map. The rest of the design journey will be about aiming toward that pin on the map. The concept statement also serves as a concise way to share an idea with others, to list a wide array of possible solutions, and to practice simplifying a concept to its most essential components.

When concept statements are used in commercial projects for entertainment, they may contain marketing language to help articulate the way the game is likely to be a success. While this serves its function, it's often too early in the design process to make these decisions.

As an example, imagine if the concept statement included the kind of hardware it would use, only to discover that after a little research, that hardware isn't available to the community the game is designed to serve. It's also common to start writing a concept statement that reads like a pitch. While it's true that a concept statement can be treated as a pitch, it's often a mistake to start pitching a game when only the concept is clear. The concept statement is really focused on computing the high-level ideas that are likely to persist for the project. Even whether or not the game is going to be analog or digital can change, but the core concept may persist.

Separating the game design from implementation details early is particularly important when doing things with games. Much is learned when iterating through possible game designs. While it's true that concept statements function as a kind of pin on a map, they are about intention not promise. Every design changes over time. Committing to delivering a virtual reality experience or a card game when all the player feedback indicates that it is a mistake is a problem. It's a problem that can persist in the project far longer than it should. Keeping a concept statement focused on goal, obstruction, and means allows the design to adapt while still meeting its goals.

By analogy, a concept statement puts a pin on the map, but it doesn't say how it's going to get there. The tendency to put marketing jargon or implementation specifics comes from a variety of prior practices. When game companies were young, people would pitch a variety of games competitively, hoping to have theirs picked. This is why a game pitch might contain some marketing. But concept statements aren't about selling a game, they're about aiming to frame a possible design.

Of course, there are exceptions to every rule. There are times when it is important to add implementation details, such as client projects that aim at specific devices. A game project might need to be implemented on specific hardware because a grant, client, or other funder needs the game to be on that device. Yet even in those cases, it should be assumed as part of the concept process that each of these game concepts aims to meet that core requirement of the project.

2.6 GAME DESIGN DOCUMENTING

After multiple concept statements have been written, there are several steps to articulating and refining a game design. Chapter 3 outlines how to design more formally, but it's important to understand how these designs will be documented to assure that the process goes smoothly.

One of the formerly common ways to record the evolution of a game is with a design document. The design document is much more commonly used in digital game design than analog game design. Typically, a game design document contains the following sections.

- Working Title

- Concept Statement

- Overview or Game Summary

- Gameplay Mechanics Description

- Interface and User Experience Description

- Story, Setting, and Character

- Level Descriptions and Illustration

- Technical Specifications and Requirements

- Art Assets, World Maps, and Concept Art

It serves as a living document, perpetually edited as projects change. For this reason, design documents can often exist as wikis or other easily edited, shared, documents.

The reality is that a game design document, even a living one, can be a bit of deprecated practice. Sometimes, game design elements are changing so often that the procedure of updating a document forms a bottleneck in the process. It can slow nimble teams. If, for example, there are only two members on a team, the infrastructure to maintain a shared document may seem unnecessary.

What game design documents do well is get designers asking questions. All of the questions. This is important, especially when designers are brand new to designing games. The formal, fill in the blank templates that are offered by a variety of online resources and printed books help to remind a designer of all the things they must resolve before the project is ready to release and sometimes even implement. The formality of a design document is quite useful for this.

The informality of other approaches, using Slack channels for updates, having sprint meetings, or the myriad of other solutions that support teams in staying focused are all completely reasonable for a modern game. The idea is simply to document in the way that is most useful to the project.

Typically, the following are common ways to document design.

- *Wireframing and flow charts*: For certain projects, it is sufficient to articulate the experience through diagrams that illustrate player flow through the experience (or use case diagrams), the key elements of a playful experience, or the main components of the playful experience.

- *Illustration and visualization*: For many projects, a series of illustrations can articulate the key elements of the playful experience. Other times, they serve as a vision for the look and feel of an experience, with design iterations moving toward that experience.

- *Slide decks*: For simple projects, a series of bullet points in Google Slides or Microsoft PowerPoint will suffice to articulate the key design decisions of a simple experience.

- *Project management software*: Project management software like Trello or Microsoft Project can aid in managing not only the design elements, but also the who, what, and when of the game project.

Obviously, these solutions can be used together or separately. It may be, for example, that a project starts as a concept statement with an animated vision of the experience. The team then breaks the needs of that project into tasks on a Trello board, before implementing it.

What's most important is that the design is documented. Taking pictures of white board notes after a conversation is a solution, if not a high quality one. The goal is to make sure that everyone involved in the project knows what's being designed. Even if it's a single team project produced over a weekend, it's easy to lose sight of the goal in the effort or implementation. Consider what happens when you go to the grocery store without a list. For simple visits, maybe it works fine. But for longer runs, perhaps when you're going to cook something more complex or new, two things happen. You either don't get all the right things, or you get some of the wrong things; for a game project, it's better to keep a list and know what you need. That way, the project doesn't waste energy on the wrong things and forget to do what's important.

As a rule of thumb, any project over one month should have some formal documentation that makes major design decisions clear to everyone on the team. Failing to do so will cause problems in the end. How that documentation is formalized is entirely dependent on the work environment and the complexities of the project.

For analog games, it's sometimes handy to document the version of the numerical balance in a game. This might be used to manage a currency system, or player advantage or disadvantage for a strategy game. In this case, a spreadsheet may be an essential part of the design document. For a party game that doesn't involve pieces or software, just players, it's useful to document in notes the goals and resulting behaviors. In some cases, more often for non-digital play, the design document may become a key element of the direction. All of the case scenarios to handle stalemates or to prevent players from cheating in a game may become handy as a guide to players in the future. While you shouldn't use other game design documentation with the intent of sharing it with players, it's useful to remember that in documenting a game, you may also be doing part of its implementation.

Also keep in mind that if versions of the document are archived, then it's easy to retrace steps and identify what changed. If a client or subject matter expert suggests a change that extends the project's timeline or budget, the versions of the document(s) can help explain the increases later. If someone on the team skips a feature of the game or playable experience, the document is the guide to keep them on track. When new members come and go from the project, they can always refer to the document(s) to understand the project. The design documents become the final word on the design and the guiding rule. This is one of the many reasons the old term for a game design document was the game bible. It's a guide to be followed for those who are responsible for following it.

2.7 PRACTICE WHAT YOU'VE LEARNED

- Generate a list of games or find a good list of top 10 games on the Internet. For each of the games, list the five essentials of games. Do the games that are more interesting have more interesting essential elements? Are you struggling to understand all of the elements for these games?

- Create a list of culturally appropriate goals from the culture you are most familiar. How can you use these to expand opportunities for other players? Are these uniform across cultures or are they an opportunity to understand some unique aspect of your culture and perhaps a unique way to play (or not play?)

- Giving yourself just 15 minutes each, write three completely different concept statements. Pitch them to a friend, neighbor, colleague, or classmate. What did they notice that you had not?

- Pick a documentation plan for your game. This can be a phased approach starting with an illustration and perhaps moving to something more formal. Try to identify a documentation plan that's most appropriate for your needs. Will a game design document count toward a class requirement? Will a slide deck presentation cover all that you need for the project? Is your game more important to document as a process (wireframes and flow charts), as an illustration (visual orientation), procedurally (perhaps as a spreadsheet), operationally (via project management software), or another way?

REFERENCES

Bizarre Creations. *Project Gotham Racing*. Microsoft, 2001.
Brown, S. J. *Field Test of Captain Novolin with 23 Children*. Unpublished manuscript. Mountain View, CA: Raya Systems, 1993.

Caillois, Roger. *Man, Play, and Games.* Champaign, IL: University of Illinois Press, 2001.

Caillois, Roger, and Elaine P. Halperin. "The structure and classification of games." *Diogenes* 3, no. 12 (1955): 62–75.

Frieberger, P. Video Game Takes on Diabetes Superhero "Captain Novolin" Offers Treatment Tips. San Francisco Examiner, (June 26, 1992), Fourth Edition, Business Section B, 1. 1992.

Huizinga, Johan. *Homo Ludens.* London: Routledge, 2014.

Meggs, Philip B., and Alston W. Purvis. *Meggs' History of Graphic Design.* Hoboken, NJ: John Wiley & Sons, 2011.

Nintendo Creative Department. *Super Mario Bros.* Nintendo, 1985.

Prensky, Marc. "Fun, play and games: What makes games engaging." *Digital Game-Based Learning* 5, no. 1 (2001): 5–31.

Sculptured Systems. *Captain Novolin.* Raya Systems, 1992.

Seanbaby. "20 worst games of all time." *Electronic Gaming Monthly,* no. 150 (2009).

Smith, Peter K. "Does play matter? Functional and evolutionary aspects of animal and human play." *Behavioral and Brain Sciences* 5, no. 1 (1982): 139–155.

Sutton-Smith, Brian. *The Ambiguity of Play.* Cambridge, MA: Harvard University Press, 2009.

Street, Richard L., William R. Gold, and Timothy R. Manning. *Health Promotion and Interactive Technology: Theoretical Applications and Future Directions.* New York: Routledge, 2013.

Van Hoorn, Judith Lieberman, Patricia Monighan-Nourot, Barbara Scales, and Keith Rodriguez Alward. *Play at the Center of the Curriculum.* New York: Pearson, 2014.

CHAPTER 3

Engagement Design and Serious Play

Until now, much of the language in this book has steered clear of emphasizing terminology. There's a reason for this. In the relatively short and recent history of digital game design, there has been a distractingly loud dialogue about the appropriate terminology for very specific applications.

There exists in the general domain of games *designed to do things* terms like persuasive play, exergaming, edutainment, serious games, serious play, gamification, docugames, purposeful game, meaningful play, social impact games, and more. Each of these terms has its champions and its critics. It also has its reason for coming to existence. Some of this reasoning is pragmatic, some of it is political, and some of it is the product of branding and marketing. In the end, from a designer's perspective, it's less important to know the terms than it is to know the science and practice of making such games. It's also important to remember that such terms come and go. Terms like edutainment, for example, are largely deprecated. Other terms, like docugames, are less often used despite the continued production of such games. It is for these reasons that it is more important to understand what is intentioned by a game's design than knowing the specific term for the design intention. Just as words like dope, bad, awesome, and amazing come in and out of favor, so to do the terms that aim to specifically describe what a game's design aims to do. These terms are useful in providing shorthand for communicating a design's intention, but they aren't necessary to the work of designing such play effectively. They help in reading literature and translating conversations about such work, but a design's intention and its ability to meet that intention are typically more important than the terminology used to describe it.

Two terms, in particular, solicit much conversation. They are serious games and gamification. The "serious games" term traces its history, in part, to the professional practice of simulation. Serious games are supposed to be games which aim to serve a serious purpose that exceeds the general frivolity of play. However, if you've been reading the previous chapters, you recognize that play has and will always continue to serve several non-frivolous purposes. Much of that purpose is serious, whether it's surviving being hunted, learning to control your impulses, practicing mathematics, or experimenting with behavioral dynamics.

What then is serious play if all play has either a serious purpose or serious benefit? There's a pragmatic read of the term serious play (or serious games) that helps posit the tension in making games about things that are considered serious. The term serious play is a qualifier, to separate frivolous play from serious play. This serious qualifier can be used to elevate it, as is necessary to promote such work among those who misunderstand play as trivial and frivolous. It is the qualifier that helps grants get funded, academic programs to emphasize their value, and to rationalize any natural exuberance for games and play.

The other way this qualifier works is to make that which is not playful, sound playful. This is the way in which a simulation, which may be specifically designed to prevent playfulness, describes itself. It is a way of aligning the prescriptive and often non-playful elements of a simulation with the character and appeal of playful experiences. This approach is a bit like the way a parent might bate a child into cleaning their room or brushing their teeth by calling such play a game, even if there is nothing particularly playful in it. It is a game in name only. But calling it a game can entice the most naive participant into perceiving it as such. Many of the simulations designed to train and evaluate fall within this category. Such self-titled serious games aim to hide practical assessments or tests under the qualifier of a game. They don't employ the play state, but they have the signs and symbols of play. They may report a score, which in actuality is really a report card. They may look and sound like a game, but lack any effort to encourage the play state. In practice, most players can tell the difference that which claims to be playful, and something that actually is playful.

Yet another common approach is to take something that is not particularly good at being a game or playful and add the moniker serious to it. This is the band-aid that popularized the term chocolate-covered broccoli. Chocolate-covered broccoli is the awkward application of something to sweeten what otherwise may not be inviting. It is an effort to cover what is mundane, tedious, or uninteresting by sprinkling it with the elements of play. Largely used as a derogatory term, it's a clear reference to the haphazard way in which such design is applied. Instead of imagining how the benefit (i.e., the broccoli) can be integrated, it remains untouched. The broccoli can't be diced into the chocolate, it must have chocolate drizzled on it. The broccoli can't be matched with the appropriate delicious accompaniment (i.e., no butter, no cheese), it must be paired with the old formula for making anything delicious. In the end, the result is worse than the two separately. Applying haphazard game elements can actually be worse than simply admitting the activity isn't playful and presenting it as such. For one, the player never feels cheated. They don't reject the experience because they engaged with it expecting play and found none.

In the last decade, the term gamification grew in favor and almost immediately became derided. The core concept is a noble aspiration. Add game mechanics or structures in a way that does not make it chocolate-covered broccoli. Integrate game mechanics to motivate, inspire, or structure player or participant actions. Well beyond incentivizing schemes, gamification aims to do more. Its aspirations, especially as ill-informed marketing jargon and sales pitch, were better than many of its implementations. That is no fault of gamification, but instead, in part, the product of the clamor of terminology. Many who offered gamification did little on the game end but were eager to attach the trendy term to their work. Just as games can be used to make something that is serious sound more interesting, gamification was attached (perhaps inappropriately) to incentive structures that had been in place for decades and weren't particularly playful. These include loyalty structures that encouraged girl scouts to sell cookies and frequent flyers to remain brand loyal. Many academic and professional treatises on the best practices of gamification can expound on the specifics of gamification. If you want to know more about true gamification, it's best to review Sebastian Deterding's book on the topic (2012).

In all of these cases, we are doing the practice of designing meaningful playful experiences a disservice. All of this work exists on a spectrum and all of it is worthy of effort. In all of this work, we are working to structure play to meet a goal beyond mere entertainment. In short, we are doing things with games. The things we do might be to educate or convince, it might be to lampoon or sadden. In the end, it's less important to worry about the label than it is the goal.

In games, we have raced to label such work in response to the myriad of challenges in getting funding and support for such work. Such labels feel like the product of a need to legitimize the practice of game design, or simply to stake our claim in a constantly evolving space. In reality, players don't really care what you call it, they just want it to be engaging. As we race to give title to the age-old practice of linking meaning and effect to games, we ignore what each of these subdomains of doing things with games knows. We aim to differentiate these areas when they've barely had time to grow into their own.

It may be simpler, more inclusive, and more productive to simply understand that serious play is all play. The difference is the intention. The designer of *Spent* (Urban Ministries of Durham, 2011), who would not have self-identified as a game designer before making the game, made an effective game about poverty in the United States. Lucas Pope, the designer of *Papers Please*, made a game that leaves people thinking more deeply about immigration policy. The intentions of these designers were to do something with games.

It may sound novel to "do something with games." The idea of working to achieve a goal through a game seems novel, but it's actually anything but new. People have been doing things with varied media for years. They've been doing things with books for years. They've been doing things with film and every other major media since they could. Songs have entertained, but they've also served as the way to set the pace of outdoor work or to rally soldiers into war. We are almost inverted in our understanding of games. We credit the Gutenberg press with print, and the resulting preponderance of literature, libraries, and so on. Play came much earlier and it served its purpose so early in our history that it is present across many mammals, not just humans. Like the invention of language, we can't pinpoint an exact date or technological innovation, but instead, we recognize the many functions it offers.

All play can serve the myriad of terms we have invented to differentiate it from the more mundane and general play. The way that happens is through design.

We can think of serious play as less of a label and more of a concept. As a designer, or someone engaged in a project seeking to employ play, you're looking to create a serious outcome from the play you designed.

Remember that designers are composers, so this is simply a convenient term to indicate that you are composing seriously. Just as Beethoven, Bach, The Beatles, or Ludacris compose music, the meaning and serious outcomes are largely a product of how those that created the music aimed their creative effort.

In his 2013 keynote at the Games for Change Festival, Ian Bogost, the very well-respected games and media scholar, highlighted an important point about serious games (Bogost, 2013). He is appropriately critical of the term. He notes that we do not champion serious books or serious films. Instead, we recognize all such work and need no distinction or qualifier.

The term serious play then functions for experienced designers not as a way of compartmentalizing one practice of play design from another. Instead, it serves as a way of reminding one of the practice itself. Just as an author writes seriously, a game designer can design seriously.

This means that there are elements of serious play in all games. Last year's best-selling games had serious play in them. There are meaningful moments in the most fictitious of games, as there are meaningful moments in the most fictitious of books, music, and film. *The Great Gatsby* is a "serious book," so too are the works of major game studios who aim to entertain first and foremost. The dystopic experiences of games like *Bioshock* have their roots in major literary works and art (Tavinor, 2009).

This is a concept that is not new to media scholars, but requires revisiting when discussing serious play. All games, like all media, have some level of seriousness within a spectrum. The most comedic works may aim to lampoon political figures. To understand designing for serious play, you must start by understanding that all play can be serious.

Dr. Stuart Brown illuminates this with repeated examples in his book *Play: How it Shapes the Brain, Opens the Imagination, and Invigorates the Soul* (2009). He connects play as an integral behavior for humans as animals. He also reiterates what Huizinga, Sutton-Smith, and others have repeated. Part of the power of play is that it is outside of ordinary life.

3.1 SERIOUS PLAY IS NOT ORDINARY LIFE

As mentioned previously, a core aspect of play is that it is outside of ordinary life. As such, it's important to note that serious play and ordinary life are not the same. The dominant framings of games put them in opposition to the mundane and ordinary experiences of everyday life. While a game's play may be part of the everyday, the play is a way of crossing the transom from the mundane to another state—a state we've been calling the play state.

3.2 MAKING SERIOUS ISSUES PLAYFUL

The obvious challenge in designing playful experiences is our innate cultural tension between play and seriousness. Philosophically, you could return to the spectrum Brian Sutton-Smith offers. Play is not the opposite of seriousness, it's the opposite of depression. If action is innate to play, then as designers, the focus should remain on the doing. We do serious things in games all the time, including killing, capturing, destroying, building, and more. The tension between seriousness and non-seriousness is not in the things we do in games, it's in the aim of the designer.

As a species, humans have been playing games for so long that we fail to recognize how much seriousness is already in the play with which we engage. In the history of chess, for example, the role of the queen changed over time in part as a response to the rise of European female queens. The game, originally from India, provided the king with the most power, but our contemporary version of chess is the result of a more recent political history in which queens had power (Flanagan, 2009).

There is perhaps no more serious topic than play. As mentioned previously, some of the history of serious play begins with military simulation. Much of the modern video game industry owes its technological innovations to the needs of the Cold War and manufacturing, as efforts to accurately simulate were started with intentions for use in modern warfare, military training, and reducing the costs of manufacturing. Simulations remained a cheaper alternative to creating and destroying planes, missiles, and related machinery.

At the forefront of this research in the United States was the Massachusetts Institute of Technology (MIT). Supercomputers at this institution were employed to do calculations for everything from NASA needs to US Airforce simulation. Yet one way I like to frame this history is to remind people of MIT's other innovation in game design. The computer scientists at MIT created one of the worlds' first computer games, *Spacewar!* (Russell, 1962). Despite, or perhaps because of, the seriousness of the scientists' everyday work, they created a game.

It's a convenient, if not overly simplified, way to emphasize that play and seriousness are not in opposition, but instead can exist side by side. It could be argued that instead of refining missiles for the Cold War, computer scientists at MIT chose to spend their time designing, developing, and playing a space shooting game in the fictional world. Where there is seriousness, there must be play. If there is no play, there is depression.

The challenge is then in making serious issues playful. We play at war all the time on computers, as children with toy guns, and by analogy through the many competitive sports which are often referred to by analog to war. The two have even informed each other. The Greek Phalanx, for example, was once a viable American football play until it was deemed far too effective. Sports teams are not mere losers, they are destroyed or even killed in the vernacular of sports culture.

One of the common ways we make comfort with playing with the seriousness of war is by flipping the serious play concept. It's play to play war, because it's just play. Adding the word play to many things explains it and disarms an activity. It is the reason we excuse awkward behavior by claiming we were just playing, or why play in front of many words makes it much more acceptable (e.g., play-fighting). If we use serious to elevate play, we use play to deescalate seriousness. It's a means of disarming a tense situation, as in don't take it to heart, I was just playing.

Play can, and should, function as a way to explore and experiment with serious topics. The human animal recognizes this, which is why courtship includes a demonstrated ability to play. Whether it's dancing, joking, or flirting, the human animal is attuned to the play that signals the serious potential of a mate. Play is not only something outside of ordinarily life, it is also a way to explore and experiment.

So, if play is fair in love and war, it's clear that we have the potential for other such couplings. It's no surprise that play touches on other serious topics, such as health. The obvious history of sports, including the Olympics, demonstrates how such play intersects with serious goals. The first marathon runners, for example, were functioning as a kind of audition to be messengers. Those same auditions existed for the early days of NASCAR, as drivers were demonstrating their ability to smuggle illegal alcohol during prohibition (hence the requirements for using production vehicles, unlike Formula 1 and other forms of car racing). That serious play continued into cigarette boat racing and a myriad of sports which functioned as a simulation or proving ground for real world, serious application.

Of course, none of that covers the core question of how to make serious topics, playful. Although it hints at a core concept that pervades much of this design. By simply taking the core task or activity of the serious subject, encapsulating it into the controlled environment, and emphasizing the opportunity to experiment (aka being playful), a serious subject can be moved toward a playful one. This process, which is one of many, can be summarized by:

1. Decanting the core verbs or actions of the activity.

2. Encapsulating those activities in a safe environment outside the ordinary world.

3. Encouraging a play state by emphasizing key elements and deemphasizing others. This often includes encouraging players to explore and experiment within the safe space.

There will be more about the verbs in the next section, but this is a simple three-step approach to turning a common, serious activity into a playful one. Step 1 is to understand the subject and determine the core actions or things players will do. Step 2 is to create an environment in which those activities can be safe (i.e., not cause real-world harm to players). Step 3 is the one that is most creative and most like being a musician. It's about turning up the volume, or emphasis of certain elements, while also lowering the volume on others.

This aforementioned three-step model works well for simulation-based play. That's play for which there is already an existing model in the real world. If such verbs exist, and players are interested in exploring and experimenting with those verbs in a safe space, it's likely a good candidate for this approach.

Another way to employ this model is to consider changing the perspective from which the player engages in the activity of play. In the relationship to war, for example, there have been several social impact games that aim to provide the play experience of war from a new perspective. For a long while, war games provided players the position of power. The core verbs involved managing armies, controlling troops, fighting hand to hand, or flying an airplane. That approach has its appeal and it also offers its own rhetoric about war and its experience. This appeal is largely centered on the power fantasy of controlling the outcome of a war.

This War of Mine (11 bit studios, 2014), however, switches the perspective, obviously switching the player's core activities (aka game verbs). Instead of being a soldier, what happens when the player is merely a victim of war trying to survive? What types of claims about war does such a perspective shift make? This is the same thing that one of the earliest self-identified social impact games, *Darfur is Dying* (Ruiz, 2006) achieves. Player goals go from prospering to survival.

There are many other ways to begin to design a game about a serious topic. The later chapters in this book cover some specific approaches for specific domains. It's important to remember that for any given process there are always exceptions. It's also important to remember that this three-step model for simulation-based play is a compliment to designing with goal, obstruction, and means. Once these few decisions are made and a few concept statements drafted, it's important to start making decisions about the five essentials of games.

NASCAR, for example, occurs on a round track, even though few rum runners evaded police by driving in circles (although pit stops were still helpful for long runs). But the circular track makes watching the race much easier. That territory decision is an example of turning the volume up on one element of the simulation, while turning it down on another.

3.3 DESIGNING WITH PURPOSE-DRIVEN GAME VERBS

One of the simplest ways to determine the "what we do" in a design is to think about player verbs. Player verbs, or more commonly, game verbs, are the actions performed by players to act in the game. They work both operationally and symbolically. So, for example, a chess piece has specific moves. As a player, each piece is simply moved by the player. Yet the patterns of each movement have symbolic meaning. As mentioned, the queen has the most variability in moves, and subsequently, offers the most power over the board. Other pieces have their own limitations, and so by design, these are their verbs. The rook's verb is horizontal movement, the bishop's is diagonal, and so on.

Game verbs are often limited by the game's platform. Board games, for example, are often limited by their physicality, which, in turn, can create unique, novel opportunities. Consider, for example, the physicality of games like Jenga, Hungry Hungry Hippos, or Trouble (aka Kimble). Often, the physical character of game elements can be employed to improve the game design, especially in toy-based designs.

Trouble's bubble shaped dice roller is interesting to press, but it also avoids some typical challenges of children's games. The die is no longer another piece to be lost from the game. There's also no more need to discuss what happens when dice roll off the board. Additionally, it serves as an emblematic element of the game, as a toy somewhat unique to the game (Figure 3.1).

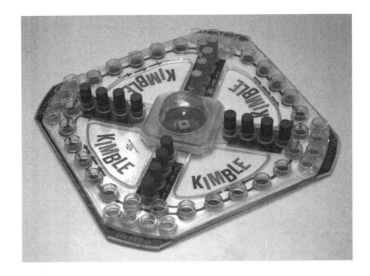

FIGURE 3.1 The distinct look and feel of the Kimble dice roller as a toy in a game. (Courtesy of Haltiamieli [https://commons.wikimedia.org/wiki/File:Kimble_1968.jpg] through Creative Commons.)

The child's board game, Hungry Hungry Hippos is a collection game. In concept, the game verb is collect. But it is the way in which players collect that appeals to the game's young audience. The toy has a unique verb attached to it—eat. As a designer, the game would be framed as a collection game, where the verb is eat, and the goal is to eat as many marbles as the player can. The obstacle is the physicality of the toy with which the player must eat. This also functions as the means (Figure 3.2).

Designing digital experiences greatly increases the potential verbs with which to play.

It's important to note that game verbs include games for which there is no physical or digital implementation. Word games, for example, have game verbs. The game verbs might be rhyme, match (as in match the first letter of each word), attach (as in attach another word with the same first letter to someone's name) argue, and so on. Obviously, games like charades employ a variety of verbs.

What's most important about game verbs in the context of purpose-drive game design is that the verbs should have a relationship to their subject. That relationship can be very close to their subject or it can be by analogy. Mary Flanagan's game *Layoff*, for example, uses the game verbs common to other match three games to make a point about corporate culture. In this case, the game verbs are not the same as decisions made when

FIGURE 3.2 The toys of the Hungry Hungry Hippos game. (Courtesy of David Goehring [https://www.flickr.com/photos/carbonnyc/] through Creative Commons.)

considering laying off employees, but in aligning the game to a match three game, the designer is emphasizing a dynamic and making a claim about the way the process works in the real world (Figure 3.3).

3.4 GAMES DESIGN AS THE PROBLEM AND SOLUTION

One effective way to understand game design in this domain is to further the concept of games as goal, obstacle, and means. Games can be understood as a series of problems and solutions. If the overarching concept statement for your game outlines a single goal and the ways in which the player can meet that goal, a game is still likely to be comprised of lots of little problems that each need their own solution.

A toy-based game, like *Bionic Commando* (Capcom, 1988), does a good job of illustrating this. In *Bionic Commando*, the player must move, not by running and jumping like other platformers; instead, the player has a grappling hook that swings them between platforms. While the goal is similar to other platformers, the individual problems and solutions are changed by this single switching of means. Swinging involves different physics, which makes movement between platforms a different set of problems to solve. The verb is swing, which is different from games with similar problems and the game verb jump.

But this is not unique to digital games. Consider the car ride game of naming things alphabetically. The concept statement is simple. Players must say a word that starts with the current letter to win each round (aka goal). Players must not use a word that has already been used by another

FIGURE 3.3 Tiltfactor's *Layoff* game uses the game verbs of match three games to make its point. (Courtesy of Mary Flanagan.)

player (obstacle). Players must speak the word as soon as they think of it to get credit for the word (means).

If the topic is animals, for example, each player must name an animal that starts with A. In the next round, it's B. This game does a couple of things well in the context of this book. First, it's a kind of education game, as it requires young players to think about how something is spelled. It also requires them to index a variety of examples for each topic. Lastly, it provides a new knowledge opportunity, in that new words may be introduced or inquiries made about the legitimacy of an answer (similar to using a dictionary to validate a word in Scrabble). But what are the problems and solutions?

The challenge to the game comes from its problems. New problems are introduced once another player takes a word before another player. So, in the animal example, Aardvark prevents anyone else from using that animal. The slowest players have a smaller set of possibilities, and thanks to the psychology of priming (i.e., encouraging people to think of something because you mentioned it), the slowest players are also challenged with thinking of something unrelated to the words they've heard. In short, the game provides one central problem, and then in playing, new problems are introduced. Thus, the pattern is that every game is really a series of problems and solutions.

This game design also affords for a bit of dynamic challenge and negotiation. Adult players might choose not to answer with the easiest solutions to increase their challenge and keep the game accessible for young minds (e.g., leaving "ant" for children and choosing "antelope" as their answer). This allows players with very different abilities to play together. In the world of digital game design, a computer can moderate these challenges, giving more challenge to high performing players and fewer challenges to poorly performing players. It's commonly referred to as rubber-banding, as it binds players together within a game with a kind of elasticity of challenge.

Game designers are tasked with designing the problems and making sure there are solutions. If there are no solutions, the designer runs the risk of alienating players. Since game design is a bit of a contract with the player, the player trusts that there is a solution to all of the problems presented. If there is no solution, or the solution is well outside of the player's offered solution space, players feel cheated or worse.

The problems and the solutions don't have to be easy or evident, but they need to be appropriate. One of the easiest ways to alienate a player is simply to offer them a problem with no solution. Consider, for example, if you were given a question in a class. You puzzle on it for a long while, proposing multiple solutions, which you are told are all incorrect. Failing to figure it out, you simply ask—what's right? The result is not that there is no right answer, but worse, simply that the person who gave you the question doesn't know it. Because games are designed experiences, not having solutions to the problems created can be incomplete and generally dissatisfying. This doesn't mean a game must have the answers, but instead, it should afford the player an opportunity at moving toward the goal.

The inverse is that open worlds and toy boxes have lots of solutions, but few, if any, explicit problems. A designer can create a playful experience by offering solutions to a set of problems that the player creates. However, that model of design is rarely exercised in the practice of making social impact games. The reason is fairly obvious. If you are making a game to address a problem, it's common to focus on the problem, especially if the solution is unknown.

3.5 GAME DESIGN MODELS

Several books, papers, articles, and videos have been produced to catalog the variety of ways in which a game can be designed. These range from the fairly methodical to the very conceptual. Some models emphasize the mechanics, others emphasize playtesting and experiential understanding of what works and doesn't work in a game's design. Since there are so many to choose from, it's typically useful to simply highlight some models that have worked particularly well for game designers seeking to make games for areas of social impact, advertising, education, and other aims beyond simply entertaining players. Each has its fit for specific design styles and needs, so there is no one-size-fits-all solution. It's also completely reasonable to blend these models to meet your own needs.

3.5.1 Playcentric Design

Offered by Tracy Fullerton at the University of Southern California, the playcentric approach champions designing in iterative circles (Fullerton, 2014). The notion is to decant the best parts of a game idea by frequently prototyping, refining the ideas, and reiterating until the best of the game can be identified. This model (Figure 3.4) has been used to create many successful games including Thatgamecompany's early successes like *Flow* and *Flower* (Thatgamecompany, 2009).

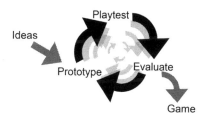

FIGURE 3.4   Playcentric game design is about iterating through a design in cycles of prototyping, playtesting, and evaluating.

3.5.2 MDA: Mechanics, Dynamics, Aesthetics

The MDA Framework (Hunicke, 2004) is a commonly referenced way to frame the design decisions between what the player experiences and the designer intends. The framework emphasizes the two-way street between the designer's process and concerns and the player's perceptions. These are framed as mechanics, dynamics, and aesthetics. The player perceives the game experience starting at aesthetics, while the designer begins the game design with mechanics. One of the key designers of this process, Robin Hunicke, was involved in the production of another Thatgamecompany hit game, *Journey*. Her continued successes both as an educator and through her company Funomena are evidence supporting the durability of this framework (Figure 3.5).

3.5.3 Affirmative Design

One often overlooked, but extremely commonly employed model is simply to affirm what has already worked. Affirmative design champions what has already succeeded and simply aims to embellish on past success. It's not as exciting or as interesting as other design models, but it does work for certain types of games. Cloning, while not particularly well respected, is the design approach that simply looks to copy what has already succeeded.

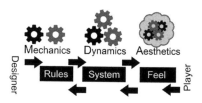

FIGURE 3.5   The MDA framework outlines the relationship between designer and player as mechanics, dynamics, and aesthetics.

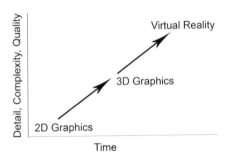

FIGURE 3.6 Affirmative design conceptually aims to improve or embellish on past functionality over time, affirming what has already been done. Moving a game from 2D to 3D and then to virtual reality would be an example of affirmative design.

Affirmative design isn't about cloning, but instead it is about moving the current trends forward. If a certain set of mechanics are popular, an affirmative design moves them forward by amplifying them in some way. It's what moves real-world tennis toward two-dimensional *Tennis for Two*, which then moves toward 3D simulations of tennis (Figure 3.6).

3.5.4 Critical Design

If affirmative design aims to continue the trajectory of design patterns. Critical design aims to critique it. Critical design is focused not on moving the conventions of game design forward, but instead about trying to offer an alternative that responds to a trend or takes the trend to its logical, if potentially dystopic end (Grace, 2012). Critical design is commonly practiced by artists and social impact designers who are looking to create games that are critical of social assumptions or system dynamics. It is most common to independent games and has found little practice in commercial game design. Some of the premier critical designers of the 20th century included Dadaist and surrealist game designers, who made a variety of analog games that offered critical reflections on society and play.

In your design toolset, you know should have the following:

- *Toy-based design*: focused on designing a game from the novelty of a specific toy

- *Affirmative design*: focused on bringing common designs to the next level

- *Playcentric design*: focused on iterating over design features to refine them

- *MDA framework*: focused on the interchange between designer intention and player experience

- *Critical design*: focused on creating a critique through game designs

3.6 STORYTELLING

Much of this writing in this chapter has focused on mechanics with little emphasis on storytelling. That's quite intentional. Storytelling has a rich history that is as old as communication itself. But storytelling games in games is often argued as being unique. There are elements of storytelling in games that are unique and many which are not.

It's important to start with the six fundamentals of a story, even if as a designer, you plan to completely ignore them. These six fundamentals of a story are setting, characters, plot, conflict, theme, and narrative arc. The setting gives the story place. The characters help carry the story, moving the plot forward. The conflict offers the drama and tension in a story, while the theme reveals what the story is really about. The entire work typically has some sort of narrative arc, with dynamics of tension on character development. In the Western storytelling tradition, there are conventions to structuring these stories, such as the three-act structure, in which every story has a clear start, middle, and end. The start typically lays out the conflict of the story (aka exposition), the middle involves some rising action, and the end resolves the story. Other stories might follow the more complex conflict structure of the hero's journey or some other conventions. Likewise, there are ways of framing stories that include more or fewer elements.

What's important is understanding that even in games, there will be an expectation that if the game has story, the story employs these conventions. It's important because, particularly in the Western storytelling tradition, players are going to start with these assumptions. They are going to expect conflict. They are going to expect a setting. It's a bit like writing a book. Following some conventions can help orient your audience, even if the aim of this book is to completely upend storytelling traditions.

As a literary example, Kurt Vonnegut's *Slaughterhouse 5* (1987) is a book that involves many futurist notions of time and place and generally subverts conventional storytelling. At the same time, it does so in a way that remains readable to people who know storytelling and those who don't.

What's important to note about storytelling in the context of social impact is its relationship to conflict, problems, solutions, and game verbs. The conflict of your game is likely to relate to the narrative of your game if narrative elements and storytelling are important to the design. That means that as a designer thinks of common narrative structures, like an inciting event and an exposition, those narrative events will need to nest with the mechanics and their meaning.

A common approach to storytelling in the purposeful design of games is to construct a narrative and task the player with moving that story forward. The answer to the question, what do I do in the game? is largely to move the story forward. This is a perfectly acceptable approach, but it will lack the sense of agency that players often seek. It does not mean that the experience won't be engaging (especially if good writing is behind it), but it does mean that the player is likely to recognize very quickly that they are being taken for a ride for which they lack control. This is what is known commonly as a story on rails. The player may need to play to move the story forward, but the story is like a train, already bound by the tacks laid before it and requiring only the effort of the player to move it in the one direction it can go.

A common solution that addresses the sense of being on rails is the application of a variety of verbs. In Molleindustria's *Phone Story*, for example, the player's verbs are four of the activities related to smartphone production (Molleindustria, 2011). This rather dark view of the world of phone manufacture and sales tells a bit of its story with mechanics. Players must harvest precious minerals in slave-like conditions, manufacture phones in an environment where workers rather commit suicide, fling the latest phone at the consumer market, and melt down the e-waste in unhealthy conditions. The story that the game tells is largely bound in the four main verbs in the game. From the game's perspective, mobile phone production is a cycle of exploited labor and coaxed consumer demand. If you've been keeping up with design approaches, *Phone Story* is a kind of critical design. As is the risk with critical designs, the game was banned from Apple's App store (Brown, 2011) (Figure 3.7).

Another trend in social impact game storytelling is to provide a means for allowing the player the ability to discover the story. *Another Lost Phone: Laura's Story* (Accidental Queens, 2017) and *Bury Me My Love* (The Pixel Hunt, 2017), both rely on the mystery structure to impart their story. A mystery structure provides the player with a problem and lets them find

FIGURE 3.7 Molleindustria's *Phone Story* depicts the dark side of mobile phone production, from the slave-like conditions of harvesting raw materials, to suicide prevention in manufacturing plants, to the electronic waste and its resulting human and environmental harm. (Courtesy of Molleindustria through the public domain.)

the solution. For each solution they find, a new conflict or question is revealed. In the old tradition of who done it in films and books, a character discovers a murder victim with a questionable piece of evidence. Perhaps there is a knife with a distinct engraved pattern. The reader wants to know the who, what, and why of the murder. The how is assumed to be "by knife wounds." In the course of experiencing the story, the reader may discover answers that only beget more questions. The symbol on the knife is a from an ancient cult, but the cult has been disbanded for years, so who? The knife might be discovered to be a stolen artifact from a museum, creating more questions. Who would have stolen it? Why did they choose such an exotic murder weapon? And so on.

Mystery structure is particularly useful in games because it provides a perpetual current of conflict and player propelled inquiry. If we understand games as collections of problems to solve, a mystery structure is an easy storytelling structure on which to scaffold play. It does so by providing players the opportunity to discover the story instead of merely pushing it forward like a locomotive. A mystery structure is the scaffold for certain types of non-digital play already. Any player of hidden object games, escape rooms, or murder mystery theater knows this structure well.

In the digital world, the two aforementioned games use some of this structure. The conflict for *Another Lost Phone* precipitates from the notion that the player has discovered a device and must learn more about the person to whom it belongs. With *Bury Me My Love*, the player is witnessing the text messaging interchange between a couple.

3.7 WHAT ABOUT FUN?

The other big element missing is the ever-important f-word. Fun. Fun is so hotly contested and so complex that it could be a chapter in its own. At times, fun is relative. Something can be more fun than something very boring, but relative to all fun things, it's really not fun at all. Fun is not only relative, it's somewhat personal. What's fun depends on age, context, and a host of other elements that are hard to pin down into very specific language.

Most design research and design methods don't necessarily start with the idea of what's fun. They instead try to narrow fun down into specific units. Is it engaging? Is it more engaging than the alternative? Is it entertaining? Is it inviting? Does it make the player laugh? Does it make players anxious or angry?

Understanding fun is best done, from a designer's perspective, as part of a spectrum. The aim is to target something that is fun, but the qualities of fun are very complex. There is hard work that is fun, such as training for a marathon, cooking, or learning a new language. Those who engage in those activities may not even perceive them as work, because the magic of fun is that it negates the work. If it's fun, it doesn't feel like work.

Remember that the opposite of play is not work, it's depression. That means that fun is perhaps not the opposite of work, but simply part of the work spectrum. Much of playing a game is a collection of tasks. Players must collect this, earn that, move here, hit that. But those tasks aren't perceived as work. They are instead perceived as play.

That is the game designer's trick. To turn work into something fun. To engage the player with the prospect of play. Play that is so good they want to engage in it more. They want to do the work of playing your game. Because, perhaps, your game is fun to them.

It is probably disappointing not to receive a formal definition of fun. In classic fashion, you could reference Merriam-Webster and learn that fun is "what provides amusement or enjoyment." The longer you design games, the more you will become dissatisfied with this definition. It is also no more substantial than the preceding explanation of fun. The next question is then, what is amusement and what is enjoyment? Do people enjoy experiences that make them anxious, angry, or upset? Certainly, as they watch films that thrill and amuse them and by the tension of an upsetting novel.

When designing, I find it useful to understand fun as simply an optimal version of the play state. If the play state is going well, it is fun. When the play state stops, or breaks, it's not fun. It's another state. Another place of being that is largely managed by the human brain and the social contract between players and the game designer. To ask for something more specific is to try to decant the magic of fun into words. Instead, as a designer, consider yourself a magician who is always practicing the art of turning work into play and play into fun. It is a practice, which is affected by a constantly changing world. What was engaging play 20 years ago may not be now. What was once dull, may become playful again. The practice of game design affords the opportunity to explore the ever-changing world of play.

For those people who desire something more concrete, I've found an understanding of player preference a good way to adjust game designs. Every player has biases toward certain types of amusement from others. To understand your own, you merely need to consider what types of amusement activities attract you and which activities sound like more work than they are worth. Crossword puzzles engage some people and frustrate others. Sudoku might be play state inducing for some players and anxiety inciting for others. Going out dancing calls some players and scares others. For every play experience, there will be people who are attracted to it and others who find nothing attractive in it at all. To understand these, play profiles can be constructed. The play profile simply indicates what players like and dislike.

Play profiles can function like demographics, technographics, and psychographics in focusing a design and its audience. Aligning a design toward the natural play profiles of the targeted player group is a shorthand way to make sure some aspects of the play designed are engaging or even "fun" to that audience. If players already have word puzzles in their play profile, then designing a new word puzzle has a higher potential of attracting the player than something that's not in their play profile. The work of Nick Yee is a good place to start in understanding player preferences for specific game elements (Yee, 2016).

Understanding play profiles can be formalized by choosing a framework. Framing of the ambiguity (Sutton-Smith, 2009) of play functions as a nicely formalized way to interpret play preferences. It can serve as a way to evaluate a play experience to understand what elements need to be adjusted to move it toward a fun experience. In his writing, he outlines a variety of ways that players engage in play. He calls these the seven rhetorics of play. They include:

- *Mind or subjective play*: Play experiences that are largely centered on the creative, imaginative experience of the brain, such as daydreaming, fantasy role play, and playing with metaphors and analogy.

- *Solitary play*: Play experiences focused on the self and self-satisfaction, such as collections, listening to music, art projects, yoga, and crosswords.

- *Playful behaviors*: Play experiences that rely on the novelty of behavior, such as playing tricks, playing a part, putting something into play, gaming a system, or playing to the system's explicit requirements.

- *Informal social play*: Play enjoyed through the lack of structure and its relationship to socialization, such as joking, partying, and touring.

- *Playful celebrations and festivals:* Play centered on ceremony such as birthdays, religious celebrations, and weddings.

- *Contest play*: Play mainly involving competition and aiming to outperform others, such as athletics, lotteries, and drinking games

- *Risky or deep play*: Play which flirts with the edge of safety, engaging adrenaline and calling players because of its inherent risk or depth of experience. These include high risk extreme sports, bungee jumping, and skateboarding.

3.8 THE RHETORICS

The seven rhetorics are progress, fate, power, identity, imaginary, self, and frivolity. They are discussed individually here, first as Brian Sutton-Smith outlines them, and then subsequently as a design orientation toward which a game design can be manipulated. The rhetorics in themselves can be understood as seven elements of a composition. Depending on the aims of the game's design, these elements can be dialed up or down to meet specifics needs. Much like authors may choose to write toward Aristotelian dramatic structure (O'Neil and Lambert, 1982) or the hero's journey (Campbell, 2008), conventional game designs can use the observations of Sutton-Smith's seminal work to design and adjust a game.

3.8.1 Progress

Sutton-Smith (2009) writes that the rhetoric of play as progress "is the advocacy of the notion that animals and children, but not adults, adapt and develop through their play." The notion is clearly centered on the notion that play is valuable because it offers some an opportunity to refine or practice skills useful in the non-game world. This is the rhetoric applied when championing a game's real-world benefits whether they are social, physical, or mental. From this perspective, sports are valued for the ways they support physical health and playing chess for its mental challenges. In the digital world, this rhetoric is most easily seen in claims around play improving hand-eye coordination (Rosser et al., 2007), language skills (Rankin et al., 2006), and problem solving (Chen-Chung et al., 2011).

For a designer, the rhetoric of progress is the dimension of that game for which players see an opportunity to adapt and develop. The lure of play from such a perspective is in its non-game value. The attraction to the play experience comes from the play's ability to help the player progress toward a specific goal. The goal may be as practical as mastering a foreign language or as abstract as gaining social capital by being the first of their social group to complete a game. The player is attracted to the game's ability to take the player from one place to another (aka progress). In these terms, progress from one place is not from the real world to an imagined one, but instead from a starting point to a hoped level of accomplishment. The progress is the movement toward an accomplishment, whether it's collecting new words in a language learning game, driving a virtual car better than before, or completing crosswords puzzles.

The sense of progress in digital games has often been expressed as level and score. Players are given a sense of their progress by some marker that helps them know where they started and where they are now. These progress indicators help them to understand how they "develop through play." These markers also include the myriad of upgrades and other unlockable items that show other players how well another player has done. The accumulation of in-game currencies, for example, allows players to not only recognize but demonstrate their progress in a game environment. The V-bucks earnings accumulated in *Fortnite* (Epic Games, 2017) are a good example, as they allow players to earn in-game currency and then display their earnings via cosmetic items for their player character and other customizations.

As designers look to balance a play experience, it's easy to ask questions about the rhetoric of progress. Does the player have a sense of progression?

Does the game provide and report progress to the player and does it do so in a way that is meaningful and easy to understand and communicate? If not, including elements that clearly indicate progress to players should improve the appeal for players who seek this rhetoric in their play.

3.8.2 Fate

Sutton-Smith (2009) defines the rhetoric of fate in direct opposition to the rhetoric of progress. He claims this rhetoric rests "on the belief that human lives and play are controlled by destiny, by the gods, by atoms or neurons, or by luck." He claims that for this rhetoric, little rests on the player other than the player's "excel perhaps through the skillful use of magic or astrology." If progress is commendable and valued in society, fate is its opposite, considered in Sutton-Smith's view to be popular among the "lower socioeconomic groups" and generally not respected by "the intellectual elites" (Salen and Zimmerman, 2004, p. 304). Although some of Sutton-Smith's framing is arguably elitist and dismissive of beliefs contrary to his own, the observations are useful in game design.

Fate as a design element is typically expressed as some version of randomization. Those who understand digital randomization understand both that computer-generated random numbers are not truly random and that each has a seed on which its randomness is based. All the same, randomization is a common element of digital games that offers not only variability, but sometimes a sense of fate. These luck-of-the-draw moments are sometimes satisfying to players, and sometimes frustrating. In player-versus-player games, it's common, for example, for players to celebrate the luck of discovering a stronger weapon, a treasure of randomly generated in-game currency, or some other element of the rhetoric of fate. In large online games, part of the randomness involves players dropping into games, while in others, it's part of the play experience. *Fortnite*'s llama loot piñata is an example of the rhetoric of fate in practice.

As a designer, elements of fate serve multiple functions. They first add variability. This variability is not merely designed variability as perceived by the player, it is variability to which the designer has ceded control of the experience to fate. In a fighting game, agreeing to fight a randomly chosen opponent is a roll of the dice that assures the chips were not stacked against the player (although obviously the bounds of this dice roll are stipulated by the design). And, if the chips are stacked against the player, it's okay because it was a random assignment anyway. The release of designer culpability is a secondary opportunity for the designer. The player rarely faults the designer for the results of a random game element, unless the bounds of randomization exceed the limits of the game.

As a game design element, it's easy to see how players who are attracted to fate-based play, like gambling, are enticed by the lure of such play in a game. The moment the field of competitors for a car racing game is randomly generated is a moment of excitement for a player. It allows them to feel good about themselves if they win and can release them from feeling bad about themselves if they lose. The roll of the dice, the whims of digital gods, or whatever other generator of fate is to blame for a loss and to champion for a win. Games that offer little fate would likely be less attractive to people who enjoy and seek such play.

If a game's experience seems too managed, too much under the control and direction of the designer, introducing fate is an easy way to cede some of that control. Adding randomness, or event and character seeds that are based on things outside the designer's immediate control (e.g., a racing simulation's track weather depending on real-time, real-world weather) is an easy way to add an element of fate. Borrowing from analog games and allowing players the digital equivalent of spinning or rolling for selections is a good way to integrate the more complex attraction of fate. By allowing players to initiatives such actions, the designer is leaving a bit of the control to the player, allowing the impression, at least, that they can use their skill to roll or spin advantageously (even if it is an illusion of control). It might increase players interest, especially if they are drawn to other fate-based play.

3.8.3 Power

The rhetoric of play as power is largely focused on contest. It is one of the ancient rhetorics, as Sutton-Smith (2009) defines them, persisting historically among much of human play. For him, the rhetoric of power is "about the use of play as the representation of conflict and as a way to fortify the status of those who control the play or are its heroes." The rhetoric is "as ancient as warfare and patriarchy … an anathema to many modern progress and leisure play."

Power demonstrates itself frequently in digital play as competitive win scenarios. Situations where there are two or more players and one must prevail are obvious applications of the power rhetoric in game design. The power rhetoric is even present in situations where the player is trying to best the computer, as in the early chess simulation *Sargon* (Spracklen and Spracklen, 1978). It's worth noting that well before digital war simulations and first-person shooters, Sutton-Smith identified the obvious link to warfare and patriarchy.

Elements of power in games are typically comparative. They demonstrate which players are on top and which are not. They illuminate the contest focused elements of the game, providing leaderboards, describing comparative performance, or shinning a light on those that win. Such play is often framed by a goal of being the best, or at least better than the rest. While in ancient terms, the Olympic Games might be a prime example of such play, the contemporary elements of comparative scores and leaderboards are good examples of such. These include, of course, reporting the number of kills a player has completed in-game. *Fortnite*'s Battle Royale and its player-versus-player eliminations is a good example of this.

Dialing up the element of power is easily done by providing feedback to the player about their performance relative to others. This drives the play toward a sense of contest, but it's not the only way to do so. Games in which elimination occurs for poor performance is also a common element of power. Getting dropped from a car racing game, for falling too far behind, or removing players each round (as is part of some card games), are other common ways to increase the sense of power in a game. Any situation in which a player is supposed to be the last person standing, metaphorically, are heavy on the rhetoric of power as a design element.

3.8.4 Identity

The rhetoric of identity is about "confirming, maintaining or advancing the power and identity of the community of players." This historically happens through the use of parades and festivities, but also through representation. This rhetoric focuses on the representational character of play. It serves to provide a link between the player and the performance of play.

Identity is interesting because as a game design element, it is one that has only lately been pushed into focus. Consider, for example, the debate around gender and racial representation in game characters (Burgess et al., 2011). Much of the concern for players is focused on the representational qualities of the gameplay experience. The stereotypes and misrepresentations of culture within games frustrate players or even infuriate them. This is evidently less of a problem when in early computer graphics representations were more abstract and difficult to attribute to any one culture or identity. However as representational complexity increases, with not only graphical simulation, but with narrative and situational complexity—the sense for the rhetoric of identity increases. Although not a unique characteristic of the game, the distinct player character identities used with custom *Fortnite* players is a good example (e.g., distinct cosmetic player elements and the representation of that character in game space).

As a game design element, it's easy to see that opportunities for players to increase their sense of identity through (or often identifying with) game characters or elements of representation. The simple logic is that if a game represents a community, players want some way to find identity with those players. This is shown not only in real-world representations of genre or race but also in fictional play. Players of *Mario Kart*, for example, choose player characters and identify with them, even if they don't consider themselves to be a real-world Koopa or Bowser (Nintendo EAD, 2017).

This is where designing for the rhetoric of identity is most useful for a designer. It is in the notion that the designer can find ways for players to find identity in a game that offers the potential for balancing a game. Allowing the player to choose and even customize characters, cars, or whatever they use in the game helps them develop a sense of a representational relationship. That identity can help move the experience from a detached experience to one in which the representational relationship encourages the player to invest. These qualities also persist in situations where players might adopt a role, such as role-playing games in which players elect to be healers or spellcasters. An easy way to consider how much identity a game design offers is to ask how much of an opportunity the designer has given the player to say—that's me, or a representation of me, or people like me in the game.

It's important to note that identity and fate can sometimes be at odds. Where identity ties the player to the experience, for some players, fate can divorce them from it. This is because for those who are not confident in fate, or those who do not believe in it, fate becomes an adversarial force. Fate, from this perspective, becomes a reminder that either fate has a representation in the game or that the player's identity is subject to fate. Good examples of this tension are moments when a player asks why is my character wearing a pink shirt or why is my car advertising dish detergent? If the game chose these random attributes for the player, they might work against the player's sense of identity. This tension is part of the art of game design, as game design requires the balance of these elements in a way that holds the entire design together.

3.8.5 Imaginary

The rhetoric of the imaginary "idealizes the imagination, flexibility, and creativity of the animal and human play worlds." It views the value of play as a creative space, in which things like playful improvisation are valued. Sutton-Smith considers the rhetoric of the imaginary to be one of the modern rhetorics, when compared with the ancient.

The rhetoric of the imaginary as a game design element is best exemplified in supporting player creativity. Open worlds and sandboxes provide good examples of such play as they allow the player to engage in improvisational play within the designed experience. *Minecraft* (Mojang, 2009), for example, with its heavy emphasis on building is a good example. So too is the play with *Grand Theft Auto V* (Rockstar North, 2013), as both are mission-based play and non-mission play afford players a relatively wide array of solutions. In the world of *Fortnite*, this is most apparent in *Fortnite Creative*, but elements of the imaginary also exist in *Fortnite Battle Royale* (organizing squads, strategizing eliminations) and *Fortnite Save the World* (collecting resources and building shelter).

In game design, it's easy to ignore the opportunities in the imaginary by failing to support player improvisation. If there is only one way to solve a problem in a game, it is likely players seeking more imaginary rhetoric will dislike it. They are attractive to the variability and the rewards of coming up with their own, imagined solutions. Supporting such play is rewarding to such players, even if the ambiguity might frustrate other players.

It's also worth noting that employing the rhetoric of imagination has an interesting interplay with the rhetoric of progress. Players of *Minecraft* note the benefits of such creative play (i.e., progress in creative problem solving). Yet, in such games, there is little of the design to give a sense of progress within the domain. At best, games like *Minecraft* indicate progress in the imaginative rhetoric through play communities which critique other people's construction in the game. This is where increasing imaginative digital play is complicated. Imagination is a hard element to quantify, so players looking for the rhetoric of power can easily become frustrated with the realities that both optimal and suboptimal solutions work in a game. This is why some games support creative improvisation with in-game achievements and style points to help indicate progress and power.

In its purest sense, a play experience that is developed around the rhetoric of improvisation may not be an actual game. It may instead be structured play, which some argue is not a game but something else. It's also easy to forget that games like *Heads Up* (Ellen Games, 2017) are heavy on imaginative rhetoric.

3.8.6 Self

The rhetoric of self is focused on "solitary activities" in which the draw of play is focused on the individual experience of the player. The rhetoric aims to provide "the intrinsic or the aesthetic satisfactions." The value is simply, how it feels to play.

This element of game design is sometimes taken for granted. Designers think critically about the experience, its mechanics and dynamics, but as the MDA framework amplifies, players start at the aesthetics. Some game designs are very heavy on promoting a solitary, satisfying aesthetic experience as most evident in Thatgamecompany's *Flower* (Thatgamecompany, 2009) and *Journey* (Thatgamecompany, 2012). The fact that the co-author of the MDA framework contributed to the design of both games is evident in the highly praised aesthetic experience of both games. These games are heavy on the rhetoric of self, offering a unique experience centered on self (although *Journey* is realistically about two individual solitary experiences).

Designers who emphasize how a game feels are often thinking about the rhetoric of self. They are asking questions about the solitary experience of play. The play experience of *Fugl* (Team Fugl, 2017), is a good example of such focus. The experience in its early iterations was merely the experience of motion in a procedurally generated, voxel represented digital world. The focus is not on besting another player, of getting further than someone else, or in being more creative. Instead, the player is merely asked to experience a procedurally generated voxel landscape through a bird flying simulation.

When designing a playful experience, it's easy to lose track of the value of the aesthetic experience. More than merely thinking about the quality of art and sound, this experience is a combination of elements spanning moth ends of the MDA framework. It's also important to recognize that sometimes the aesthetic experience is intentionally broken. Games like *QWOP* (Foddy, 2008) are inviting because they are clunky and uncomfortable. Clunky and uncomfortable are part of their aesthetic or feel. The humor of the experience is also part of its solitary experience.

3.8.7 Frivolous

The last of Sutton-Smith's rhetorics is the rhetoric of the frivolous. Frivolous in this concept is "foolish," "idle," or the "puritanical negative." Such play is dismissed and valuable only in its escape. In its historical use, such play exists to juxtapose work, to offer the out-of-ordinary experience.

The frivolity of a game element is something that some designers easily forget in the formality of evaluating and iterating on a game. It is the element that is least formal in its execution and analysis, but one distinct to games. It is so informal that outlining elements of frivolity is awkward in writing. It is perhaps more appropriate to remind designers that the foolishness of play, or its whimsy, is an element that must not be ignored. Failing to apply may be the difference from that which is playful and that which is not (or at least not perceived as such).

As a designer, recognizing these types of play can help in adjusting the appeal or potential fun of any designed experience. It's important to understand that any designed experience can incorporate multiple elements of each of these. If a player experience offers multiple elements, it may also offer an opportunity to widen the audience.

Consider many widely appealing play activities, like professional sports. Professionals sports not only offer contest play as one team works to best another. They also offer a sense of playful celebration, with the ceremony of the start and the ending of play, which may include parades and other ceremonies distinct to the sport. Watching sport on television can be solitary play or group play, as contrasted by watching it at home in the solitude of a den or live in the clamor of a stadium. Audiences maintain fantasy teams (imaginative play), dress in the colors and costumes of their teams (playful ceremony), joke about the opposing teams (informal social play), and remain captivated as injured players are carried off the field (risky play). Such play is not limited to the people playing the game, it extends to the audience that watches its play. It inspires others to play, such as little leagues and game watching parties. I would argue that one of the best ways to inspire a wide impact with a playful experience is to design an experience that affords for the widest inroads for each of these elements.

If you were to try to determine why widely engaged play activities are fun, it's likely you'd find different answers from the play community. Some players like the strategy of the experience, others like the element of imagination or the risk of the experience. This is true for play experiences as seemingly widely divergent as the Eurovision Song Contest to the United States' Super Bowl.

In addition to understanding the fun derived from these individuals appeals and play profiles, it's useful to consider how play is embraced by players. Brian Sutton-Smith offers another useful set of categorizations for this need. He describes them as the rhetorics of play. These rhetorics are the claims for the value of play in society, but they also function as a way to adjust a game to appeal to potential players. They include:

- *Play as imaginary*: Play's value is in its ability to unearth the unexpected or support improvisation. Such play is useful and appealing because it brings out something otherwise hard to extract from people. Hence, people play with ideas.

- *Play as self*: Play value comes from the solitary joy of the experience itself. It is appealing to bang a pencil on the table or kick a ball because it simply feels good.

- *Play as frivolous*: The value of play is a product of its mere entertainment. Play is good for its entertainment and the frivolous juxtaposition to that which is non-frivolous.

- *Play as identity*: Play is important because it is part of the player's identity. A former football player continues to be a football fan because they play is part of their identity.

- *Play as progress*: The notion that play is useful because it is a way to practice. Play is valuable because it is a way to practice, such as playing an instrument to become better at it.

- *Play as fate*: The idea that fate is in itself an interesting thing to play with and perhaps even a system that can be guessed or divined.

- *Play as power*: Play is valued because it supports demonstrating who is best. It appeals because such a comparison is valuable and winning or being better than another is important, in the least as a proxy for power.

These rhetorics can function as another way to evaluate a playful experience's appeal. They nest with aforementioned types of play to offer a way of framing elements of a playful experience formally. If, for example, people with a play profile biased toward gambling are not interested in a design, it might make sense to add more chance. If players don't feel enough sense of self in the game, adding customization is an easy way to potentially increase the appeal for those players.

Thinking critically, this is a way to explain the national appeal of the Olympics which serve as a way to address so many of these rhetorics in one set of play-focused events. The contest is play focused on power, with one nation winning over another. The ceremonies, from the parades to the medals, are part of its link to the rhetoric of identity. Elements of fate exist in everything from varying weather conditions to who competes each year and all the other variables that are not ruled against in such play.

It's then easy to see how making something fun, especially across a wide audience, is often about making sure the elements of play touch upon the varied interests of the players.

3.9 PRACTICE WHAT YOU'VE LEARNED

- Practice the many different design methodologies on a small-scale design task. Revise a simple game like catch, tic-tac-toe, or tag through these designed experiences. Or take an early 1980s game and apply the design methodologies to them. How does each design method shape the game?

- Practice drafting concept statements for existing games in the social impact space. Apply a few of the design methods to adapt new concept statements for the games. Have you improved the game or made it worse?

- List the many ways that work tasks become fun. Where is the border between work, play, and fun crossed and what helped move the work through the stages?

REFERENCES

11 bit studios. *This War of Mine*. 11 bit studios, 2014.
Accidental Queens. *Another Lost Phone: Laura's Story*. Accidental Queens, 2017. http://anotherlostphone.com/.
Bogost, Ian. 10th Games for Change Festival. 2013. https://www.youtube.com/watch?v=GBduFJUdoog.
Brown, Mark. "Apple bans Phone Story game that exposes seedy side of smartphone creation." *Wired Game| Life* (2011) https://www.wired.com/2011/09/phone-story/.
Brown, Stuart L. *Play: How it Shapes the Brain, Opens the Imagination, and Invigorates the Soul*. New York: Penguin, 2009.
Burgess, Melinda C.R., Karen E. Dill, S. Paul Stermer, Stephen R. Burgess, and Brian P. Brown. "Playing with prejudice: The prevalence and consequences of racial stereotypes in video games." *Media Psychology* 14, no. 3 (2011): 289–311.
Campbell, Joseph. *The Hero with a Thousand Faces*, Vol. 17. Novato, CA: New World Library, 2008.

Capcom. *Bionic Commando*. Capcom, 1988.

Deterding, Sebastian. "Gamification: Designing for motivation." *Interactions* 19, no. 4 (2012): 14–17.

Ellen Games, *Heads Up*. Warner Bros., 2017.

Epic Games. *Fortnite*. Epic Games, 2017.

Flanagan, Mary. *Critical Play: Radical Game Design*. Cambridge, MA: MIT Press, 2009.

Foddy, Bennett. *QWOP*. Bennett Foddy, 2008. http://www.foddy.net/Athletics. html.

Fullerton, Tracy. *Game Design Workshop: A Playcentric Approach to Creating Innovative Games*. Boca Raton, FL: AK Peters/CRC Press, 2014.

Grace, Lindsay D. "Critical gameplay: Designing games to critique convention." In *Proceedings of the 20th ACM International Conference on Multimedia*, 1185–1188. ACM, 2012.

Hunicke, Robin, Marc LeBlanc, and Robert Zubek. "MDA: A formal approach to game design and game research." *Proceedings of the AAAI Workshop on Challenges in Game AI* 4, no. 1 (2004): 1722.

Liu, Chen-Chung, Yuan-Bang Cheng, and Chia-Wen Huang. "The effect of simulation games on the learning of computational problem solving." *Computers & Education* 57, no. 3 (2011): 1907–1918.

Mojang. *Minecraft*. Mojang, 2009.

Molleindustria. *Phone Story*. Molleindustria, 2011. http://www.phonestory.org/.

Nintendo EAD. *Mario Kart 8 Deluxe*. Nintendo, 2017.

O'Neill, Cecily, and Alan Lambert. *Drama Structures*. London: Hutchinson, 1982.

The Pixel Hunt. *Bury Me, My Love*. Dear Villagers, 2017. http://burymemylove. arte.tv/.

Rankin, Yolanda A., Rachel Gold, and Bruce Gooch. "Evaluating interactive gaming as a language learning tool." In *Proceedings for ACM SIGGRAPH Conference, New York*. 2006.

Rockstar North. *Grand Theft Auto V*. Rockstar Games, 2013.

Rosser, James C., Paul J. Lynch, Laurie Cuddihy, Douglas A. Gentile, Jonathan Klonsky, and Ronald Merrell. "The impact of video games on training surgeons in the 21st century." *Archives of Surgery* 142, no. 2 (2007): 181–186.

Ruiz, Susana, Ashley York, Mike Stein, Noah Keating, and Kellee Santiago. *Darfur is Dying*. 2006. http://www.darfurisdying. com.

Russell, Steve. *Spacewar!* Steve Russell, 1962.

Salen, Katie, and Eric Zimmerman. *Rules of Play: Game Design Fundamentals*. MIT Press, Cambridge, 2004.

Spracklen, Kathe and Dan Spracklen. *Sargon*. Kathe Spracklen and Dan Spracklen. , 1978.

Sutton-Smith, Brian. *The Ambiguity of Play*. Cambridge, MA: Harvard University Press, 2009.

Tavinor, Grant. "Bioshock and the art of rapture." *Philosophy and Literature* 33, no. 1 (2009): 91–106.

Team Fugl. *Fugl*. Kotori Studios Ltd., 2017. http://fuglgame.com/.

Thatgamecompany. *Journey*. Sony Computer Entertainment, 2012.

Thatgamecompany. *Flower*. Sony Computer Entertainment, 2009.

Urban Ministries of Durham. *Spent, the online game about surviving poverty and homelessness reaches its millionth play and invites Congress to accept the challenge* [Press release]. 2011. http://www.umdurham.org/assets/files/pdf/SPENT1mmRelease_FINAL.pdf.

Vonnegut, Kurt. *Slaughterhouse 5. 1969*. London: Triad, 1987.

Yee, Nick. "The gamer motivation profile: What we learned from 250,000 gamers." In *Proceedings of the 2016 Annual Symposium on Computer-Human Interaction in Play*. ACM, 2016.

CHAPTER 4

Educational Games

A s mentioned in Chapter 2, one of the most obvious purposes of play is education. In animals, play can serve as training for serious skills like hunting or experimenting with learning how to gather food. It is no surprise then that structured play, or games, can serve the same function.

Games designed to serve educational needs form a sort of foundation for the many ways we aim to do things with games. At the heart of most games, there is some form of learning and assessment. For any game, designers must communicate the rules in a way that makes them understandable to new players—this is a kind of teaching goal. Games also often require players to practice them, learning the nuances of their rules sets, and experimenting with how they can perform within the rules of the game. Many games are also built around rigid assessments that require the player to perform well enough to remain in the game. A baseball player, for example, gets three attempts to hit the ball before they lose their opportunity to be a batter. In arcade car racing games, there's often a timer at checkpoints. Failing to make it the checkpoint in time may result in the game being over. Digital games also have a kind of matriculation schedule, where the better the player gets the more ability they earn in the world.

As a designer, to give a player an enjoyable experience, you may want to skip what they already know and move right to what they don't. So, for example, if the player is already comfortable with the rule set or actions of the game, you don't want to bore them with a tutorial explaining what they already understand. To do so, you need some way of assessing their current skills. This is likely some basic form of assessing the player's ability and understanding of the game rules. The player may be required to do something in the game to skip through such explanation. In some car racing games, for example, players unlock licenses to earn better cars. This achieves two things that improve the player's experience. First, it gives them a sense of progress. Second, and more importantly, inexperienced players avoid the frustration of not being able to control cars that may require more driving skill than they have. It's a bit like the height requirements for amusement rides. Until the player has reached a certain height, the experience will not be very good for them.

Other times, the designer may simply be trying to make the design as engaging as possible by employing the right balance of skill and mastery. If a player is tasked with too many up-front challenges, the game can quickly become overwhelming. Think of the experience of sitting behind the cockpit of an airplane. All the buttons, levers, and switches can be intimidating. They would be less so if the first time you sat behind the cockpit, only the flight yoke was available. Once you were able to master the yoke, other switches and buttons would be unlocked. This isn't just good design, it's good education. Introducing algebra and trigonometry in your very first math class can be intimidating. Instead, you started with the basics—counting. This approach is common in many game designs, whether it's about killing dragons, making new animal friends, or learning a language.

As an example, consider the standard design of an action video game. The player plays with a set of abilities, perhaps shooting from a spaceship. When they demonstrate, in game, that they can do that well, the challenges increase, but so to do the opportunities. The more the player does well, the more opportunity or ability the player is given. The laser gun will have a missile added, the player's speed increases, and so do the number of enemies. This is a very common formula for making play engaging.

While there are many ways to describe the way psychology and education intersect to make this happen, one model has demonstrated clear application in game design. Named by Mihály Csíkszentmihályi in 1975, the flow state model outlines the balance between challenge and skill to support optimal performance. In short, as a designer, one way to think about the ramp-up schedule of challenge and skill expectation is to think of it in terms of Csíkszentmihályi's flow. If there is very little skill and very little challenge, the player may be apathetic about the entire experience. If too much challenge is required for the unskilled player, they may become anxious and overwhelmed. Your goal is to balance player

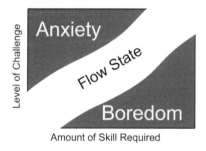

FIGURE 4.1 Csíkszentmihályi's concept of a flow state is a way to design games that can balance player skill and challenge.

skill with the tasks the game requires. Doing so helps the player fall into a rhythm, the zone. It's worth mentioning that this is not only a pattern put forth by Csíkszentmihályi. It's also a pattern common to a variety of practices about peak performance and state, including Buddhism, Taoism, and some forms of yoga (Figure 4.1).

4.1 FEEDBACK SYSTEMS AND ASSESSMENT

Many games, particularly digital games, are perpetual feedback systems that are continually assessing, reporting, and responding. If the player does well, then the challenge is increased. If the player is doing poorly, the play might be adapted accordingly. Games like *Super Mario Kart* (Nintendo EAD, 1992), for example, are very good at assessing individual player performance and adjusting play accordingly. In the game, if a player is doing well, the kinds of power ups, or potential aid they get from the game's system are pretty low impact. If the player is doing poorly, they can get some exceptionally powerful power-ups. The decision as to who gets the magic bullet, one of the most powerful power-ups, which pilots the player toward the middle of the pack, is really about who needs it the most.

This balance of performance and support is commonly called rubber-banding. It happens in non-digital play too, often as a set of negotiated rules between players or as part of a rule system designed to bring all players into competition. In non-digital games, it comes in the form of exceptions allowed for younger players, as handicaps in scores, or as age group and experience divisions in a race. Setting classes of players, such as age groups in races, is a way of rubber-banding the experience. In some races, there are literally calculations for these balances. In autocross car racing, for example, cars are classed based on their performance, and race times are multiplied by this value. So, for example, when a Class A Ferrari finishes two seconds ahead of a Class F Toyota, the calculated times may result in the Toyota winning. The idea is that if the same driver was behind both cars, they actually performed better in the Toyota (given the car's limitations). This is a way of not only balancing the competitive play space, but also of allowing widely disparate players to inhabit the same virtual play space or territory. It provides feedback to the players that encourages them to play together. Without such calculations, the individual cars perform so differently that the players wouldn't really be playing together. Yet with these calculations, the players are pulled back together into the same playing space. The calculation is the rubber band that binds them.

Rubber-banding, or leveling the game's experience so that amateur and pro can play together, is a very simple example of how games are often assessing player performance to create a better experience. The elements of a game add a layer that pulls the play experience of players together. It does so mainly in the way it assesses players. It is why there are bantamweight and heavyweight champions and why contests have levels of competition. It helps players understand how their performance will be assessed, and often we feel best when we are compared with a performance similar to our own. This is the reason Csíkszentmihályi's flow matters. Even when players are competing at different levels, the impression that the challenge and the skill are appropriately balanced matters. Few people like to play unwinnable games, just as few people want to take a class they are sure they will never pass. That exercise in assessment is an important one, as it is a common focus in educational games.

4.2 GAMES AS EDUCATIONAL SYSTEMS

But assessment is not the only way games integrate with educational goals. Games are also information-rich environments. They encourage players to learn about large sets of information, respond quickly, and learn their rules, sometimes in real time. It is for this reason that games have also been championed as opportunities to educate.

The usual examples of players learning in games that were not intended to be education include the vast array of characters a young Pokémon (Creatures Inc., 1996) card game player might memorize, or the many rules and statistics players of role-playing games learn and process to make appropriate in-game decisions.

At the same time, games based in the real world have provided players with lots of information about the world they depict. The historically accurate architecture in *Assassin's Creed 3* (Ubisoft Montreal, 2012), for example, has been credited with providing a kind of special knowledge and appreciation for architecture.

There are many different ways to learn and discuss educational games. There are games that are designed to provide information, through repetition, exposure, or experience. There are games that are designed to assess, either as a self-assessment or to feed a system that aims to gauge a player's understanding, attitude, or ability.

4.3 GAMES AS TEACHERS

One way to frame the design of games is to consider them as a kind of teacher. If you understand the framing of games as a set of problems, then it is clear that games introduce fundamental approaches to problem solving and conflict resolution. The designer writes the problem and offers the possibilities for solutions. It could be argued that each game is merely a test. Or that each game is an opportunity for a player to experiment in a physical, digital, or conceptual lab designed by the game's designer. In this way, games could be understood as a teacher. When games are properly designed, they task the player with demonstrating understanding by solving problems and practicing specific skills.

It's reasonable to frame most games as educational. Games require players to learn their rules, and by playing, they prove their understanding of them. The learning curve experienced by those who have not played specific games demonstrates the fundamental knowledge required to play them.

This knowledge extends beyond the motor skills needed to succeed at an action game, the physical prowess required by sports, or the focus of a poker player. Depending on the context, it includes technical knowledge, historical knowledge, and some scientific knowledge. Learning the difference between a solid wooden baseball bat, a hollow corked bat, and an aluminum one is a lesson in physics and history (corked bats have been used to the embarrassment of major league baseball cheaters). Drafting behind another player in a racing game is an application of basic physics, reducing the effort for the follower. Learning how to organize a raid in a role-playing game is a combination of teamwork and leadership, which requires players to index appropriate spells and skills. Calculating probabilities in blackjack or learning the language of poker are all kinds of learning and practice.

Of course, the one obvious drawback of such learning is that much of it is focused on the rules within the game. It is learning that is useful to the fiction of the game, but not necessarily to the world outside the fiction.

Learning the lineage of characters in *The Hobbit* (Tolkien, 1937) series, for example, does not make a person a real-world historian.

In other instances, the knowledge gained from playing video games is not limited to fiction. Players of simulation games learn a significant amount because a simulation is based on real-world elements. Consider the example of *Gran Turismo* (Polys Entertainment, 1997), a franchise which has gone through several iterations and spawned a collection of other racing simulations. The game employs a competency-based system of matriculation that allows players to graduate through race car ranks by proving that they can master skills in acceleration, breaking, holding a racing line, and other fundamentals. In *Gran Turismo*, objective matriculation through the system is augmented by the creative problem-solving skill set employed by purchasing the appropriate car for the track and modifying the race car through true-to-life principles of physics. The game goes so far as to allow players to modify camber, drag coefficient, and others—all very technical elements in modifying a car to adjust its physics around a track. Now consider that people who have driven cars for decades know less about camber than players of games like *Gran Turismo*.

Simulations, such as *Torcs*, an open-source game, have proven useful in a variety of research studies. For players though, it is not merely an exercise in turning when appropriate, it is a world that requires engineering knowledge and skill to navigate. This is one way, particularly with simulations, where games function as a kind of teacher (Figure 4.2).

What is remarkable about games in this context is that they apply learning as a necessity that compels the player. Educators often discuss

FIGURE 4.2 Car racing games like *Torcs* contain a kind of rubric for car racing. This particular car racing game is open source and is useful for doing a variety of academic research. (Courtesy of berniw, torcs [https://sourceforge.net/projects/torcs/] through the GNU Public License.)

the challenges of making course content relevant. Yet relevance is, in such games as these, immediate. Students of any car racing game will literally be left behind if they do not succeed. Yet, like a good instructor, evaluation in the game world is consistent, perpetual, and objective.

A quick glance at the game mechanics and game objectives of any car-racing game indicate some clear learning outcomes. The competencies for any car racing game might read:

- Understand the mechanical use of specific items in the car: throttle, breaking, gearing

- Understand the physical properties of drag, weight, and raw materials (e.g., carbon fiber, aluminum) as they relate to high speed vehicle performance

- Recognize the model, make, shape and performance characteristics of international vehicles produced Ford, Honda, Toyota, and others

- Understand the core racing classes, licensure, and track locations

- Increase understanding of driving control and strategy

These objectives read as though they were ripped from a course syllabus on technical driving. Each is an independent concept that would require hours of disciplined study to master. Yet, even if studied in a traditional classroom, the instruction would lack the practical application that many students desire.

However, these learning objectives are met, demonstrated, and reinforced during gameplay, which is paced for the student's specific needs. The play experience necessitates the educational experience. The player cannot play well until they understand, and the more they understand, the more they get to play.

4.3.1 Understanding versus Reporting

This is also a fundamental difference between education in many school environments and education in the game world. In the game world, there is a need for understanding, not just simple recitation. You cannot succeed in most major games by memorizing vocabulary or having the ability to report back what you just heard.

If you are to beat someone in an FPS, you must understand how the weapons work, where the weapons are most effective, the geography of the space, objectives, and others. This character of games distinguishes it from a variety of other forms of entertainment. While it is common for a sports fan to earn the respect of their peers from the ability to recall specific statistics or to report scores, it is rarely the place for earned respect among the game-playing community. This recitation of statistics is instead often eclipsed by evaluation of a player's performance in the game world.

It may alternatively be argued that games that follow the Simon says game template of listen and repeat are exercises in recitation. These games include the well-established *Dance Dance Revolution* (Konami, 1998) game type and the musical *Rock Band* (Harmonix, 2007) franchises. It is fairly true that these games employ a mechanic that simply requires the player to follow directions, but these games are perhaps better diagnoses as exercises in following direction, anticipation, and timing.

To succeed in these games, it is not enough to repeat the material provided. The player must be able to respond at the appropriate time and under the appropriate context. In this way, the games are more akin to exams in geography that require great memorization, but also contextualization. They are more like an oratory recitation, in which good performance is not merely repeating the content, but knowing the content so that it can be reported back with the right emphasis (e.g., in the tradition of oral recitation of great Latin speeches). It can also be argued that the exergame *Dance Dance Revolution* is in itself a physical education, practicing specific muscle groups similar to techniques in an aerobics class.

4.4 VIEWING PLAYERS AS STUDENTS

As many educators have written before, it is not enough to simply tack on education and it is not enough to hope that the merit of being merely educational will allow the game to be a success (Gee, 2005). In reality, most games are not intended to be educational games, they are intended to be entertaining.

What's useful to a designer is to think of the player like a student. What does the student need to succeed at any given point? Which tests are too hard and which tests are too easy? What really needs to be tested and what is perhaps a distraction? These questions, borne from framing the player as student, help the design of a game.

The core concept is rather simple. As a designer, you are not only evaluating the player through play, you are scaffolding an experience. The scaffolding forms a complete experience. The experience may be entirely new to the player, requiring the designer to introduce elements methodically to avoid an overwhelming or intimidating experience. The experience may be familiar, at which point the designer is trying to structure the experience in a unique and interesting way.

Framing players as students also puts a significant onus on the designer. Designers aren't teaching players directly, they are designing the systems that make teachers. Like teaching, the player's failure may be due to the teacher's failure to structure the right educational experience through the game. If few players can get past a challenge the designer added to the game, then there may be a problem with the way the game is teaching the player to achieve (assuming that the game is designed to be won). If the teacher must meet the needs of the students, then the game must meet the needs of the player. If you design games, you must understand how to read player needs and adjust the game accordingly.

Many designers don't actually recognize that this is what they are doing. But thinking critically about the many ways that games are designed, the dynamic of teacher and student becomes evident. In iterative game design practices, where the designers are created, played, and evaluated, the focus is on getting feedback quickly to refine the experience. It's like writing a test, checking to see if it's too hard or too easy, and refining that test again. Or, it's like being in a classroom, reading the experience of the students and adjusting the assignments based on student performance and experience. In order to do so, their needs to be clear feedback systems to which the designer responds.

4.5 FEEDBACK SYSTEMS AS DESIGN MODEL

An easy way to understand the dynamic of a game is through a feedback system. Players provide input and the play becomes output. What is output depends on the game and its structure. A game of tic-tac-toe takes marks on a paper (X or O) as input. The output is the resulting set of possibilities. Play is perpetuated by the loop between input and output. The play signal, that indication that an invitation to play is being accepted, is a two-step feedback system. First, a player indicates they want to play, then the other player responds in kind. It is a dialogue common to all play and a shorthand for understanding what needs to be designed.

Games are designed to provide input and output. The games players practice in-game are their input in the game world. The results of their play are the output. Whether it's the reaction of a ball hitting a bat or the button-press that fires a weapon at an alien, there's typically some action and some reaction. Since game designers are creating the entire set of actions and reactions, inputs and outputs, they are designers of a feedback system.

Game design uses the feedback system to teach its play. If the system is effective, the student understands it. If it is designed well, the student seeks more of its experience, attempting its challenges and interrogating it for more and more output. A good design is one that propels players to engage with its feedback system repeatedly, providing input and seeking output. The complexity of that system varies greatly and is largely dependent on the needs of the designer.

4.6 KNOWING INPUT AND OUTPUT

If games are considered complex feedback systems with input and output, then educational games can also be framed by these two types: input and output. It's useful to think about a game focused on providing information as an output game. It functions like a broadcast, pushing its voice out with the hope that the player listens.

At the other end is an assessment game, which focuses on input. The player plays, and the assessment game takes the play as its input. The game's focus is not on sending information, but is instead on collecting information. The play may be used as a replacement for a test, and it might be used to gauge a more accurate or unique kind of input. Yet, like input, it's important that what is collected is useful. Assessment, or an input-focused game, is only as good as the data it collects.

This dichotomy of input and output, or information and feedback, is not a common way to discuss educational games, but it is a useful one from a design perspective. Many people in educational games have specific terms for the aim of their work. While the specifics of this terminology will change over the years, it's useful to form some basic concepts to help differentiate educational intent. While it was important to understand what is meant by such terminology, from a design perspective, it's also useful to simply know the primary goal of the game. Is it intended to impart information, evaluate information acquired elsewhere, or both? This simple distinction will dictate the variability of the experience, the best verbs, and the kind of goals that need to be met for both the team that wants to create the game and the players.

4.7 INFORMATION GAMES

Information games abound. The earliest digital games in the education domain were largely information games. They sought to provide players with a resource and often merely encoded what was available elsewhere, turning a book chapter or encyclopedia article into a playable experience.

Information games are based on a broadcast feedback model, where information is imparted, and little is requested back. The feedback is simply a ping back to the game system indicating that the broadcast was received. This is the model of a game that aims to teach players a bit of information, such as vocabulary or geography. The games are often most focused on providing the information than assessing whether or not it was understood. More advanced information games might expose student-players to a new way of understanding a problem, a new perspective, or a new process. A game that focuses on the day in the life of an unfamiliar animal might be much more focused on information than assessment. It merely aims to expose, not evaluate.

4.8 ASSESSMENT GAMES

Assessment games on the other hand focus on the evaluation of the player's performance. They may expect that the player already has certain competencies. If the information game is the study sheet, the assessment game is the quiz. Assessment games give immediate feedback about the player's performance and place evaluation as their primary goal. Where an information game may allow a player to say, that's nice, tell me more, an assessment tells the player far more than it asks.

Where exposure is the aim of an information game, an assessment game assumes exposure and looks to evaluate understanding. Does the player understand linear algebra or can they accurately identify the branches of government? The goal with an assessment game is, as you'd expect, assessment.

4.9 MIXING INFORMATION AND ASSESSMENT GAMES

Games that aim to provide information and ask players to practice are often a mix of both information and assessment games. In reality, very few games are entirely just information games or assessment games. Instead, they mix the two, and as mentioned previously, adjust the game's challenge. This distinction, or the false dichotomy, is more a way for you, as a designer, to frame the primary aim of the game. It allows you to point the needle in the direction you plan to head, with an understanding that you'll probably be somewhere between the two.

Adaptive testing was all the rage when it was first introduced, but in reality, many games had been designed around adaptive testing for years

FIGURE 4.3 A typing game, called *Letter Blaster*, which uses the incremental and adaptive challenge to meet the player's ability, balancing skill and challenge to work toward a flow state.

previously. A good example of an older digital game is a typing tutor, like *Type Attack* (Sirius Software, 1982). In these games, the player is asked to type a letter to shoot down a specific falling letter. Similar to the mechanics of *Space Invaders* (Taito, 1978) or *Missile Command* (Atari, Inc., 1980), the letters fall toward the player and failure to type the right key means the destruction of the player's space. The common algorithm for this type of game is to start simple and expand the available letters as play proceeds. The player starts with the letters ASD (the letters where the left hand should be for traditional typing training). If the player succeeds, then letters from the right hand are introduced (e.g., JKL). The longer they play, the more exotic the keystroke, until the entire keyboard is engaged in the pattern (Figure 4.3).

Another more contemporary example is *Guitar Hero*. Unlike the typing tutor game, however, *Guitar Hero*, *Rock Band*, and all of its equivalent clones do something different. Instead of increasing the challenge dynamically based on performance, the challenge remains pretty much the same during play. The player selects or is given a song at a particular difficulty and the difficulty remains the same during play. Lower levels involve using fewer buttons on the guitar controller, although the dynamics of a song do affect the game's challenge.

Instead, to offer more challenge, the player is rewarded visually and with points when they do the work of the game well. They gain recognition for 72 notes in a row without an error, and they unlock opportunities to score even better with a correct note streak. This approach is simply a complement to the aforementioned approach. Both work, and both have their advantages and disadvantages

One of the caveats of a game that perpetually increases its challenge is that it can be fairly unforgiving. Players must perpetually perform better to expand their experience. Likewise, as a feedback system, players are fairly aware of how they are doing. This is good, in that it's honest and fair, but it can also be disheartening and critical. By analogy, think of it as a teacher who asks you interesting questions until you get one wrong. Once you get one wrong, the questions get simpler and simpler until you are not particularly interested in any of the questions being asked. As a student, you are aware that something is going wrong, and the reward for trying is something simpler and simpler. It's like being offered training wheels the first time you fall off a bike. Keep falling off and you may find you're switched to a tricycle.

On the other hand, self-selected, non-dynamic systems can be frustrating because they can produce a very flat experience. The player must wait until the task is complete, such as a 4-minute song, to get the full experience of an interesting experience. That can be pretty frustrating to the player too. Especially for players who are not good or do not know how to self-assess (Figure 4.4).

FIGURE 4.4 The game *Function Force*, produced at the weekend-long White House Game Jam, does a good job of providing feedback to players and balancing its challenges. It aims to assess student understanding of linear functions and was produced by Dr. Josh McCoy, Dr. Mike Treanor, and Chris Totten in 2014. (Courtesy of Josh McCoy, Mike Treanor, and Chris Totten.)

4.10 INFO GAMES: INFORMATION THROUGH PLAY

One of the things you've likely started to notice is that the definition of an educational game is fairly broad. That's because a variety of games that aim to educate aren't always labeled as educational games. If a game is designed to sell players on the prowess of a certain car, for example, it would be considered an "advergame." But, at the core of that advertising is education. The designers of the game want players to learn the merits of their product. This is why, for nearly all designs that seek to deliver information, educational game design is foundational. As you'll read in a future chapter, educational game design also comes with some ethical and moral responsibilities, but for now, it's simply useful to remember that the rules and aims of providing information with an educational goal are part of not only games for the classroom, but for a variety of non-classroom uses.

Typically, when people talk about educational games, they refer to the collection of games that are directly linked to formal education. These are often games designed around specific curriculum and training. They might include a game for training emergency medical staff, explaining surgery, assessing a middle school student's understanding of linear equations, and more. In common parlance, this is useful, like other titles, as it helps focus the discussion and tasks at hand.

As you now no doubt realize, games in education have been around for a very long time. They certainly predate the notion of a game designer. However, if you've ever suffered through a poorly constructed educational game, you'll also recognize why game designers can greatly improve the play experience.

Consider the rather widely praised educational game, *Oregon Trail* (Rawitsch, Heinemann, and Dillenberger, 1974). The game was originally developed to teach school children about the realities of 19th-century pioneer life in the United States. It was produced by the Minnesota Educational Computing Consortium in 1974. The player assumes the role of a leader of a caravan of settlers traveling from Independence, Missouri, to Oregon's Willamette Valley in 1848.

As practice for understanding the design, it's useful to dissect the elements of the game that compel learning. Applying the pattern of goal, obstruction, and means to achieving the goal, *Oregon Trail* is pretty easy to understand.

- *Goal*: Get to Oregon by crossing the American West

- *Obstruction*: The challenges that faced settlers of the day, disease, hunting, raids, finances, etc.

- *Means*: Careful planning, spending resources, packing appropriately, accepting tradeoffs, a little luck, and some skill

As an educational experience, the message of the game is immediately clear. Getting to Oregon takes careful planning, accepting tradeoffs, a little luck, and some skill. The game itself creates the environment and emphasizes the lessons it seeks to provide. As any player of *Oregon Trail* learned, it was not improbable for a traveler to die of dysentery.

The way this kind of design works so well is evident in its structure. It selectively simulates. The design selects the elements that are both interesting to play and important lessons in the larger understanding of the game world. The player makes decisions that affect the health of the individual party members and their progress toward a single destination. It exposes the challenges of life on the trail, but only the ones that seemed important to the designers.

It's important to note that, for example, the game does little to acknowledge the tensions of race in Oregon or the source of tension between native populations and the settlers. It does what many designed experiences do. It emphasizes only the elements that seemed appropriate to the designers at that time. More recent evaluations of the game are critical of the game's interpretation of settler life.

4.11 FIRST STEPS IN DESIGNING WITH EDUCATIONAL GOALS

To create this kind of design, it's important to outline your learning objectives. It's best to start from the top and then work your way down. First, what is the primary goal of the entire experience? These primary goals might be as general as teach Japanese, or as specific as helping someone memorize the elements of the periodic table. The primary goal of the game is your design, the metric by which you will evaluate your success or failure. The goal should be chosen carefully and should be appropriate to the scope, scale, and resources you have. That doesn't mean a small budget can't shoot for a big goal. As you'll learn, good game design can bridge the gap between large and small budgets through effective design.

Once that primary learning goal is chosen, the next step is to subdivide that goal into smaller sets. For some domains, like language learning, educators have already constructed a variety of ways to teach the material. There are idiom and phrasal models, there are vocabulary models, and so on. Regardless of whether or not you think there's already a framework for delivering the education you hope to provide through the game, you should check. Sometimes allied fields offer useful models. For many disciplines, particularly in formal learning, there are learning progressions. These are maps of what students should master at which level of their education. Learning progression can sometimes map neatly to a set of game activities.

When doing anything with games and any form of education, it is important to learn about the discipline, product, or subject. It would be foolish of any game designer to create an educational game without either working with a subject matter expert in education or studying the topic. Every game does not require in-depth knowledge of its subject, but failure to get some exposure is naive at best. You wouldn't paint mountains without having seen them, and you wouldn't make claims about what your game will do without some sense of how it has been accomplished in the past.

When working with subject matter experts in education a variety of core concepts are likely to arise. When doing things with games, there is always a level of research. Even if what you are doing has never been done before, parts of it have. To return once again to the music analogy, every note has been played, but your job is to arrange them in a way that's new and interesting for your audience.

Regardless of whether or not models for subdividing the topic exist and prior examples of work have been completed, it's important to select the sub goals that will lead to your primary goal. These are the learning objectives that will feed your long-term learning goal. So, for a Japanese language learning game, the sub goals might be to recognize numbers, recognize colors, and respond to greetings. These are merely a subset of the entire goal of teaching Japanese, but they help focus your efforts as a designer. The subset makes the larger goal not only achievable but assessable. They are smaller bite-sized achievements that allow you to make progress toward your larger goal. At the very least, they serve as helping you as a designer know how your project is progressing. They help you know if you are 30% of the way there or almost done.

As you've likely guessed, each of your learning objectives, or sub goals, will help focus your design. With a long-term goal and a set of learning objectives, you have the basics to start designing an educational game. But how?

One first step, but certainly not the only one, is to start thinking about appropriate game verbs that match the learning objectives. For recognizing color, for example, an easy game verb might be matching. The player may need to match the English language color to the appropriate Japanese language color equivalent. Since there are many matching mechanics, from the card game Uno (Mattel, 2014) to the mobile mechanics of match three games like *Bejeweled* (PopCap, 2001), it should be easy to see how game mechanics can come from a match verb in a language learning game. Likewise, simply asking the player to match the sound to a color would work for a game that's about hearing instead of reading the language.

An alternative first step is to consider how the sub goals could work in unison. So, for example, could they be tied together with a narrative or a situation? In this approach, the result might be a game in which a player must meet a goal unrelated to language learning, which requires them to learn the language to meet their goal. Consider a game in which the player must move from one place to another, but do to so, they must read or listen to Japanese to make their movements. This is the kind of design that's at the heart of many game experiences.

In the end, there's a reason this book is more than four chapters. The chapters that follow aim to cover some examples, best practices, and design guidance for doing specific things with games. These all have some aspect of both providing information and assessing player performance. They all have a bit of educational game lineage in them. As you navigate the rest of this book, think of the following chapters as deeper dives in specific distinct areas of practice for game design. The chapters are set up to stand alone so that you can revisit them when new projects arise or hop around as your interests change. They also work as a good way to introduce a topic to a potential collaborator, client, or stakeholder. If you find yourself needing to teach someone about the work you're about to begin, you might want to send them to a chapter in this book instead.

4.12 PRACTICE WHAT YOU'VE LEARNED

- Check the Internet for a list of the best and worst educational games to date. What do these games have in common and how do they differ? What lessons might you learn about their success and failure? How do they fit into the frameworks given in this chapter?

- Pull together a small play diary of the kinds of games you play. Try to identify the moments in those games where you have entered the flow state. Examine what the designer did to induce that state? How did they balance your demonstrated skill and the challenge presented to keep you in the optimal performance zone?

- Find a list of ten educational games or revisit some that you've played in the past. How do these games sit in the spectrum of information or assessment focus? Draw a spectrum and place each of the games relative to each other on that spectrum.

- Outline an educational game goal and sub goals or find a learning progression for the kind of experience you'd like to design. What are the core items you must impart or assess to make that final learning goal work? Where are there some likely stumbling blocks? Is the game goal too big or too small?

REFERENCES

Atari, Inc. *Missile Command*. Atari Inc., 1980.

Gee, James Paul. "Learning by design: Good video games as learning machines." *E-learning and Digital Media* 2, no. 1 (2005): 5–16.

Harmonix. *Rock Band*. MTV Games, 2007.

Konami. *Dance Dance Revolution*. Konami, 1998.

Nintendo EAD. *Super Mario Kart*. Nintendo, 1992.

Pokémon [card game]. Creatures Inc. 1996.

Polys Entertainment. *Gran Turismo*. Sony Computer Entertainment, 1997.

PopCap. *Bejeweled*. Electronic Arts, 2001.

Rawitsch, Don, Bill Heinemann, and Paul Dillenberger. *Oregon Trail*. MECC, 1974.

Sirius Software. *Type Attack*. Sirius Software, 1982.

Taito. *Space Invaders*. Taito, 1978.

Tolkien, John Ronald Reuel. *The Hobbit*. London: George Allen & Unwin, 1937.

Ubisoft Montreal. *Assassin's Creed 3*. Ubisoft, 2012.

Uno. Mattel. 2014.

II

Application

CHAPTER 5

Changing the Body and Mind

G AMES HAVE BEEN EMPLOYED to affect people's thinking and cognitive processes for years. After reading the previous chapters, it should be clear that play does some really interesting things to a player's brain. It triggers a special mental state—the play state.

The play state is an exceptional mental space that allows players to focus, to be creative, and to engage differently than the everyday state. Historically, the play state has been described in many different ways. From some perspectives, it's similar to the concept of the magic circle, commonly associated with Huizinga (2014). Biologists note that the play state is an important part of development, encouraging animals, including the human animal, to take risks and experience life differently. Others, like play anthropologist Brian Sutton Smith, emphasize the many ways players engage. In the domain of mental play, Sutton Smith reminds us of the ways that we play with an idea or engage in mental play games like word games or name calling (1999). These multiple perspectives inform the sense of games as a mental activity.

Because we often witness play as physical, such as playing with a ball, we forget how much of play is mental. Sports are playful experiences that often engage the physical body. However, people who engage in sport will also emphasize the mental demands of those activities. Whether it is focusing on the challenges of the sport or keeping the drive to practice and improve, there is a clear interchange between mind and body in all such play. The motivations for engaging in the activity, the intrinsic and extrinsic rewards player seek, and the kinds of feedback players seek are all tied to who they are, where they've been, and what matters to their own minds and communities.

Game designers largely work to get and keep people in the mental state of play. This is why understanding players, their needs, their wants, their desires, and their motivations can make game designers more effective.

5.1 DEMOGRAPHICS, TECHNOGRAPHICS, AND PSYCHOGRAPHICS

When thinking about design, many people involved in human-interaction design consider three factors. These are demographics, technographics, and psychographics. These are shorthand ways of understanding players from distinct characteristics.

Demographics describe basic characteristics like the player's age, gender, and background. Clearly designing an experience for a 2-year-old means that, on average, they will have limited abilities to count and communicate. This is because, on average, the human brain has not developed those skills particularly well yet. For the demographics of 2-year-old players, certain design constraints will inevitably be present because of the characteristics of that population. Some of these constraints are mental (e.g., counting and language skills), some are physical (the height and weight proportions of the average 2-year-old), and some are a combination of both. Gross and fine motor skill development for a 2-year-old child are different from a 10-year-old, and different from a professional gymnast or concert pianist.

Demographics can aid in making some assumptions about the needs of the player. If designing games for 5-year-olds in Mexico, it is likely that players will speak Spanish, for example. It would be safe to assume that some instructions in Spanish will be understood. If designing a card game for players in Asia, they may be more familiar with the rules of Mahjong than Old Maid.

This is in part because there are many cultural and community elements to the games we play. Some games are largely universal, such as versions of tag; others are much more distinct to specific communities of players. Old Maid has a Victorian history traced to the British Empire, while Mahjong is a Chinese card game from the Qing Dynasty. Even references change in culture and language, as people who play Old Maid may only know it as *Schwarzer Peter* (German language) or *abanuki* (Japanese

FIGURE 5.1 The game *Schwarzer Peter*. (Courtesy of Ji-Elle [https://fr.wikipedi a.org/wiki/Utilisateur:Ji-Elle] through Creative Commons.)

language). New designers often make the mistake of designing from their own demographics instead of understanding their audience's (Figure 5.1).

There is nothing wrong with designing with your own demographics in mind. It can, however, limit your design. The trick with design, any design, is to recognize your proximity to and your distance from your intended audience. There are some universal tendencies between players, and there are some that are very distinct. Building the perfect game for yourself does not guarantee it will be at all interesting to others. Understanding your audience helps you prevent the mistake of designing for the wrong people.

This mistake is particularly easy to make when considering the language of image. Symbols are often localized in their meaning and are rarely universal across cultures and communities. A careful examination of the image depicting the *Schwarzer Peter* game illustrates this point. The characters depicted are likely to be offensive and uncomfortable in a contemporary context in this vintage version of the game. Before the game is even played, its images conjure meaning informed by a player's history with similar images. This is a history the designer may or may not recognize, which is why it is important to get feedback on a design frequently and well before it is released.

As a more contemporary context, the two vertical lines, | |, refer to absolute value in mathematics. In computer programming, they mean the logical "or" (as in this or that), containing an entirely different meaning. Even among people who come from the same culture, their professional background may change their understanding of game rules, relationships, and goals.

Demographics, then, serve as shorthand for understanding some of the physical, behavioral, and psychological attributes of your players. Five year olds may not have the attention span for long and complicated rules, but 25-year-old players are more likely to accept those terms. Games that offer rules based on capitalism may be more or less interesting to people who have direct experience with capitalism. These prior experiences shape the experience of the game, so it is important to know what experiences the players already have. Those prior experiences can also be used as a shorthand to involve players in a game sooner. Framing the game relative to a game that players have already played means they will typically spend less time learning the rules of your game. But if only a portion of players in your target audience have played the game, it could result in a disproportionate advantage for those who have played similar games to those who did not.

Of course, with all demographic considerations, it's also important to avoid stereotypes or other incorrect assumptions. The easiest way to do so is to do some research. This research could come in the form of personal interviews, advice from subject matter experts, or through co-design. Co-design allows the designer to work directly with the audience it is intended for and can do a really great job of unearthing biases, cultural differences, and nuances that may not come through in a traditional interview or discussion.

Demographics provide a broad lens that can be used to form an archetypal view of players. This includes some information about their mental state and capacities. All people go through developmental stages as they age, and those stages have distinct characteristics. The research of developmental psychologists involves understanding these phases. It is of course important to note that these phases are not only about moving from childhood to adulthood, but also part of the many phases of adulthood, from early adulthood to old age.

5.2 TECHNOGRAPHICS

However, demographics are just one lens. The way people process information and how they are or are not excited about something is also shaped by technographics and psychographics. Technographics are used to describe the technical characteristics of their interactions. Technographics segmentation is relatively new, introduced in about 1985.

Technographics can be used to describe and understand groups of people by their access and history with specific technologies. Instead of understanding players by common, readily identifiable characteristics like age and gender, technographics seek to identify people by the technologies they use. Frequent mobile device users may be more comfortable with certain interactions than those who rarely use the technology. Likewise, someone who has 20 years of history using a rotary phone, may have different expectations and interests than someone who has always used a smartphone. The technologies with which a person is familiar help shape their expectations of future interactions. In this way, technographics are like demographics for a person's technical identity and history.

But familiarity is not the only technographic consideration. Access to technology can also factor into technographics. Designing games for mobile devices makes sense only if player communities' technographics include easy access to mobile devices. Knowing technographics helps to shape design constraints as well. It also affects player psychology.

Imagine, for example, the cognitive challenges of reading small print on a small screen. Or the challenge of trying to hear instructions on a device that is not loud enough. These are cognitive challenges introduced by technographic limitations. The more good designers consider the many ways in which an idealized design is influenced by both demographics and technographics, the more the designer recognizes the interplay of these factors into the success of their game.

It is also tempting to think that technographics only apply to digital games. This is not entirely true. A technographic history plays into all sorts of understandings. The language in your game might be confusing to someone with a different technographic experience. Mentioning a smartphone, telling people to go online, or referencing common technical parlance may be more confusing than helpful.

While these things may be the result of demographics, there are lots of ways designers can unintentionally alienate players with technical references that do not meet their personal experience. As an example, we created a game that was labeled Tinder for News. To understand what that means, you would have to know what Tinder is (a dating app for mobile devices). To give it more meaning, you'd have to know that the game involves swiping right for people you like and left for people you don't. While Tinder for News means plenty to those familiar with the app, it means very little to those who don't. It's especially confusing because tinder is the word for anything that burns easily. Now also recall that if Tinder is not available in your country or that older people don't use it, you fall out of the group who understands the reference.

These types of mistakes happen more often in subtle ways that people don't recognize until they test their game with audiences. They happen in question cards that seemed smart at the time, or interface elements that are informed by interactions outside the technographic range of your players. It is easy to misunderstand player experience and make mistakes by failing to recognize the specialty knowledge in your target audience's experience. Designing a game for sailors, that references the left and right sides, instead of port and starboard, would likely be a mistake. Designing a simulation game for surgeons and oversimplifying the language is another way to quickly alienate your players. It can be very problematic to use the wrong technical language because of a misunderstanding of technographics.

5.3 PSYCHOGRAPHICS

The last category to consider is psychographics. Psychographics are typically used to describe the interests, activities, and opinions of individuals. In their most basic form, they can help match the subject to play preferences. A digital game about skateboarding is more likely to appeal to people who have skateboarding in their psychographic. Psychographic data in marketing research is often referred to as IAO data—interest, activities, and opinion data. This IAO data is often used as a way to link content in ways that will immediately encourage interest from distinct psychographics.

Designing a game that plays to the popular interests of teens can be aided by analyzing the psychographics of a possible play community. The demographics will help to narrow the community of players, and the technographics can help shape the specifics of the game's implementation.

But psychographics can also be used to describe a psychological state. The concept of universal accessibility aims to design experiences that are accessible to as wide a set of users as possible. The term is borrowed from human–computer interaction. It is used to help guide designs for people who may have motor skill impairments, color blindness, or a variety of other challenges that could affect their ability to interact with a system. The concept champions the idea that a good design can meet everyone's needs. If someone can't see, a universally accessible system will still allow them to interact with it. If they can't hear, they will still be able to understand the instructions.

What's important here is that universal accessibility is not about disability. The player whose device isn't louder than the clamor of a crowded train is temporarily experiencing a kind of technographic deafness. The player whose device isn't bright enough to show clearly against the glare of the sun is also experiencing a kind of technographic blindness. Universal accessibility helps everyone. It's a simple way to evaluate your design. Will it work without the audio? How much of it will work if the player can't see? Are there redundancies that will help the game become more universally accessible? In some environments, such as apps and games for federal contractors or private foundations, games are required to meet stringent requirements that make sure the final product does not exclude players unnecessarily.

But accessibility is not only about physical characteristics. The same is true of psychographics. Creating a stressful experience can drive players toward a psychographic shift. The stress can prevent them from performing well. It can impair their cognitive abilities. The source of stress can come from a variety of factors. Of course, the challenge of playing can cause stress or boredom, as illustrated by the notion of flow, discussed in Chapter 4. Recall that flow is really about mental states and anxieties created in games. If the player is too anxious or not engaged by the game, their mental state will change.

But stresses can also be triggered by predispositions and history. Early in the history of computer games, people who were predisposed to seizures were affected by the experience of video games. The stimuli would cause players to have epileptic fits in basic entertainment games. This was a common enough risk that some game manufacturers included a warning, one that persists for some types of play now. The seizures were a problem distinct to a psychographic segment that the designers had not considered. The results were catastrophic for the players and detrimental to the industry.

Players also have their own individual histories. These histories might include traumatic experiences they do not want to revisit. They can include phobias, which can be triggered by game content. When designing game experiences, it's important to recognize that individual play experiences can be improved or worsened by these psychographic histories. Content that can remind players of their past or current depression, for example, might be useful in aiding or worsening their experience. Each player has their own psychographic experience.

While it's not common to consider psychographics in this way, for the practice of game design it is quite useful. As more designers aim to affect the mental state of players, they must be aware of the interchange between demographics, technographics, and psychographics. It's also important to consider any ethical considerations when creating such work. While it might seem like a good idea to induce extreme stress among a population, it may not be ethical. As the discussion moves toward influencing player behavior, the question of ethics becomes even more pronounced.

5.4 GAMES TO AFFECT BEHAVIOR

Understanding that games can change the way the human mind operates, there has been a clear history of games designed to change human behavior and even improve mental health. One of the early, large-scale successes in this space is a game called Re-Mission. Re-Mission was designed to change the behavior of young cancer patients. The game provided reinforcement of the core idea that adhering to a medical routine, including taking medications appropriately, would improve outcomes. In controlled studies, the game demonstrated that it improved the cancer outcomes of the patients who played it. It was a remarkable finding, and one that resulted in newspaper headlines championing a game that cures cancers (Kato et al., 2008).

For any kind of work that looks to change player behavior, it's important to begin with a basic understanding of the demographics, technographics, and psychographics. Understanding where the player is beginning will not only help in assessing their progress, it will also help in creating some kind of trajectory for that change. People are very complex. The way they think, the way they form opinions, and the kinds of activities that change that behavior are equally, if not more, complex.

Changing people's behavior is the focus of entire industry and research areas, from marketing to psychology. It is not a trivial task to get people to change their opinion or behavior. Especially if that change is to last beyond the few minutes of the experience. Long-lasting change is distinctly nontrivial. In the early work of games designed to change player behavior, expectations were very high. The hope was that the mere power of games and play could turn 10-year smoking addictions into afterthoughts in hours. The reality is that no single game has yet to demonstrate an ability to undo years of habit in a few hours of gameplay.

To date, there is no formula for creating such change. Instead, there are some concepts and case studies. The concepts borrow from a variety of allied areas. They take concepts from psychology or marketing and adapt them to the propensities of games. They employ demonstrated strategies to help change player behavior through play.

The passages that follow highlight the key concepts in this domain. They don't make promises about the one key to creating change in players. Instead, they show how practice has been moving forward on turning play behaviors into positive behaviors.

5.5 PERSUASIVE PLAY

The concept of persuasive play is one way to consider the power of play to change people's minds. With persuasive play, the notion is simply to change a player's opinion through playful experiences. Companies do this work through advergames, where a play experience is meant to encourage players to view the product differently. Non-profit organizations do this work though games that seek to inspire empathy in a player or to show the many sides of an argument. There are several books on persuasive play. The gist of this work is simply that play behavior can shape non-play behavior.

The idea is simple: If a player can do something in a game, they may be able to do it outside the game. This may be linked to solving a problem, practicing a skill, or understanding something differently. In advertising contexts, this may be as simple as reminding people that the product even exists. In psychology contexts, it may focus on treating post-traumatic stress disorder, helping people deal with their anxieties, or addressing the challenges of depression.

The simplest experiences in this domain are about providing a simulation. Driving a Mini Cooper in a game, it is hoped, may help future car buyers recognize what a wonderful car it is. For this reason, there has been a large and profitable market in placing car brands and models in popular racing simulations. This approach to persuasive play is simply a playable product placement. Much like seeing a hero drink a popular soft drink in a movie, these games play toward the power of association and simulation to change player behavior. They attempt to inspire the kind of thinking that gets consumers saying to themselves, "the world's most desirable cars in this racing simulation are like the cars I can buy down the street." Car manufacturers like Ford and Jeep have used versions of these playable experiences for years, aligning their product brands with racing, status, and exploration. The simulation bolsters the brand and aligns an experience with what advertisers hope is a new behavior (i.e. buying the product).

These placements not only demonstrate, they align the product. While a Mini Cooper might not be the fastest car in the game, it's listed among some of the most race-worthy cars in the world. This aligns the product with others, attempting to encourage players to associate the product with others. These alignment strategies have been employed in other mediums for years. Such games are really an adaption of what has been employed in the past.

Aligning product and product association are core to the notion of advertising in games. Many major games, particularly sports simulation titles, contain some form of in-game advertising as a strategy. The notion is that, while scoring that touchdown or making that goal, seeing the virtual sign for a specific product will help align the experience with the brand or product advertised. This is more than merely increasing awareness; this is an effort to pull the identity of what's advertised toward the play experience (Figure 5.2).

While in-game advertising is a huge industry in itself, it's not the only way that behavior is affected via advertising. Creating specific games that focus on specific products or brands is also common practice. Many companies that make soft drinks, candy, chips, cereal, and other low-cost foods also create advergames. These games combine both alignment of the brand and simulation. They have historically been aimed at children between the ages of 8 and 16, although advergames have also been made for adult players.

FIGURE 5.2 In-game advertising (IGA) for the United States Air Force in the game *Anarchy Online*. (Courtesy of Sebquantic [https://commons.wikimedia.org /wiki/User:Sebquantic] through Creative Commons.)

Advergames are widely distributed throughout the world and have proliferated as the largest effort of persuasive play. While most of these games are not typically considered social impact games, the many case studies they provide are useful to those who want to do things with games.

Since there's much more to learn about persuasive play, Chapter 7 focuses entirely on it. If you need more than what you just learned, you may want to skip there now or at the end of this chapter.

5.6 EXERGAMES: PHYSICAL HEALTH THROUGH GAME PLAYING

While games are often considered a leisurely activity, it's important to understand that leisure contributes to social, mental, and physical health. In the relatively recent history of digital games, the notion of exergames has been proposed. Exergames aim to encourage players toward positive physical activity. Such games might encourage a physical therapy patient to do their exercises or get a sedentary person to become more active.

In the simplest understanding, the original exergames were sports. Sports are simply games that encourage players to be active, often requiring them to exercise to perform better in the game. Sports also have a practical need at many of their roots. The Olympic marathon was a way to test potential couriers. Even NASCAR racing started as a way to test the driving skills of smugglers of illegal alcohol in the prohibition-era United States. The relationship between play and specific societal needs is clear.

But exergames intend to do more than sports have historically done. They aim to change the behavior of the players in long-lasting ways. They do so by employing the incentives of games and tie in-game performance to a player's physical efforts. This is emphasized by a game's ability to track performance and improve the routine. If a typical action game requires players to repeat an action over and over (aka button mashing), then a good exergame can do the same toward the benefit of physical health.

These games also often aim to address the needs of those who are not performing at the level of an athlete. So, for example, someone recovering from an accident, fighting the effects of a degenerative disease, or someone struggling with obesity. The games raise what might be a boring or even dissatisfying activity into the level of play. They turn the much-needed bike around the neighborhood into an inspiring bike through the Andes Mountains or an intergalactic pedal-powered space ship experience. They do what much play does, turning work into something enjoyable, engrossing, and well, less like work.

These rehabilitation games function differently from sports. A sport typically sets a standard across a variety of players, requiring them all to meet the core needs of the sport (e.g., run 26 miles). However, exergames are adaptive, customized to the abilities of the player and able to adapt as the player becomes better. They make the work of rehabilitation, for example, feel more playful. They can also employ the flow state to adapt to the player's varying needs or to adhere to a regime that a physical therapist or other medial professional sets forth. They can serve as entertainment, performance tracker, and trainer.

To date, these games have been demonstrated to improve outcomes for players struggling with a variety of health issues. Most notable are obesity (Staiano et al., 2013) and visual attention (Shawn and Bavellier, 2003).

The improvements that these games yield in the physical body have an obvious relationship to a player's mental health.

5.7 GAMES TO AFFECT MENTAL HEALTH

Any discussion of mental health should really be done with the consultation of mental health professionals. The complexities of both the practice of mental health treatment and its diagnosis are not to be taken lightly. While most work aims to produce a positive effect, it is possible to create its opposite. As you will read in Chapter 11 on evaluation and ethics, the first rule of any such work is simple. First, do no harm.

At its simplest, it's easy to claim that any game that has an educational goal is also a mental health game. If a game educates, it may be assisting a player's mental health. However, this is only reasonable at the surface. In reality, mental health games aim to do far more than educate players. They aim to create a lasting, positive effect.

Creating such an effect requires not only an understanding of the player demographics, psychographics, and technographics—it also requires an understanding of mental health. The co-dependency between designer and subject matter expert is one that all people who aim to do things with games become comfortable with. It's not practical to expect to create change without understanding the mechanisms that affect mental health.

It's important to note that sometimes merely inspiring empathy will assist another player's mental health. Letting players know that they are not alone or helping those who do not face the same metal health challenges, it helps to understand that those challenges can create a positive effect. Such games are discussed in Chapter 8 on empathy and games.

5.8 NEUROSCIENCE, MEDITATION, AND HABIT

One promising area of mental health research in games combines neuroscience and games. The work of Adam Gazzalley is worth highlighting. As executive director of Neuroscape, the research team works to apply game design to improve brain disorders such as attention deficit hyperactivity disorder (ADHD), autism, depression, multiple sclerosis, Parkinson's disease, and Alzheimer's disease (2018). This work is generally regarded as the pre-eminent effort to bridge the physical science of mental health with the propensities of games. They have demonstrated effects through play and neuroscience that show promise for clinical treatments (Angueara et al., 2013).

On the other side of the mind–body relationship are games that aim to help players practice the mindfulness of meditation. Some people would place Flower and Journey as games in this category, although more recently, designers have been creating more games around mindfulness and taking care of oneself. One such game is *#SelfCare* (TRU LUV, 2018). The game focuses on virtually decompressing by allowing the player to imagine they have been in bed all day. Games like *Critical Gameplay: Wait* is another example. In the game, players must balance seeing and doing. As the player moves, the world disappears, but as they wait, more of the world reveals itself. Trees, flowers, butterflies, and more start to appear. Players earn points, signified by a single modulated tone, for seeing these things. However, each time they move toward them, they disappear. Players must practice slow, concentrated efforts instead of the fast-paced experience of many games (Figure 5.3).

FIGURE 5.3 *Critical Gameplay: Wait* requires players to slow down, encouraging a different mental practice than is typically present in arcade games.

5.9 THE NEGATIVE EFFECTS OF MENTAL HEALTH AND GAMES

Of course, if games are going to improve mental health, it's also important to ask if they can harm mental health. While the focus of this book is on the positive outcomes possible through effective game design, it's worth explaining the persistent discussion of negative effects of video games in particular.

While the arguments against analog games have been relatively scant, there have been some people who have claimed unhealthy mental repercussions form playing certain types of analog games. The most obvious of these is of course gambling. Gambling addiction, like shopping addiction and substance abuse, is diagnosable. There are resources and treatments available for people who have a gambling problem.

But the critique of analog play is not limited to games of chance. A variety of sports have been identified as unhealthy and damaging to the mind and body. Even non-sports, such as Dungeons and Dragons, have been identified by some as potentially mind-controlling (Martin and Fine, 1991). While much of that critique has been dismissed, there remain people who are critical of this play behavior because of its purported potential to change the way people think.

Most recently, there is a growing body of research that links aggression in games to aggression in the real world. It aims to prove that by playing violent video games, players carry those aggressions into the non-game world. In short, the research aims to prove that playing violent video games makes for violent players. This is a hotly debated topic with many champions on either side. Annually, a new researcher or group announces a definitive answer to this debate. Shortly thereafter, another announces contradictory evidence.

Less hotly debated is the occurrence of game addiction. Game addiction is primarily focused on video games and internet games, but research seems to indicate there is a small percentage of players who can be identified as problematic game players. Generally, those labeled as problematic gamers are male (Wittek et al., 2016) and the range of people with problematic gaming range between 1.4 and 10% of all individuals who play games consistently.

While it is important to remain vigilant to any mental health concerns around game playing, it's also important not to give way to a fad. In the history of nearly every new medium, those who do not engage in the activity have identified the mental health risks of engaging in that activity. From jazz, to dancing, comic books, dime store novels, surfing, skateboarding, motorcycling, shooting, basketball, and more—many leisure activities have had their moment of being accused of the mental and moral destruction of their contemporaries.

In understanding how games can influence mental health, it's important to do as professional researchers do. Objectively collect the evidence, practice proving and disproving, and make judgments when there is conclusive evidence. There is a substantial effort to employ the power of play toward the benefit of society. It's obviously important to support such efforts in the pursuit of a better experience for people in their daily interactions. The opportunities continue to outweigh any potential challenges.

5.10 PRACTICE WHAT YOU'VE LEARNED

- Play five advergames online and see if you notice any patterns. Are the five essentials of these games similar? Do the games have competition, inventory, territory, implements, and rules? Are these games interesting? What do they do that you didn't expect?

- Collect five research studies on each side of the game addiction or game aggression argument. What do these studies demonstrate about the understanding of how games may change people's behavior? What are your personal critiques of the work? What questions do you have or want to investigate?

- Review the collection of social impact games at the GamesForChange.org. What are some patterns for the games engaged in addressing psychology, mental health, and related work?

REFERENCES

Anguera, Joaquin A., Jacqueline Boccanfuso, James L. Rintoul, Omar Al-Hashimi, Farhoud Faraji, Jacqueline Janowich, Eric Kong et al. "Video game training enhances cognitive control in older adults." *Nature* 501, no. 7465 (2013): 97.

Green, C. Shawn, and Daphne Bavelier. Action video game modifies visual selective attention. *Nature* 423, no. 6939 (2003): 534.

Huizinga, Johan. *Homo Ludens*. New York: Routledge, 2014.

Kato, Pamela M., Steve W. Cole, Andrew S. Bradlyn, and Brad H. Pollock. "A video game improves behavioral outcomes in adolescents and young adults with cancer: A randomized trial." *Pediatrics* 122, no. 2 (2008): e305–e317.

Martin, Daniel, and Gary Alan Fine. "Satanic cults, Satanic play: Is Dungeons and Dragons a breeding ground for the Devil?" *The Satanism Scare*, Edited by Joel Best, New York: Taylor and Francis,1991, 107–123.

Neuroscape. https://neuroscape.ucsf.edu/.

Old Maid [card game]. https://www.bicyclecards.com/how-to-play/old-maid/.

TRU LUV. *#SelfCare*. TRU LUV, 2018. http://truluv.ai/selfcare/.

Sutton-Smith, Brian. "Evolving a consilience of play definitions: Playfully." *Play and Culture Studies* 2 (1999): 239–256.

Wittek, Charlotte Thoresen, Turi Reiten Finserås, Ståle Pallesen, Rune Aune Mentzoni, Daniel Hanss, Mark D. Griffiths, and Helge Molde. "Prevalence and predictors of video game addiction: A study based on a national representative sample of gamers." *International journal of mental health and addiction* 14, no. 5 (2016): 672–686.

CHAPTER 6

Defining Newsgames and Its Complements

A T THIS POINT, IT should come as no surprise that games can and have been used to raise awareness about current topics. In the early 2000s, this idea was introduced formally by game designer and researcher Gonzalo Frasca, as newsgames (2003). Since then, Sicart has provided a thorough and engaging explanation of newsgames (2008) that rounded out the potential and laid the foundation for early understanding. In this original framing, newsgames were about sharing or explaining the news through games.

The concept is fairly simple. Each time there is a new or newly popularized broadcast medium, it's reasonable to expect that that medium may be used to share the news. When the radio became popular, there shortly followed news radio. The same is true of television and the Internet. With the rise of games, so to would there be the opportunity for such news focused games.

Many people consider one of the first digital newsgames to be *September 12th* (Frasca et al., 2003). The game depicts a Middle East city over which a reticle sits. The city is initially populated with varied civilians and the occasional terrorist, depicted as carrying a gun. Using a mouse click, the player can choose to fire a missile when they see a terrorist. After the missile is fired, it kills the terrorist. However, the missile creates collateral damage. That collateral damage results in death and the creation of more terrorists. The pattern continues repeatedly with no clear end (Figure 6.1).

FIGURE 6.1 *September 12th*, one of the original digital game news toys. (Frasca et al., 2003. With permission from Gozalo Frasca.)

The reality is that *September 12th* isn't the first newsgame. By the designer's own description, it's a toy. It's a thing with which players engage to understand or explore a news topic. From Chapter 1, it should be evident that toys are right in the middle of the spectrum between a non-playful interactive and a true game. It should also be clear that news toys have been around nearly as long as Internet news; however, their playfulness has varied greatly.

Nevertheless, the term newsgame is a handy one for understanding how to do things with games. It is useful in providing an umbrella term for the efforts of designers to afford people the ability to play with a variety of news centered experiences. In reality, much work in the social impact domain could be considered a newsgame. The well documented game, *Darfur is Dying* (Ruiz et al., 2006), a game about the conflict in Darfur, is a clear example of a social impact aimed game that can easily fall within the newsgame category.

But newsgames don't have to be about a contemporary topic to still be considered a newsgame. Around the same time as the rise of the newsgame term, other researchers and designers were championing the potential of a docugame. In short, docugames are to the general category of games as documentary films are to the general category of film.

Docugames look to take the documentary perspective, tradition, and semi-objective journalistic lens and apply them to a play space. It is arguable whether any true docugame has been created, or if one can be created, but it's useful to understand that docugames are a way of framing games about specific topics. Examples of docugames include *JFK Reloaded* (Traffic Games, 2004), a game that allows players to reenact the assassination of the President of the United States. The game received much criticism. Its design goal was to offer historical simulation, a common aim of many docugames.

In the early days of digital docugames research, the focus was on authenticity of simulation (Grace, 2011). Much of the research offered a sense of possibility in providing historical simulation and versions of realism (Bogost and Poremba, 2008). These games aim to recreate a moment in history and allow the player to play through them.

This kind of historical simulation is, of course, also familiar. Anyone who has witnessed or participated in war reenactments or visited a theme park that aims to provide an authentic glimpse into the past recognizes its characteristic.

It's reasonable to ask why docugames and newsgames should be grouped together. Or why games with a specific social impact agenda should also be grouped into the newsgames category. The easy answer is simply that all of these games aim to collect information, in much the way a journalist does research, and then report it. In the docugames examples, designers collect historical data and then create some version of a playable version of that data. In social impact games, the players are engaging in, at the very least, an interpretation of the data.

As has been written in other parts of this book, nomenclature is not nearly as important as design and intention. All sorts of things are called newsgames, or social impact games, or docugames. Players couldn't care less what they are called, they simply want to engage with the final product. Naming, categorizing, and differentiating is a useful academic pursuit, because it helps explain patterns, formalize concepts, and distinguish areas of practice. As a designer, these things matter far less than intention.

Good designers work toward goals. As a designer, you don't need to know that you are designing a social impact game or a docugame. Aiming toward the strict definition of these may actually prevent the designer from doing their job well. It might also distract from achieving the goals that the project needs. This is particularly true in emerging practices like these, where the terminology is in constant flux and where the borders between such categories are still being actively negotiated.

Think of the distinct names for games about things as a way to short-hand the work. But note too, that the people who are often doing the most interesting work in these spaces are also working between the defined spaces. They create social impact docugames or some other combination.

6.1 DESIGNING NEWSGAMES

There is an excellent book on newsgames, authored by Ian Bogost, Simon Ferrari, and Bobby Schweizer (2012). The book differentiates between the many categories and catalogs of newsgames. It helps the reader understand the difference between games that function as infographics, puzzles, or as reports of current events. It is clearly useful to understand the many ways in which games or toys about news topics can be created, but as mentioned previously, categorization is not nearly as important in the context of this book. Instead, work to understand how to design and implement such games as they relate to intention. What is it that the project requires and how can the implementation of a game help meet that need? Are there ways in which the news is not being currently understood and that a game or toy can help? Is there an opportunity for improving engagement, perspective, or some other element of the current solution?

For this reason, this section of this chapter attempts to explain the common ways such work is designed. Instead of categorizing such games by their implementations to help steer the design process, it's useful to think about models of design practice. Generally speaking, there are a few common bases for the design of such games and toys. They vary by the source of their design and the process that frames their creation. While it's useful to know about the many games available, it's common for people to ask—how. How are such designs derived? Where do these ideas come from and how can I, as a designer, come up with my own? The following pages are aimed at helping designers answer those questions.

6.2 The Model-Driven Toy

Some newsgame designs derive from turning a model, theorem, or hypothesis into a playable experience. These games or toys take something that is abstract and turn it into a collection of interactions that help players experiment with it.

One of the masters of this work is Nicky Case. Nicky Case creates explorable explanations, turning models of systems into playable experiences that serve as explanations. Working with Vi Hart, the game Parable of the Polygons is an excellent example of this type of work. In this toy, players

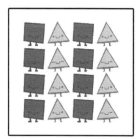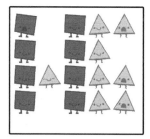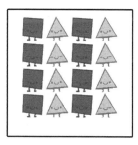

FIGURE 6.2 Parable of the Polygons introduction, which helps players understand the neighbor preferences of the game's characters. (Courtesy of Vi Hart and Nicky Case through the public domain.)

move triangles and squares apart and together, which in itself is very easy to understand. But the dynamics between the game elements are dictated by a paper written by Thomas Schelling's 1971 paper, Dynamic Models of Segregation. Schelling's paper offers a mathematical model for discriminatory individual choices. The game somewhat condenses 44 pages of abstract study and models into a simple to play experience. This experience explains Schelling's models without the need for language (Figure 6.2).

There are many reasons that this toy works so well. Aesthetic decisions like choosing to make the non-player characters not only color distinguished but shape distinguished, improves accessibility across a wide audience (e.g., color-blind players can play). It's delivered via a single-page website, requiring little investment in setup time from players. The experience offers playful cues (the expressions on the characters, the wiggle when the player interacts with the NPCs, etc.) on a serious subject. The content is introduced concept by concept, so players aren't overwhelmed by the final larger experience (Figure 6.3).

To design a model-driven toy, it's obvious that the design needs to start with a model. In the world of news, these models may come from recently proposed solutions or newly published research. They may be quantitative or qualitative. In the world of politics, for example, it's common to report on how tax revisions will affect the general population of readers. In a newspaper article, the explanation is often abstract and perhaps overly general. The revisions typically have some formula behind them. If readers were allowed to play with the revisions, to try one politician's proposals against another, readers may form a new understanding. In this situation, the reader, or player, is not learning from a report, they are learning from experience. They experience two different models and their effects in the

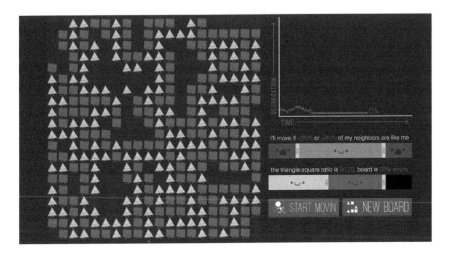

FIGURE 6.3 Parable of the Polygons complete game. (Courtesy of Vi Hart and Nicky Case through the public domain.)

simulated world. Perhaps players can put in their own income and find out what the annual tax change means for them individually. At the same time, this toy might share how each can influence the larger economy.

While the model may form the basis for the design, the designer is charged with turning something that may not be easily understood into something that can be experienced playfully. Converting the nuances of US Federal Tax law into a playable experience, for example, is not merely about letting players manipulate variables.

This is where things become much more complicated for the designer. Too many variables would be overwhelming to a player, too few might be read as oversimplification. Either way, achieving the balance offers something unique. It offers the reader/player an opportunity to make a decision based on their experience. This is, in an ideal world, the kind of objectivity that reveals information without telling the player how to think. They are provided with the model, or an approximation of it, and then allowed to explore the concept on their own.

This is the power of model-driven toys. Whether the model indicates financial repercussions, the tensions of different political or religious views, the effect of meat production on the environment, or the best way to save money on a commute—it's merely exposing data and the relationships in that data. Some types of researchers are perpetually making and revising models. They create formulas to describe financial markets, international relations, and a variety of other dynamics. A quick search on the Internet reveals models for a wide variety of things, from the world-changing to mundane. This means, in terms of resource, there are many places to go to get the basis for a model-driven toy. There's a lot of raw material with which a game designer can work.

Once a model is chosen, the design task is often finding a way to make it playable without destroying the model. It's easy to haphazardly put together something playable based loosely on the research. But doing so may disrespect the work, embarrass the designer, or result in dismissal.

The other caveat in using models is to recognize the expectations of players. The results of playable models typically must have a tight feedback loop, where players can quickly discern the effect of the decisions that they make. Often, designers of such playable models also need to learn the model well enough to design some version of it. This means that there is a high chance of error, as a rushed design may result in an incorrect derivation of the model. Likewise, many such models aren't necessarily appropriate for playful designs, because they don't afford much variability.

For this reason, when possible, designers of model-driven toys work with a subject matter expert to create these experiences. The subject matter expert checks the fidelity of the experience to the original model and can also help designers identify unintended results in their creations. Think of the model as an interview subject. If taken seriously, the designer should really aim to understand the model. Portraying or presenting a model inappropriately can be a dangerous mistake.

6.3 THE PLAYABLE SIMULATION

Another common approach to designing newsgames is to create a simulation that offers players a peek into the reality of its given subject. This model is often less about designing something new as it is about designing something that is faithful to the events as they occurred.

These are considered playable simulations because the player is supported by some playful experience. Perhaps the initial setup of the experience is true to real-life events, but the player is allowed to change them. Or the player is allowed to explore in a way that encourages play. The experience is designed to engage players in the experimentation or exploration state.

For many years, the company Kuma Reality Games created playable experiences based on the official reports of military operations (2008). Their *Kuma\War* games, for example, allowed players to play monthly episodes from military operations in Afghanistan, Iran, South Korea, Vietnam, Sierra Leone, and Mexico. The episodes work like a docugame, based on specific data about the event, which allows the player to relive the experience through first- and third-person shooter mechanics.

Playable simulations don't have to represent their subjects aesthetically. The game *Budget Hero* (Wilson Center, 2008), for example, allows players to simulate balancing the national budget of the United States. As a playable simulation, it has models about the United States federal budget behind it. Players are allowed to make choices that influence where they would spend money. The experience of the game allows players to not only see the outcome of their choices, it also allows the makers to collect information about player preference. It serves as simulation and as a way of polling players. Since budgets can be very complex, it contains some simplification, but it is balanced appropriately for a wide demographic.

The trick to designing playable simulations is to find the appropriate elements that will be playable and that which must remain true to the subject. To do so, it's useful to determine the aim of the playable simulation. Is the simulation created to explain what happened and why? Is it created to engage the player in a newsworthy event?

The virtual reality experience, *Ferguson Firsthand*, is a good example of a playable simulation on a current news topic (Empathetic Media, 2015). In *Ferguson Firsthand*, the player is allowed to experience the events of the Ferguson, Missouri shooting from the perspective of eye-witnesses. Players quickly realize the ambiguity and complexity of eye-witness testimony while also recognizing the travesty of this shooting (Figure 6.4).

FIGURE 6.4 A screenshot of the *Ferguson Firsthand* experience. (Empathetic Media, 2015. With permission from Empathetic Media.)

It's important to note the difference in the critical reception of *Ferguson Firsthand* and *JFK Reloaded*. With more than a decade between both experiences, the criticisms changed. Where *JKF Reloaded* angered some by its depiction of historical events, *Ferguson Firsthand* did not. While analyzing the reasons would be worthy of a chapter in itself, it's worth highlighting a few differences. *Ferguson Firsthand* emphasized its journalistic aspirations and the merits of virtual reality as a way to transport players to a more realistic work. It played to the notion that virtual reality can be an empathy machine. Its developers were a company known as Empathetic Media. It also never emphasized its character as a game, even though it was built with a game engine for a largely game-focused platform. There are no points in *Ferguson Firsthand* and its production incorporated a news organization, Fusion (a joint venture between major news and entertainment companies).

The dichotomous reception and press around the two games offers lessons to be learned for anyone designing such playable simulations. Involving subject matter experts, like journalists, and aligning the experience appropriately to the seriousness of the topic can clearly help. Failing to do so can be highly detrimental. It's also worth appreciating that in the 10 years between the games, players and audiences seem may have developed a better sense of ludic literacy. They may have, thanks to the many games on serious topics that preceded *Ferguson Firsthand*, been ready to accept that something that looks like a game does not necessarily trivialize an experience.

While a playable simulation may seem simple, as it is foundationally a reproduction of the news event, it is often more nuanced than that. Any designer of a simulation must decide which elements are to be simulated and which are not. Even the most faithful simulation remains an exercise in selection. These selections could be considered editorial decisions, as they determine what's worth simulating and what is not worth simulating. Forgetting that such selections may be perceived as a bias would be a mistake. While everything from the real world can't be included in a simulation, paying attention to what the design leaves out as well as what it puts in will assure that the quality of your experience is appropriate.

6.4 PLAY BY ANALOGY AND ABSTRACTION

While most games represent their subjects in a way that abstracts them, some do so in more substantial ways. Instead of looking to turn an abstract model into something playful or to provide a real-to-life simulation, another common design model is simply to abstract out as much of the representation so that what remains is a relevant, abstract analogy.

The game *Lim* (Kopas, 2012) is an excellent example of such an experience. In *Lim*, the player controls a small square. The square moves through the maze and has one additional game verb—blend. Pressing the space bar lets the square change to the colors of its nearest neighbors. If the player fails to blend, the other non-player squares in the game seem to become aggressive to the player character. The player character is knocked about the board and sometimes out of the maze entirely. However, blending doesn't always work or persist. The player is left to traverse the maze with a heightened level of anxiety. The game works beautifully as a playable experience in bullying and otherness (Figure 6.5).

Games like *Thomas Was Alone* (Bithell, 2012) do an excellent job of reminding players that literal representation is not the only way to understanding or explain. The game is often referenced as having a remarkable ability to turn its extremely simple animated characters into characters that players connect with and care about. In a Kotaku review of the game, Evan Narcisse writes "Amazingly, I felt more connected to *Thomas Was Alone*'s colored, polygonal blocks than I have to most human characters in recent games. Part of the game's genius is how attached you feel to

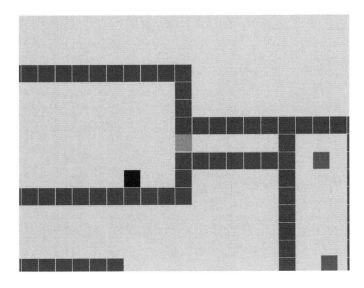

FIGURE 6.5 *Lim*, an excellent example of designing meaning by abstraction. (Kopas, 2012. Courtesy of MKopas.net.)

Thomas, John and the other tinted, four-sided personas you encounter in Mike Bithell's indie platformer" (2012).

The opportunities in high levels of abstraction abound. They cost less to produce but allow players to project their sense of self on them. Players don't look at a small blue block and say that doesn't look like me, the way they may with *Tomb Raider*'s Lara Croft or *Street Fighter*'s Ryu. Instead, players can understand that that character, if done well, is merely a placeholder for them in the game world. A placeholder that represents their actions, goals, and obstructions.

This is not a surprise to designers of analog games. Abstract game tokens are common, as wooden cubes represent everything from armies to riches. The challenge for some digital game designers is to remember the lessons present in analog game design. Distinct characters can be charming, but they aren't always necessary. The iron or car for Monopoly players do nothing to develop a sense of character or player investment in characters, but they function to distinguish players on the board.

Simulation by analogy and the use of abstraction offer the opportunity to open the play experience to other audiences. It is no surprise that games like *Thomas Was Alone* became popular at the same time that researchers and the general play community started questioning diverse representation in games.

Abstracting aesthetically or through mechanics can allow games to be about wider subjects. In the world of digital games, it's easy to fall into the trap of simulation. To think that more literal is better. But, as the lessons of the Uncanny Valley teach us, it's important to recognize that on your way to realism, designs can actually alienate.

Consider, for example, how representation in games affects players. If the player character in a game does or does not look like the player, they may feel more or less invested. They may say, hey that's me on the screen, or they may not. If you're making a game that aims for empathy, the empathy can easily be affected by representation. One of the oldest tricks in the design book is to handle representation by removing it. With an appropriate level of aesthetic abstraction, for example, one size can almost fit all.

Analogy, on the other hand, allows players in games to be about something without explicitly announcing it. This is an old trick of science fiction and fantasy books and films. The struggles of the X-Men feel similar to the struggles of anyone on the outside. They remind players of something they feel but may not want to deal with directly. A superhero comic is not about racism, it's about the secret powers unleashed when the hero is left un-subjugated. The children's movie is not overtly about the power of unions to overcome aristocracy, it's about insects coming together to do good for the entire colony.

Analogy in games, as it is in other mediums, is an opportunity to make something about something feel like it's not about anything at all. That's an important opportunity. It means that the game can broach sensitive subjects, allow players to play with things they might not normally, and still remain comfortable.

A common mistake in creating playable experiences is to forget the opportunities in analogy and abstraction. It's the kind of mistake that has people making playable experiences or serious games about sexual abuse stuck. How do you discuss the topic without showing it? How do you make such content available to minors without harming them in the process? More often than not, the solution is found in abstraction and analogy.

6.5 THE GRAND FEATURE: AAA GAMES ABOUT NEWS

It could be argued, under this broader interpretation of newsgames, that many games not typically considered newsgames actually qualify as such. The *Call of Duty* (Infinity Ward, 2003) series, for example, goes through painstaking detail to create the events of past world wars. Their historical accuracy is a key element of the engagement in their play. The games have large audiences and large communities. They are without argument, successful at what they do.

By the aspirations of many early docugames, such big-budget games are a clear achievement. It is a mistake not to recognize this and appreciate that while these games rarely attribute themselves to the community of social impact games, they actually share many of its design aspirations. At the least, they share an appreciation for historical simulation.

For as much attention as *JFK Reloaded* attracted, it was a sliver of the content and detail provided in the considerably larger budget of the *Call of Duty* games. While the politics of these games are worthy of critique, the effort and examples they provide are certainly useful to game designers looking to create newsgames. The design process and retrospective analysis from the teams involved in the production of these games are readily available in trade publications, industry conferences (particularly the Game Developer's Conference), and promotional pieces associated with these properties.

The tips, tricks, and how tos for such work could easily fill an additional book. Instead, it is useful to note that if the budget and project timeline for a planned newsgame can support work as detailed and substantial as historical war games, there are resources to support such development outside of this book. Those resources are worth reviewing, in much the way the independent film-maker with a $50,000 budget can learn from blockbusters with much larger budgets. Learning how they engage players, what those players are seeking, and noting the trends of general play are all useful. Even if you are wholly opposed to such play, ignoring it is a mistake.

Of course, it's important to note that such games have also been the subject of social impact discussion. The International Committee of the Red Cross (ICRC), for example, has championed the notion that major developers should integrate international humanitarian law into their gameplay experiences (Crescente, 2011). The critique by some is that war crimes are evident in games, and that designers and developers ignore the morally appropriate representation of rules of engagement in games. This is the burden of simulation.

Their argument is simple. The play in these games is so real, and at times so historically accurate, that it makes sense to also integrate the realities of combat. These experiences could be used to document, share, and critique newsworthy events. Such games, for example, could be used to explain violations of international humanitarian law via modified versions.

At the least, what such play affords is an opportunity for discussion, critique, and even modification. As games age, they are sometimes provided to their communities for modification. The reality of old versions of major franchises leaves a foundation from which new designers can build.

6.6 WHERE TO BEGIN AND WHAT TO DO

While designing newsgames shares attributes with many other ways someone can do something with games, there are a few things to keep in mind. Newsgames are often time constrained games. Particularly when dealing with current topics, newsgames share similar design constraints with editorials and other journalistic practice. This means that as a designer of newsgame there may be a tension between fast and accurate.

An inaccurate newsgame, like an inaccurate article, can be faster to create, but it's also going to be wrong. This tension is particularly true in games that are trying to avoid editorial bias. These are what some researchers call reportage games. Reportage games and toys try to be unbiased reports of data. While the process of abstraction, creating mechanics and generally designing something playful means that changes or filters occur, the general goal is to report. Such games aim not to sway their audiences one way or the other, but instead to simply impart information.

Editorial games, or games that explicitly aim to provide bias or slant in the way they frame their subject, are less likely to feel the tension of accuracy, but that doesn't mean they should ignore it. If the editorial game is based on erroneous claims, the entire basis for the game could be invalidated.

It is thus important to begin with the most basic decision—intention. What kind of newsgame is going to be made and why? Is it designed to increase a player's empathy to a situation? Is it aimed at demonstrating an otherwise hard to understand model? Is it designed to bridge a language or cultural gap by explaining something through play? Each of these goals requires a specific approach.

If the game is intended as an editorial game, it's going to borrow substantially from the patterns of persuasive play and empathy games. These are discussed in detail in other chapters. Suffice to say that the intention of the game dictates much about who is expected to play it, what format it will be delivered, and what play experiences will be most attractive and engaging.

At the start of any news focused play project, it is important to understand the claim to be made and how the game's experience will make that claim. It all starts with intention. A good editorial game does what it intends, just as any good newsgame hits its intended design target.

If the game is based around demonstrating a model, it's essential to gather a full understanding of the model. Some teams choose to partner with a subject matter expert who thoroughly understands the model and can validate the final game design. When there isn't a subject matter expert available, the next best approach is simply to educate the team or individual about the model. This may involve learning about the model through a variety of media—perhaps a reading, perhaps a short film. In this way, a model-based game design incorporates elements of games education, as the player will become the student of the designer's created experience. A review of Chapter 4 will help focus your efforts here. Much of game design orbits elements of educational game design, so understanding how your player will learn or how to structure their learning will help you structure a good playable experience.

For simulation work, the intent comes from understanding why a simulation is an appropriate choice. Determining why a simulation is needed will help focus on what needs to be simulated. If the goal is to simulate a complex system, it doesn't mean that all of the complexities need to be simulated. Instead, a subset of the complexity might suffice to meet the intent. Most games take longer to make and use more money than expected, so aiming to simulate everything in a given scenario is often an elusive and unrealistic goal. Instead, understanding intent helps aim efforts toward the most important elements.

The second step is to aim toward a minimally viable product (MVP). An MVP is the least amount of project needed to get the results you seek. This MVP helps assure that the game will meet its deadline. Since newsgames are always a tension of speed and accuracy, aiming toward the minimum amount of publishable game early assures that when the project is completed it has at least met its intents. A really good-looking game that fails to make its editorial claims or simulate what it intended is useless. Since much of newsgames is about utility, the intended purpose of the game, meeting its aim should be a prime element of the game's MVP. Targeting MVP core requirements well before their actual due date is also important.

In 2017, our team created a game about all the rash of sexual harassment cases against famous men. The aim was to remind players of the systems in reporting such violations. Based on Maggie Farley's concept, we created a game in which players had to tip the scales of justice by getting enough women to speak about their experience. The MVP for the game was something we made in less than 48 hours. It was a web and mobile playable game where players tapped the bubbles that prevented women from speaking about their experience. Once the bubbles were popped, the women would fall and tip the scales, hurling the harasser off the screen (Figure 6.6).

Lastly, it's important to get approval quickly and frequently when developing a newsgame. If the game is aimed at a particular publishing venue, such as a newspaper, it's important to make sure that the editors feel comfortable with the content and that they understand what will be produced. Iterating through a game's design may result in a variety of seemingly innocuous changes.

However, once an editor sees such changes, they may have clear objections and disagree with what seemed to be innocuous. As such, routine interactions, including sharing the state of a game is important. For professional teams, more than one newsgame has been buried on page ten (or never published) for unexpected derivations, discontinuity between editor expectations and final product, or simply because what was envisioned didn't match expectations.

FIGURE 6.6 *Hurl the Harasser,* a game on sexual harassment made in a weekend for the University of Miami Newsjam.

As a process, these are the basic steps to making a basic newsgame:

- *Establish intent*: Determine your basic aim so that you can get the right subject matter expertise. The intent may change after working with a subject matter expert, in much the way a journalist may discover a new, better story while researching another.

- *Collect, organize, or otherwise align subject matter expertise*: This may be as simple as reading the research or more commonly involves partnering with the person who knows the content best. That person may the primary researching journalist, a first-hand observer, or someone trained in the area. It's important to recognize that working with communities and doing what is known as participatory design is included in efforts to work with subject matter experts.

- *Specify design*: Try to outline the core elements of your design, understanding what is required of an appropriate MVP and what features are ideal but not essential. The design can be specified a variety of ways from game design documents, to video demonstrations that imitate the final product. Some teams prefer to use intranets, wikis, or cloud shared documents to allow changes to be tracked and current design specifications to be shared across teams that may be globally distributed.

- *Review design with the client, stakeholders, and/or decision makers*: Try to be explicit as possible about what will be made and how it will work. Imaginations run wild and what is imagined by some may be very different than the final product. It's important to listen, but also recognize that reviewers may not have spent as much time with the material and wrestling with the specific challenges.

- *Iterate and implement*: Once the green light has been given, it's time to start making the game or toy. The process for implementation will vary, but typically iterative approaches that allow for feedback as the project takes shape take into account the most adaptive design process.

- *Pre-publication review*: Share the final project before it goes live to make sure there are no objections, concerns, or oversights.

- *Publication*: Send it on its way and pay close attention to the unexpected, as surprises often come in the first period the project is launched. Be ready to handle them but also be ready to answer press inquiries and other requests.

It's evident that despite typically having less time to make newsgames, the steps for such games can be more substantial than personally developed art games or other projects. This is perhaps one of the many reasons that there are a variety of newsgames that are actually created independently of their subject matter experts or publication specialists. That's because while the above model is commonly executed, it is not the only way to make newsgames. There is a whole collection of independent newsgames which work like small publications in themselves.

6.7 INDEPENDENT GAMES AND NEWS

Some game designers find themselves so compelled by a new topic that they create their own newsgames. They often do so without the pressure or expectations of a newspaper team or subject matter experts. Instead, they work like artists have worked historically, learning about a topic and then producing creative work that reflects on the contemporary. This has been true of musicians who write music about contemporary news, of playwrights who focus the themes and events of their work on current topics, or artists who paint moving images of the challenges of the day.

As an example, independent game maker Lucas Pope created a game called *The Republia Times*. The game takes aim at news as a kind of distraction. In the game, the player manages the front page of a newspaper. At the request of the game's fictitious government, the player must placate its readers by choosing front page articles that do not make the government look bad. With each iteration, through the front page, the player adds distracting headlines about celebrities and other fluff, ignoring the realities of economic woes and political scandal.

The Republia Times (Pope, 2013) was produced without the guidance of traditional subject matter experts or the expectation that it would be published alongside an article on journalism and corruption. Instead, the designer was moved to make such a game and in so doing highlights a real problem.

Assuming the political freedom to do so, there is nothing to stop anyone from creating their own newsgames. In a free society, such work is similar to the license of artists and other creatives. Many of the most interesting games in the newsgame space were designed just this way. The example that started this chapter, *September 12th*, is an example of a game made like this.

6.8 THE CHALLENGE OF LUDO-LITERACY

One of the societal challenges that have hindered the growth of newsgsames is something commonly referred to as ludo-literacy. It is the idea that in order to play and play well, players must understand how to play. Ludo-literacy, stemming from the Latin for "I play" (ludo) is about general society's ability to "read" or understand such games. In their brief history, many mistakes have been made that are likely related to ludo-literacy.

In the early history of radio, Orson Welles' 1938 radio play adaptation of *The War of the Worlds* (1898) alarmed the world. The story goes that the adaptation was broadcast live on the radio. The play focuses on an invasion by extraterrestrial aliens. Unfamiliar with the difference between news radio and radio dramas, or perhaps unable to read the differences over the air, audiences believed there was an actual extraterrestrial invasion

(Koch, 1970). The drama was a kind of on-air radio simulation. The fact that it went 30 minutes without a commercial interruption furthered the illusion of reality. Critics days after its transmission called for regulation that prevented such misleading content from being broadcast again. This is a particularly apt example as you read about alternate reality games in later chapters.

Likewise, early in the history of film, a clip of a train moving on a collision course toward the camera alarmed audiences so much so that some jumped out of their seats. This was a new experience. An experience that didn't translate well to an audience that was still trying to read the language of film.

These are all examples of a kind of literacy. In these cases, they are radio and film literacy. Particularly in digital games, this literacy is still developing in the general audience. While many of the conventions of gameplay are completely natural to gamers, they may not be to the average newspaper reader. It is this challenge, this difference in ludo-literacy that continues to be a challenge for newsgame growth.

At its worst, it can actually lead to a misinterpretation of the game entirely. There are, for example, still many people who are surprised to discover that games can be about things other than frivolous escapism. For these audiences, it may even be offensive to make a game about such a topic (e.g., *JFK Reloaded*). To do so, in their view, is to trivialize something that may not be trivial.

This is a challenge of ludo-literacy for the designer. Such players would have a hard time interpreting the medium, engaging with the appropriate frame, and experiencing it as needed. The language it uses, the language of play, is uninterpretable, hard to understand, and perhaps even too much work to be worth the effort.

It's important to recognize that some players may not be ludo-illiterate, but instead, they are simply only able to read a certain narrow type of play. Much like entering a foreign country and only knowing the greetings or daily use words, such players have enough literacy to get the basics done but not enough to have the kind of meaningful conversation that synthesizes new ideas and understandings.

To tackle this challenge, designers have a few options. Simplified play is often an easy one. In much the way that international airport signage depends on convention and pictographs over regional specific language, a design for low ludo-literacy is likely to be simple in its expectations of players and the depth of experience.

Another approach is to avoid the label of "game" entirely (e.g., *Ferguson Firsthand*). Ludo-literacy is play related and context specific. If a user is told to play with something, they become a player. If a user is told to interact, they remain a user. While the distinction is minor, framing a game or playful experience first as an interaction disarms any anxieties players may have about playing.

This can be done both in the language around the game or toy and in the ways in which it affords play. Providing a highly structured, less playful initial experience may give an audience the scaffolding to quickly move from low ludo-literacy to high ludo-literacy. This can be done by limiting initial affordances in the experience and expanding them as the player successfully engages with it.

In the end, it's important to understand that ludo-literacy exists in everyone. Psychologists identify an ability to engage in play as a prerequisite to disorder. Normal human development involves play, and as such, it means that nearly every person who engages in an interactive experience has the potential to recollect that ability to play. The addition of a digital experience to the play experience can be seen nearly as augmenting any and all past play experiences they have had.

6.9 PRACTICE WHAT YOU'VE LEARNED

- Visit the Games for Change archive (http://www.gamesforchange. org/games) and identify games that are newsgames. Where do they fall on the spectrum between editorial and reportage? How do they work and what is their intent? What makes some feel better than others?

- Play the games listed in this chapter and take notes, deconstructing their elements. What is the concept statement for each? What is the goal, obstruction, and means to accomplishing the goal? What are the five elements of the game and what makes the experience unique from others you have played?

- Review a popular newspaper or other news outlet and identify the hot topics of the day. What are people debating, what are they struggling to understand? Practice designing by outlining a few concept statements for games related to the topic. What would you need to know more about to get it right? What kind of subject matter expert would you need? Do you think there's potential in the games you've started to design?

REFERENCES

Bithell, Mike. *Thomas Was Alone*. Mike Bithell, 2012.

Bogost, Ian, and Cindy Poremba. "Can games get real? A closer look at 'Documentary' digital games." In *Computer Games as a Sociocultural Phenomenon*, 12–21. London: Palgrave Macmillan, 2008.

Bogost, Ian, Simon Ferrari, and Bobby Schweizer. *Newsgames: Journalism at Play*. MIT Press, Cambridge 2012.

Crecente, Brian. War Crimes in Video Games Draw Red Cross Scrutiny. Kotaku. December, 11, 2011. https://kotaku.com/war-crimes-in-video-games-draw-red-cross-scrutiny-5863817

Empathetic Media. *Ferguson Firsthand*. Empathetic Media, 2015. http://www.empatheticmedia.com/virtual-reality/.

Frasca, Gonzalo. Simulation versus narrative: Introduction to ludology. In Mark J. P. Wolf and Bernard Perron (Eds.), *The Video Game Theory Reader*, 221–235. New York: Routledge, 2003.

Frasca, Gonzalo, S. Battegazzore, N. Olhaberry, P. Infantozzi, F. Rodriguez, and F. Balbi. *September 12th*. Newsgaming.com, 2003. newsgaming.com/games/index12.htm.

Grace, Lindsay. "Gamifying archives, a study of docugames as a preservation medium." In *Computer Games (CGAMES), 2011 16th International Conference*, 172–176. IEEE, Louisville, 2011.

Infinity Ward. *Call of Duty*. Activision, 2003.

Koch, Howard. *The Panic Broadcast; Portrait of an Event*. Little, Brown, New York, 1970.

Kopas, Merritt. *Lim*. Games for Change, 2012. http://www.gamesforchange.org/game/lim/.

Kuma Reality Games. *Kuma\War*. Kuma Reality Games, 2008.

Narcisse, Evan. *Thomas Was Alone*: The Kotaku Review. 2012. https://kotaku.com/5929049/thomas-was-alone-the-kotaku-review.

Pope, Lucas. *The Republia Times*. Lucas Pope, 2013. http://dukope.com/play.php?g=trt.

Ruiz, Susana, Ashley York, Mike Stein, Noah Keating, and Kellee Santiago. *Darfur is Dying*. http://www. darfurisdying. com. 2006.

Sicart, Miguel. "Newsgames: Theory and design." In *International Conference on Entertainment Computing*, 27–33. Berlin, Heidelberg: Springer, 2008.

Traffic Games. *JFK Reloaded*. Traffic Games, 2004.

Wells, Herbert George. *The War of the Worlds*. London: William Heinemann, 1898.

Wilson Center. *Budget Hero*. Wilson Center, 2008. https://www.wilsoncenter.org/budget-hero.

CHAPTER 7

Persuasive Play

T HE TERM PERSUASIVE PLAY is shorthand for a variety of playful experiences designed to persuade players toward a specific claim or perspective. The idea is that games, like other media, can be persuasive. Like a well-written speech, a compelling documentary film or a convincing book, games can make arguments, and in so doing, persuade their players.

The original concept of persuasive play is credited to a few people. Ian Bogost's seminal work on persuasive games, encapsulated in his book by the same name (2007), clearly lays a foundation for much of the contemporary work in persuasive games. This well referenced work provides, in the author's own words "an exploration of the way videogames mount arguments and make expressive statements about the world that analyzes their unique persuasive power in terms of their computational properties." It is this perspective that informs much of the digital and non-digital design of persuasive games.

However, persuasive play has many trajectories from which it has formed as a practice. It's also the product of a long-running research trajectory across educational game design. Educational games often endeavor to help people learn. The learning topic isn't always science or math, sometimes it's about teaching people the value of something they may not have thought was valuable, or in helping them understand a new way of approaching problems. It is this thrust of the educational game design practice that also helps fuel the development of persuasive play.

A third trajectory of persuasive play is games designed to sell. Most often such games are created to sell products or to enhance a brand by aligning it with playful experiences. Much of this work is labeled as advergames, a collision of advertising and games. Unlike other areas of persuasive play, much of the work in advergames is done without an academic research underpinning. Instead, many advergames, especially those with corporate origins, are made with a strong focus on the methods of traditional advertising.

Any effective designer of persuasive play practitioner should be aware of the many ways in which these games are designed, implemented, and tested. There is good persuasive play happening in very different places, from the web to conference show floors. The term persuasive play can be used very loosely to cover all forms of play in which the designer or facilitator of the play is hoping to meet a persuasive goal.

More practically, persuasive play is often much more blunt and directed. It comes in the form of games like *Spent*, which sets players up with the challenge of surviving poverty and homelessness. Players must make hard choices related to health, housing, and employment without going broke in a single month. Players are soon persuaded toward understanding and perhaps even becoming a bit more empathetic toward the challenges facing impoverished people in the United States.

Another example is *Commuter Challenge* (Figure 7.1), a game in which players must try to keep their low-wage job while struggling to rely on unreliable public transportation in Washington, DC. Or the often-cited *Darfur is Dying*, in which players try to meet basic daily needs while avoiding the threat of the Janjaweed Militia.

What all of these games have in common is a clear persuasive message. They aim to help players understand a situation that they may not have understood otherwise. This is the main claim of the power of persuasive play. That it can transform a player's understanding, perspective, appreciation, or other qualitative factors about the subject of the game.

7.1 ANALOG GAMES HISTORY

Most effective histories of persuasive play start with a common game that few recognized started as persuasive play. In 1903, Lizzie Magie set out to change the way people understand the practices of landlording. She wanted people to understand the problems apparent with landlording. Her concerns were based on a model of economics, known as Georgist economics. She set the game's case study as Atlantic City, New Jersey, and called the game The Landlord's Game. In no uncertain terms, the game was designed to help players support anti-monopoly sentiments. Magie didn't support monopolies (Figure 7.2).

TIME:
90 MIN

MONDAY

MONEY:
$187.25

Luckily, cleaning up is undramatic and you leave work on time.

Head for the train.

Try something new today.

Treat yourself to a car service to day care, a 30-minute trip for $22.

LATE: 0

RESTART

FIGURE 7.1 *Commuter Challenge* was designed to help players understand the problems with being a low-wage employee when public transportation is unreliable.

Years later, through some changes and adaptions by Parker Brothers, the same game would be adapted into what most people know today as Monopoly. For more than 50 years, the game was offered in only two versions until changes in marketing and intellectual property opened the game to many localized, ironic, or demographic specific versions.

From an historical lens, Monopoly might be the most important persuasive play game in the canon of such work. Magie made some impressive decisions that are perfectly in line with what we know about games now. We know, for example, that people often understand experiences better than reports. This is one of the claims for the power of persuasive play. It is more compelling to show someone how something works, or let them experience it for themselves, than it is to merely tell them about. In an era of soapbox speeches and formal persuasive intent, Magie offered an experience that aimed to make an argument through play.

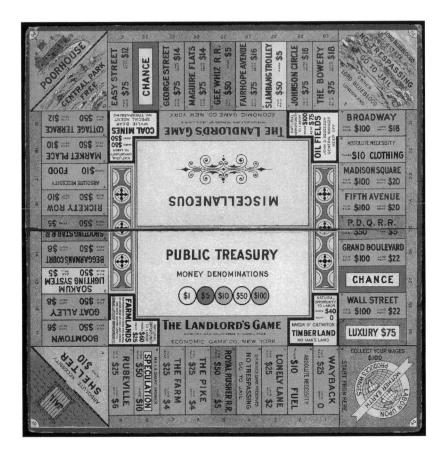

FIGURE 7.2 Magie's The Landlord's Game was one of the most widely recognized games in the United States, which was designed to persuade players toward anti-monopoly sentiments.

Her design did something else that other persuasive mediums did not—it entertained. Even if you weren't interested in the claims about Georgist economics, the game was interesting to play. Even if you differed with the claims, you could still enjoy the game.

While much attention for persuasive play focuses on the digital, there is a long history of trying to impart knowledge or claims about what is important through play. Since 1952, for example, Avalon Hill (formerly the Avalon Game Company) has endeavored to make analog strategy games on a variety of topics. The company, based in Baltimore, Maryland, is a mere 60 miles from the nation's capital, Washington, DC. They have produced a variety of military simulation games as well as other simulation and relatively instructive games with varied levels of persuasive content in them. They have made games about the rise of the Roman Empire, about being a train barren, and how to beat inflation.

Although a blip on the radar of classic board games, Avalon Hill's Beat Inflation Game is a novel piece of a persuasive play in itself. It is a game based on a financial model. The goal of the game is to make a profit while inflation rises and falls. Players do so by buying and selling real and paper assets. The game's argument is about strategies to race from $100,000 to $1,000,000 as quickly and effectively as possible. It was one of the company's least successful games (Figure 7.3).

Why would Avalon Hill's Beat Inflation Game fair so poorly, and Lizzie Magie's The Landlord's Game do so well? They both aim to make claims about economic models. They both aim to persuade players on the merits or detriments of specific practices.

In the end, every review, and my personal experience, point to one obvious difference. The Beat Inflation Game is simply not interesting. It's a lesson people forget quickly. Being persuasive on its own is not compelling. The game needs to be interesting too.

This is why, for example, some of the most effective persuasive play in the analog space is role play. Role play is powerful, as it forces people to take on new perspective and own it. This is one of the reasons why Model United Nations is such an effective educational experience.

From a global perspective, the history of persuasive games has not always had a positive trajectory either. Some of the more infamous board games in history had the intention to argue for a specific world view or set of values. One such game is Juden Raus, a game designed during World War Two and offered to the Nazi regime as early as 1938. The anti-Semitic game was actually rejected by the SS publicly but aimed to promote its anti-Semitism all the same (Schädler, 2003).

7.2 DIGITAL PERSUASIVE PLAY

In the history of digital persuasive play, one of the first notable projects was *Pepsi Invaders*. *Pepsi Invaders* aimed to boost the morale of Coca-Cola employees by offering a clone of the successful *Space Invaders* game. In *Pepsi Invaders*, commissioned by Coca-Cola, players would shoot the words Pepsi out of the sky as the descended on the player character (Djiato et al, 2011).

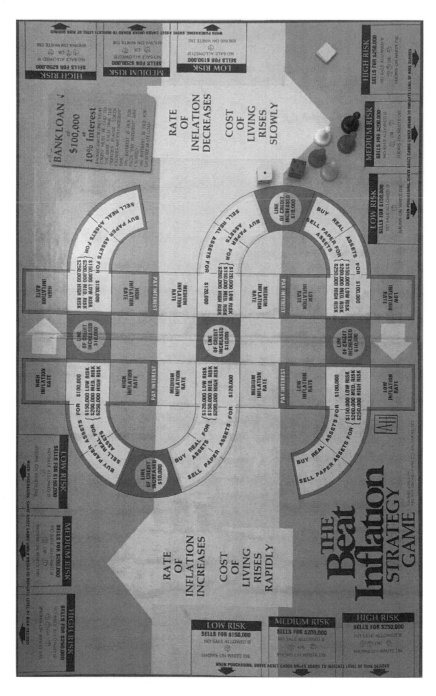

FIGURE 7.3 The Beat Inflation Game is another board game based on a financial model.

7.3 WHY GAMES?

The obvious truth is that there are lots of ways to persuasive people. There are already books, films, theatrical performances, speeches, diatribes, and more. What then do games offer that these others don't? The core claim is that games offer the ability to do. Players don't hear about the product or message, they play it. If play is practice and laboratory, then play is a great way to gain experience with the product or idea. Are you not sure it's important to brush your teeth three times a day? Play a game that helps you understand what happens if you don't. If you're not sure how climate change affects the planet, play with this to understand it.

In the early chapters of this book, it was explained that for each medium there is a core verb. Readers read books. Filmgoers watch a film. Audiences listen and so on. The unique characteristic of games is that players are focused on what they *do* in a game. This is not only how players perceive games, it's how we experience them. A common start to explaining any game begins with "you must" or "your goal is." It is this sense of ownership that the player's actions affect the game world, and the game world is dependent on those actions, which makes the potential for persuasive play so promising.

Once a movie is started, it will continue until it's stopped. With a game, nothing happens unless the player does something with it. This is an exceptionally powerful attribute. It creates a kind of contract between designer and player. If the player agrees to play, the designer agrees to entertain. It also means there's a shift in perspective. The game is about what the player does, not what the player is told.

In film, for example, watching often means going on the journey with the films' subject. While watching the film, we may want the protagonist to do something or we may hope for their success, but control is ceded to the filmmakers. In games, players feel that they are in control. The actions of the player character or avatar are their actions. The virtual car crashes, it is their fault. The level is not complete and the game's hero failed—the failure is with the player. Assuming the game can be won.

Players own the mistakes and successes that occur in a game. In games without player representation on screen or on a board, the actions they make are their actions directly. This is an essential difference in games compared with other media. It is a difference of participation.

If the player becomes rich with Monopoly money, they have done so. They do not impart their relationship to the story of their experience of someone else's experience.

This is even further emphasized by the general feedback loop of all games—digital or analog. Generally speaking, a game ceases to be played when people cease to interact with it. This is not true of film, which will continue even if every audience member walks out of the room.

Traditional theater, that which does not aim to break the fourth wall by supporting interaction with the audience, also continues regardless of the audience's engagement. In a funny twist of tradition, the mantra of theater is that the show must go on. The performance proceeds regardless of the audience situation around it.

Of course, all of this is a generalization of the medium. Choose your own adventure books, for example, do support reader choice in sculpting the story. Interactive theater requires audience interaction; 360-degree film requires some exploration by its audience too. Likewise, there are undeniably games that can continue, to a limited degree, without being played, but these are all the exception to the rule. You can puzzle on the philosophical conundrum, is a game truly a game if no one plays it? Is it not simply a rule set or a document until it is played?

What is clear is that games require player action. So, the notion that players *do* the game is the starting point for knowing how to construct persuasive play. Remember, readers read, viewers watch, players do.

The second core concept is the idea that what is possible and the results of action in a game are the product of the game's design. The game determines outcomes by structuring rules. The game invalidates or validates player choice and action. These decisions are how the game's persuasion is designed.

Much like any creative work, a game's design is a collection of choices. These design choices emphasize what is important and what is not. If a board game contains fake money, it's safe to assume that money is an important part of the game. If the game has dice, it's safe to assume that chance matters in the game. Every decision in a game is a claim about what's important and what's not. At least it should be, when a designer is making conscious decisions about the game they are designing.

If every decision is a claim about what's important and what's not, it's also a framing for the player. To do anything in a game, players must start by accepting the rules of the game. This may be via the social contract of an analog game, or through the restrictions provided by the code of a digital game. The result is that to play, the player must accept the designer's decisions about what's important and what's not.

Game design is then about constructing worlds. It's about constructing the world of the game, whether that's a party game about avoiding taboo words or the exotic adventures of Lara Croft. The core claim about the potential power of persuasive play lies in the idea that designers construct worlds and give players the ability to experience them. The rules of that world, the experiences in it, the possibilities afforded the player are all dictated by the design.

That means that instead of trying to persuade people by saying, "suppose you were poor and you are trying to live on a tight budget," we can instead make the entire experience for them. We can leave out the suppose, and simply design experiences that make the player poor and give them the goal of trying to keep as much money as they can. This is why games like *Spent* offer so much potential.

The concept is simple. Players own the actions they make in games. Game designers design the rules and systems that dictate what is valuable and what is not. Playing a game is a way of practicing and exploring a designer's framing of what matters and what doesn't. Every game design is a curated experience. The designer has considered what is important and what is not. That curation is in itself an argument about what matters.

7.4 ADAPTING THE LIMITATIONS OF GAME DESIGNS

At first, it can be intimidating to think that every choice must be made. Building worlds, even the smallest of them, can be a very large responsibility. One that could have you questioning absolutely everything and making little progress.

It's a bit like designing a house. You could start with every element, evaluating the materials of each element from roof tiles to plumbing. But starting with all the questions, the really small ones and the really big ones, is the wrong way to go. Instead, you need to start with a few basic questions, like location, size, and for whom it is being built. Many decisions precipitate from those answers, which is why understanding demographics, technographics, and psychographics can be so useful. It's also useful to remember that many decisions come from using what has already been successfully done before.

This is why once a core persuasive intent is decided, it's often smart to adapt existing gameplay experiences. Employing the rule sets of a gambling game might map well to certain persuasive intents. Using the conventions of a digital platformer, also give both designer and player a familiar starting point. They provide a kind of archetype or template from which the game design can derive its unique, new experience.

By analogy, if you want to have a specialized dialogue with someone, you don't start by defining the language, you start by using familiar language and defining the few key terms that let you get at the specifics. In game design, it's the same. Instead of defining an entirely new way to play, often it's about adapting familiar ways to play and making a few key decisions that change the experience toward that persuasive intent.

This analogy to language is quite intentional. Playing games requires a kind of ludo-literacy. A kind of understanding of the language of play, the conventions of play, and the general rhythm of its dynamics. Just as certain types of poetry have specific meters, or certain types of music have distinct beats per minute or instrumentation, games and playful experiences have both rhythms and a kind of language of play. The conventions of sport, with competing teams, time limits, and other elements are part of the language of play. So too are the distinct ways that the games are communicated to players and their audience. Baseball runs or the American football field goals, are different ways of describing how points are earned in their games. They represent both the particular language of the sport, and also the goals and focus of the playful activity. Success in baseball is the product of the number of times the player runs past the home plate. Runs are a way of describing points and the unit of performance inventory. Games that use runs as their indication of progress are part of the ludo-literacy of baseball players and audience. Those people know runs and are likely to understand them in derivative games.

That means that when a game departs significantly from the norm, it's often harder for people to understand it. If you design a game in which field goals are achieved by running past home plate or by collecting money every time the player passes go on the board, you'll likely confuse players. For those who know American football, the conventions of play and the terminology of the game influence the perception and expectations of future games. If your persuasive intent is to critique the conventions of other games, such terminology might be effective. If your persuasive intent has nothing to do with the play standards of such a game, the game may be very confusing to players.

This becomes particularly difficult when designing games for people who have less experience with games. Inexperienced players may have little ludo-literacy. They may have a hard time reading the experience of your game, ultimately preventing them from understanding it. Much like a person may be literate in English, but not in Mandarin, the best poetry in a foreign tongue is often lost by someone incapable of reading it. It's important to know the audience and to make sure that the way meaning is being conveyed in a game is matched to player ludo-literacy.

This is also why some persuasive games are more effective at their intents than others. At first glance, it might seem that a game about matching candies might be more effective at selling candies because it is a literal representation of those candies. But how does matching candies relate to the increasing desire to buy more candies? What does the core action of the game, matching, have to do with eating or enjoying them?

Matching game verbs to persuasive content is one way to support designer intent and ludo-literacy. Common game verbs like match, collect, build, destroy have clear meanings in analogy, offering plenty of opportunity for certain types of persuasive content. The game verb collect, for example, is useful for inspiring consumer behaviors. Collecting all of a set, as a playful experience, is at the heart of activates like card collecting (e.g., baseball or Pokémon cards). Building is a part of Lego, where the play itself is facilitated by collecting useful pieces.

The application of game verbs across persuasive intents affords an opportunity to provide analogy as well as literal persuasive content. Collecting knowledge is a common first draft game verb for a variety of persuasive intent experiences like treasure hunts (e.g., for exploring the wonders of a space or for team building by relying on the skills of individual members) to social impact games that employ quiz mechanics (e.g., unlocking new areas of a game by answering questions).

Such examples are fairly literal because players are collecting what the playful experience argues is valuable. Not all persuasive play game verbs are literal. They may rely on easily translated analogy as well. Some rely on no direct relationship to the game verb. Instead, they aim to leave the player with a sense for a product or situation, or an impression that may carry into a behavior change.

You might not think a game about a long-jump version of hopping in your car could help sell a specific brand, but it may. The brand, Mini USA, for example, offered a game with this basic structure, *Mini Jump* (Mini USA, 2005). To explain how water consumption and the foods people eat relate, the John S. and James L. Knight Foundation funded team at Jolt created a card game. The game focused on players constructing a dinner plate with the least amount of environmental impact. Players quickly

FIGURE 7.4 A card game about water consumption and food choices, made by a team of students at the American University Game Lab.

learned that certain foods, like meats, cost many more resources than others (Figure 7.4).

The literal experience is not always the one that's most persuasive. If you doubt this, consider how often a car is marketed through attributes most people will never use. Viewers are shown a car careening down a race track at 105 MPH and skidding through a corner. At the very bottom of the advertisement is a warning—professional drivers on closed track, do not try this yourself. The appeal of driving that way, or having that potential is engaging, but the reality is nothing like it. That car will likely spend most of its time circling the block looking for an appropriate parking spot, stuck in bumper to bumper traffic, or resting, unmoving in a garage. What sells, or what persuades, one of the largest purchases people will make is the idea. The feeling or sense of the vehicle. The idea of it.

That's what persuasive play does too. Mini offered a suite of online games when it first launched in the United States. The games had almost nothing to do with the car, but they felt like the playful, whimsical, oddball brand they were building. The games and playful experiences were interesting in the early days of advergames on the web. They created a stopping point. A place for people to send their friends for a collection of interesting little games featuring the car. If you were interested, you could even shop for the cars online and see the possibility space. The collection didn't take itself too seriously, persuading you to do the same. Perhaps, on a whim, you'd just go ahead and buy one of these vehicles because you like the site, a bit free spirited, young, and willing.

The truth is that often games can do more in creating a spirit or sense of product than merely reminding us of its existence. This is what many of the most effective persuasive play games do. They don't always simulate the product; they simulate an aligned emotion or sense of product. They offer less literal experiences.

This is also true of effective social impact games. It's not always about inviting the player to experience the frustration of poverty, the detriments of an unhealthy lifestyle, or the problems with the many things that you, as a consumer, are doing to the planet every day. Instead, if you want to draw players in, offer them the chance to show how they can beat the system and break the cycle of poverty (even if the game won't let them). Invite them to see what their current lifestyle will do to them in a few years or give them a chance to explore how a few changers could change that trajectory. Instead of aligning them with the problem, help them explore a world of solutions. Play is far more inviting when there is an opportunity to win, not an opportunity to lose less.

Consider Tiltfactor's game, Awkward Moment. The team describes it thus:

> Awkward Moment® puts 3–8 players in terrifically awkward social situations! Players gather a hand of Reactions and together face hysterical, embarrassing, or stressful events. How Awkward! Taking turns as "the Decider," players use Decider Card to determine the basis for a winning Reaction. Players try to impress the Decider by submitting the best response from their hand of cards! Awkward Moment is a 20-minute game for middle and high school students (3–8 players ages 12 and up). (Tiltfactor, 2019.)

Nothing in that invitation or explanation of the game hints at the game's intent. The game is really about broadening participation in science, technology, engineering, and math fields (STEM) and reducing gender biases. Awkward Moment was designed to apply psychology that strengthens associations between women and STEM and to inspire greater assertiveness in confronting social bias (Figure 7.5).

It all seems quite obvious from the outside, but it's hard to do well. This is why game design is a practice. To do this kind of work well takes practice. Once you've become really good at it, something will change, and you'll have to keep practicing to continue to be good at it.

FIGURE 7.5 Tiltfactor's Awkward Moment employs psychology to address social bias. (Courtesy of Mary Flanagan.)

7.5 SIMULATION

Often, when people are first thinking about persuasive play, they think of simulation. They hope that by designing a digital petri dish of the problem or by simulating the experience, they will persuade people toward the game's intent. This is possible, but it's not always the easiest way to go about it.

Consider, for example, the conventions of a first-person shooter game. If a game is realistic, it might limit ammunition, as ammunition is limited in the real world. But, in so doing, the game may be rather dull.

Of course, what's important and what's not can be a product of fun or practical needs. Sometimes, a designer leaves out or adds features or elements simply because they support the practicalities of a game. In reality, any kind of fragmentation wound or deep flesh wound, common to some forms of real-world war, is going to slow a fighter down. But having to deal with such realities in a game is more than most players are willing to deal with. If a game is too close to reality, it may cease to be interesting or engaging. Spending 15 minutes eating dinner in a space shooter or tending to a wound that occurred 4 hours prior can feel pretty tangential to a game about saving the world from imminent destruction.

Simulations, even the best of them, are still an exercise in selection. There is curation. Some things must go and some things must stay. While this is a practical reality, it's also an assumption by players and the product of a designed experience. The designer can't put every element of the subject of simulation in the game. The player doesn't expect everything to be simulated. When the designer chooses what stays and what goes, they are making a decision about what's important and what's not. They are also communicating with the player about what's important and what's not. Like any communication, there is an agreed upon language—that language is ludo-literacy.

This is one of the reasons why persuasion via simulation is not always easy. The practicalities of simulation can interfere with the designer's intent to communicate what's important and what's not. The language of play is not without its ambiguities. For players, distinguishing what the designer chooses to do and what's a practical limitation is not always easy.

If, as a player, you are offered a simulation of a car by a car manufacturer, you may appreciate how the car looks and how it handles. You may think, sure this is a great car. But you know you're being sold to, so you're also quite aware that you're not getting the entire experience. You know some things are being hidden from you, and you might even start looking for them. You might notice the simulation doesn't show how inefficient the car is or how little leg room is in the back. You realize quickly that you have more questions than answers because the simulation simplified your experience.

Now take the same aim in a contemporary space. No one tells you they are looking to sell you a car. Perhaps you're excited about cars and play a lot of racing simulations. Your current racing simulation includes a variety of cars, some are the rarest and most beautiful in the world. In addition, there are a couple that you've seen on the street. Two years later, when you're buying a car, some of those brands you played might just stick with you. You might not even realize why, but you've got some innate feeling that certain brands are sportier than others. Or more rugged. You didn't sign up to be persuaded, but you were persuaded all the same.

This is why, for example, auto manufacturers want their cars in racing simulations. In the early 1980s, designers were begging car manufactures to allow them to use their brands: 25 years later, the car manufactures are paying to be in the games (Wilson, 2012). Similar to the brand placements movie viewers have seen for years, this is perhaps the cleverer way to integrate persuasive content, to sell consumers on something, than merely giving them an opportunity to try it.

Selling cars or their brands are good examples, because they involve not only current buyers, but aspirational buyers. Brands like Porsche and Ford are very much aware of this. The *Ford Racing* game franchise ran from 2000 (Elite Systems) to 2008 (Razorworks). When the Porsche Boxster was first offered, the PlayStation game *Porsche Challenge* (SCEE Internal Development Team, 1997) was released. Such games not only align the brands with racing, they also feed aspirational buyers (e.g., young people who aren't old enough to drive yet).

7.6 CRITICAL PLAY AND CRITICAL DESIGN

Of course, all of this is discarded when the player engages in working to game the system, actively working against the rules of the game for their own goals. Players are always free to engage in playing with a game contrary to its intended play. Engaging in a war game, as a pacifist, can be a way to make claims about what the game designers intended. This kind of critical playing is not often a design consideration, but more often serves as a way to think critically about what a designer can do in their dialogue with the player. What happens when a game isn't played as intended and what meaning does that leave?

While it may be impossible to play the entirety of a *Call of Duty* game without shooting a virtual gun, what does it mean to never fire a single missile in the *September 12th* game? How does the game support or prevent such play? Likewise, what meaning is left when the player engages in critical play?

While not often the focus of design activity, thinking about critical play can aid in completing the persuasive intent of a game. What happens when a player does nothing with a game you've designed? Or what happens if they do something unconventional but likely? Does your game design about feeding the poor allow the player to starve them for profit?

Just as players might subvert expected interactions, designers can do the same.

Designing persuasive content around subverting player expectations or assumptions is part of the design practice of critical design. Critical design often aims to subvert player expectations. If play is built on an archetype of familiar game experiences, critical design can provide an opportunity to create critical distance between player assumptions and the game's reality. Perhaps players assume points are the way to win, but the designer wants to subvert that expectation to make a persuasive aim. A clever designer might, for example, create a board game with a lot of paper money only to have the player discover that while they were worried about collecting money, they were actually losing the game.

Critical design often aims to exploit the "aha" moment of player surprise. If a player is engaging in familiar activities and something goes

FIGURE 7.6 Molleindustria's *The Best Amendment*, a game offering a distinct argument about gun rights. (Courtesy of Molleindustria through the public domain.)

wrong, they are often left asking a simple question. What did they do and why didn't it work (this time)? That moment is the key to encouraging the player to think critically about their behavior.

A good example of this is Molleindustria's *The Best Amendment*. Molleindustria produces games that are labeled as radical games. They are often critical of society, current news, or concepts. In *The Best Amendment*, players are offered a typical, casual shooting game. The player proceeds as expected, shooting their enemy. Later rounds grow to more and more enemies, increasing the challenge. What players fail to recognize until they play is that each level is simply an instance of the player's last round. When the player is shooting, they are shooting at themselves, folded over time. It is critical of the notion that the best defense against guns is more guns. It is, by the designer's own language prefacing the game "An unofficial NRA game about gun control, tactical shooting, and 4th dimensional thinking. Be the good guy with a gun! Stop the bad guys with guns! But will that make you a bad guy in the eyes of somebody else?" (Molleindustria, 2013). The suggestive forms of the characters (somewhere between bullets and white hoods) and the rattling banjo background music further emphasize the creator's commentary (Figure 7.6).

7.7 PROCEDURAL RHETORIC

Such designs can serve a persuasive aim (such as encouraging players to avoid the lure of chasing that paper money), but they also create a very real challenge. If a game aims to persuade by lying to a player, or tricking them, it's often a single shot experience. Such games are similar to scams, they can be run once before they need an entirely new audience to be effective. This is the problem with employing some surprise trick in a game's design. Once the trick is known, its opportunity to have an impact is greatly diminished.

That's very different from a game that employs some persistent, repeated, and ideally enjoyable message through a full gameplay experience. If play is practice, then a game that asks a player to do something repeatedly might feel like a repeated practice. In theory, if a game rewards the player for repeatedly saving the bulk of their in-game currency, they are learning behavior that will transfer to the real world.

The reality of this theory is not as direct or as simple as claimed. Players practice shooting in first-person shooter games, for example, but there is no evidence their aim improves. For all the racing games in the world, there are lots of bad drivers and plenty of first-time drivers who still need practice with real cars.

Beyond the tradeoffs of simulation, it's also evident that practicing in games doesn't make people experts. Instead, it gives them an opportunity to play with a set of rules that the designer constructed. These rules have a sense of what's important and what's not.

This is the core concept in procedural rhetoric. If you need some degree of ludo-literacy to understand the language of a game, then you may also need it to understand the claims a game makes about the world it simulates, references, or otherwise constructs.

This is because when designers craft a game, players are asked to subscribe to the rules of the game to play. The rules of play, the things a player must accept, and the relationship of play elements are part of this rhetoric. The designer, by creating the game, is making a claim about how the parts should fit together. If the player wants to play, they need to accept those terms (if they are not playing critically).

If aliens are invading earth, the designer constructs the means for dealing with those aliens. If the designer gives the player a gun, and only a gun, they are making claims about how to handle the problem. If the player is given a stack of cards to translate to understand what the aliens are attempting to communicate, that's a different claim. That's a different rhetoric on what matters and how the game is won.

Procedural rhetoric is important for understanding persuasive play because it helps frame the arguments the games makes. If a game offers only one way to solve a problem, then its argument is fairly narrow about the problem and its solution. A typical shooting game, for example, often has the same basic argument. If there is a problem, eliminate it to get past it.

Knowing the game verbs in a game helps unpack the procedural rhetoric of the design. If a shooting game provides a player with one bullet and 30 enemies, it might be making a claim about the balance of power or the value of that bullet. Perhaps one bullet at the right target is more important than 100 bullets for 30 enemies. Perhaps the bullet isn't intended for the enemies at all.

Procedural rhetoric is useful for aiming persuasive play designs toward their goal. What are the procedures for solving the in-game problem and what do they claim? In a game about contemporary politics, rewarding players for their vocal volume says a lot. The procedure to winning the game might not be the quality of the arguments the candidate makes, but instead how loud they resonate. The way the game is won can make an argument about the way the game world works. For some designers, the hope is that the way the game is won makes arguments about the way the world works.

7.8 ASSESSING IMPACT

Core to the draw of persuasive play is a sense of efficacy. In short, a persuasive game that is not persuasive is simply a game. That means that unlike some other ways people do things with games, persuasive play is very much tied to analyzing impact. It's a practice that is very much tied to efficacy. How effective is the game at what it aims to do? What specific measures matter?

Impact assessment occurs in a variety of ways. Most of these are informed by older traditions in assessing efficacy. They are informed by educational assessments analysis, which aims to assess growth in knowledge or changes in perception. Marketing practices have effective ways to assess how people have changed their interests, activities, or opinions. Psychology likewise has formals ways of assessing intended change.

The optimal means for assessing impact is heavily dependent on the design and its intention. Requesting that players complete a pre-test, play a game, and then complete a post-test is a nice structure for researchers but a somewhat impractical one in the crowded space of mobile applications. Although some notable games like *ICED: I Can End Deportation* (Breakthrough, 2008), used such structures to collect feedback and understand player knowledge growth, it's not ideal. In modern games, this type of feedback is better collected through tracking the player's in-game performance in logs. Doing so is often less obstructive to the play experience, although the ethics of doing so without explicit knowledge or consent of the player are clearly up for debate.

Often, it is useful to assess the effectiveness of a design in iterations. Producing multiple prototypes and refining them is an appropriate way to both design and assess some types of efficacy. Since design is a practice, it should not be a surprise that is refined and evolved as people do it.

Effect is best assessed when it's defined and specific. Broad aims are often large but hard to pin down for the formal process of assessment. This is because most assessments aim to isolate the effect by understanding where the player was before they engaged in the designed experience and after.

Aiming to change the way the player thinks about everything is obviously too broad. However, some designers similarly have broad aims. Undoing some well-formed opinion or changing the consumer behavior of someone with 15 years of shopping experience is not a trivial effect.

It's important to be realistic about the expected effect of a design. A single person's life is full of many experiences. They learn from these experiences. As a game designer, the aim is to create new experiences that they may also learn from. These experiences are often much smaller than the myriad of real-life experiences that have helped them form their interests, activities, or opinions. Game experiences can be very effective, because heuristic learning, learning through experience, is one of the many ways people acquire knowledge.

The challenge is in designing an experience that will create the desired effect in a measurable way. Measuring effect broadly is difficult and often inaccurate. There are ways to measure a broad audience, but broad effect is a bit harder.

This is why, especially for new designers of persuasive play, aiming at an assessable effect is one of the best ways to start well. Assessable effects might be narrow in their aspiration (e.g., get a very specific audience to change a minor behavior) or incremental (e.g., move players toward a minor behavioral improvement).

Measuring long-term effect is even more complicated than short-term effect. This is why many games are often focused on the long term. Others are content with the hope that they change long-term behavior. There is, for example, no widely published study of the effect of *Porsche Challenge* on the car-buying habits of players over 10 or 15 years. For some types of efforts, the hope is enough.

The formal practices of testing and assessing game efficacy are offered in Chapter 11. Generally, when designing persuasive play, it's often important to make sure that there is some type of measurable aim. The appropriate tools and methods depend largely on the scale, scope, and subject. It's also important to recognize that some persuasive content is created with not specific expectations of assessment. Art games, personal projects, and others may never be assessed, or they may be assessed by other researchers who do not have a relationship with the design.

As with any assessment, supporting objectivity, managing elements to avoid misrepresentations of data, and other experimental designs practices are essential for credible work. Good experimental design, conducting focus groups, market research, and other established practices are beyond the scope of this chapter. It should be sufficient to understand that the aim is design and experience that can be evaluated for its effect when appropriate.

7.9 PRACTICE WHAT YOU'VE LEARNED

- Choose five games that you've played before. Identify the ways in which their procedural rhetoric is apparent. How do they reward players? What elements did the designer choose to simulate and which were left out?

- Identify five common game archetypes that seem outdated or contrary to your current views. Write a few concept statements that outline a critical play or critical design version of the game. What portion of the game's conventions or current gameplay would be subverted and what argument would result from the new play experience?

- Choose a persuasive play intent (e.g., get people to eat healthier food or understand one brand as better than another). Identify a collection of game verbs that align with that intent. Write out a few simple concept statements that require players to adopt the persuasive aim of your design. Test those concepts with players. Which ones are easiest to understand, and which ones are difficult?

REFERENCES

Bogost, Ian. *Persuasive Games: The Expressive Power of Videogames.* Cambridge, MA: MIT Press, 2007.

Breakthrough. *ICED: I Can End Deportation.* Breakthrough, 2008. http://www. icedgame.com/.

Djaouti, Damien, Julian Alvarez, Jean-Pierre Jessel, and Olivier Rampnoux. "Origins of serious games." In Minhua Ma, Andreas Oikonomou, and Lakhmi C. Jain, eds., *Serious Games and Edutainment Applications*, 25–43. London: Springer, 2011.

Elite Systems. *Ford Racing*. Empire Interactive, 2000.

Mini USA. *Mini Jump*. MiniUSA.com, 2005. http://www.gamesbob.com/minijump.

Molleindustria. The Best Amendment. Molleindustria, 2013. http://www.molleindustria.org/the-best-amendment/.

Razorworks. *Ford Racing Off Road*. Xplosiv, 2008.

SCEE Internal Development Team. *Porsche Challenge*. Sony Computer Entertainment, 1997.

Schädler, Ulrich. "'Juden Raus!' (Jews Out!)—History's most." *International Journal for the Study of Board Games CNWS* (2003, 6): 47.

Tiltfactor, Awkward Moment, 2019. https://tiltfactor.org/game/awkward-moment/.

Wilson, Mark. 2012. How Do Real Cars End up in Video Games. https://www.fastcompany.com/1669990/how-do-real-cars-end-up-in-video-games-and-does-it-help-the-brands.

CHAPTER 8

Empathy Games

T HE NOTION OF CREATING empathy through games has seen its peaks and valleys. There have been scholars who have championed games as the next great empathy medium and those who have countered this by decrying such work as a myth. Generally, research indicates a potential for the ability of games to increase empathy (Greitemeyer et al., 2010). This chapter aims to outline some of the core discussions about creating empathy in games and the central concepts of designing with empathy in mind.

At its core, the notion of empathy is about the ability to share and understand the feelings of one another. Games seem like a great opportunity to develop empathy within players because we know that games often place players in someone else's role. If a player must overcome the challenges of a nurse in an emergency room or a soldier in World War Two, the logic is that they will help understand some of the feelings of real people in those roles.

Accept that we also understand that games are separate from real life. Games typically simplify the experiences of the real so that they are entertaining. Playing a video game in the role of a World War Two soldier doesn't involve all of the experiences of a true soldier. Some people argue that games dissuade empathy, as is much of the focus of those who feel games encourage violent behavior by desensitizing players to violence. This logic reads that they are reverse empathy machines, discouraging players from feeling empathy toward their victims while simultaneously encouraging players to act in such ways without developing remorse for their actions. This is, of course, problematized by the fact that the link between game playing and violent behavior is tenuous, and the vast majority of players never develop such insensitivities.

In previous chapters, we've discussed the idea that designers select what to simulate, what to dissimulate, and what to simply leave out of a game. Ideally, if designing with the goal of achieving empathy, a game will emphasize the elements that develop those specific empathies. Turning up the volume on the elements that encourage emotional understanding, while dialing down those that do not, is a delicate balance. The harmony of a game can quickly be destroyed by over-emphasizing a specific element.

This is where the tension in empathy design exists. If players engage in an FPS, there is no guarantee that they will develop the same kind of emotional affinities that a real person in the same situation develops. Players of war simulations, for example, are not typically supposed to develop post-traumatic stress disorder. Players of murder mystery games are not in need of psychosocial support for the traumas they have witnessed. Not only are games by definition not real life, they are not supposed to be. How then can players be expected to understand real emotions or the psychology of others?

Games are separate from real life, but empathy games seek to develop, at least temporarily, real emotion in players. Similar to persuasive play, the games aim to help players move from less of a shared emotional understanding or feeling toward more of one. Despite the break from reality that games offer, this is not too far-fetched.

First, consider that many players already share an emotional connection to the stories they experience. Avid players of the *Final Fantasy* (Square, 1987) franchise share the emotional highs and lows of that designed experience. Amateur and professional sports players share the highs and lows of victory and defeat, of training and strategies. These communities share some emotion even though each is coming from a different real-world experience and a different background. Being able to share those emotions across instances of *Final Fantasy*, or the sports field, can help to develop a sense of empathy in players. They begin to understand each other's emotions. When a professional team loses a game with a near-miss, the amateur player knows, perhaps at a lesser scale, the emotion attached to that loss.

In this way, all games offer some element of empathy. This empathy might be shared across a play community, or it may simply be propagated by each play instance. It's the designer's goal to develop those elements of empathy to do what is intended with the game.

8.1 SCALING EMOTION

This is the first hint at the potential for empathy games. Empathy games can, in theory, provide a scaled opportunity to experience the emotions of another. They can do so through the kind of curated experience designers create. Just as World War Two simulations decant the elements that are most entertaining by focusing on the action of the battle or the clamor of war, an empathy game can focus on those elements that create other emotional responses.

As an example, consider a game that focuses not on the power fantasy of being an invulnerable soldier, but instead, a very vulnerable refugee. The scale of action might move from killing 50 soldiers on your way to a base to evading soldiers in the dark of night and scrounging for food. The emotions as a refugee might be tied to finding out that a missing relative is alive, traveling a distance that would have once been trivial in ordinary life, or simply making a friend. The scale of the experiences is much smaller than that of the traditional fighting game, but the emotional scale of those experiences may be much greater.

For empathy games, one common approach is to reposition the emotional meter of the experience in order to help players build an emotional understanding. Some games do this by finding analogy to common in-game or real-world experiences. Many games employ the mechanics of hunting for something. In *Oregon Trail*, it's hunting wild animals for food (MECC, 1985). In so doing, the player realizes how non-trivial it was to eat when traveling the US frontier. The emotional understanding is eased by the player's previous experience of being some version of hungry in the past. Ideally, the player's emotional understanding is heightened. They increase their empathy for the need to hunt and the precariousness of life and death on the trail. What such designs do, is start with a familiar emotion and scale it for effect. The effect, it is hoped, is greater empathy.

The collect mechanic is common to games as widely divergent as *Pac-Man* (Namco, 1980) to *Grand Theft Auto* (DMA Design, 1997). Players know how to collect and recognize it as an experience. The emotional understanding comes then from the ways in which it scaled. In the game *Darfur is Dying* (Ruiz et al., 2006), players are tasked with collecting water. First, for the audience the game was designed for, this is a relatively trivial task. Turn on your tap and pour, or walk to the nearest store and buy a bottle of water. In the game, getting water is a dangerous effort in running and evading. The player must find the well, fill their water tank, and return without getting caught by Janjaweed militia with guns on the back of a pickup truck. The scale of the game is small, but the cost and emotion are much larger. The player character, on foot, is facing low odds and high risk for a relatively small need—water.

This is a good example of how empathy can be dialed up simply by changing the scale of the player task. Many players will empathize with the need to fulfill a fairly basic human need, water, with enormous challenges that seem unnecessarily unforgiving. By design, the experience is frustrating and alarming.

But, creating empathy is not always about representing a player on screen. The game *Hush* (Antonisse and Johnson, 2007) focused on the 1994 genocide in Rwanda, creating empathy experientially. The game tasks players with quieting a baby to avoid detection by nearby militia. The player does so by typing the letters on screen at just the right moments. The rhythm of play is tense, juxtaposing the effort to calm with the impending threats of the outside world. The player sees nothing of war or its realities but feels the tension. This tension is raised as play continues and it is designed to scale emotion to create empathy.

In designing games that seek to scale emotion, one of the easiest places to start is with familiar emotions and familiar mechanics. Just as in other chapters, the merits of starting with familiar experiences can create a lower barrier for entry when new players engage with the experience. The mechanics of *Hush* are common to typing games. The emotional content comes mainly from the situation explained, instead of the depiction on screen.

Scaling a familiar emotion is much easier than scaling an unfamiliar one. Many emotions are universally experienced, so designers can assume players have felt happiness, sadness, irritation, fear, and others. But scaling them, either by intensifying them, or showing how these emotions are felt by others, can support the aim of an empathy focused game. Creating a game that gives players high and low emotions is already part of the standard experience of games. Players know what winning and losing feel like, but the designer must find a way to scale them to meet the empathetic goal. Such designs are much like telling a story that begins, "remember when you were really frustrated, that's how this person feels." Of course, the challenge there is a common challenge to empathy games. How do you invite people to experience an emotion they don't necessarily want to feel?

8.2 SHIFTING PERSPECTIVE

Another way the designers aim to develop player empathy is through a shift in perspective. This second approach doesn't merely give the player a glimpse into the feelings of another, it tasks the player with owning the perspective of another with the aim of developing their empathy. Instead of being the soldier, what happens when you are the citizen in a war-torn country? More aptly, what happens when your perspective shifts, between the needs of the soldier, the politician, the citizen, and each of the individuals who have specific goals and needs in the middle of a conflict.

This second approach, a shift in perspective, is focused on the power of role play. The player must own the role they have been given. In the most aggressive attempts at empathy games, the player is given a perspective highly divergent from their own. Such a game aims to communicate the emotional experience of being a transgendered person in a world favoring cisgender like the game *Mainichi* (Brice, 2012). Others aim to remind players of the downsides of the experiences they enjoy.

This is the aim of a game like *This War of Mine* (11 bit studios, 2014), which tasks players with surviving war not as a soldier, but as a non-combatant. The game aims to develop empathy in players by relinquishing the power fantasy of many war games, by instead showing the reluctant challenges faced by living in a war-torn environment. The title of the game hints at this notion of perspective—emphasized in the inclusion of the word, mine.

This role play provides an opportunity for players to not just feel emotions, but understand them. Some games help players feel, others explain where those feelings come from. If the verbs in the game are designed to create the emotional experience of frustration, they can also be used to explain the source of that frustration. Such games aim to help players develop an empathy that is both emotional and logical. The player ideally walks away from the game with a new understanding.

The understanding comes in part from a new goal orientation. A soldier in a war game must kill all combatants; the goal is clear and direct. A non-combatant in a war game has many different goals. Survival is the one that most often arises, but it should be quickly evident that survival is a very ambiguous goal. Do players kill to survive, do they barter, do they flee? The confusion about what to do next, which goal is the right goal, can be employed to create the same sense of confusion a non-combatant might have. In this way, the player is getting an emotional education and learning empathy through experience. They are moving toward understanding why the emotions are present.

It's important to note that when the perspective shifts, so too does the emotional meaning of the decisions the player makes. The player, when assuming a role, owns the game verbs. The game's design may reward or punish certain emotional states that guide the player toward empathy. In the game *Hush*, for example, the player is rewarded for acting calmly, but the game punishes key presses that are both too early or too late. The balance of timing is an important tension design for the experience.

Hush also provides evidence that a game verb does not have to align directly with the focus of empathy. The game wants the players to feel empathy for victims, but the verbs which focus on quieting a baby are not directly aligned to the game's focus. When people think of war, they don't often think of such a tiny moment. However, it's that simple role play that affords an opportunity for an empathetic experience. Just as emotion can be scaled for empathy, situation can be too. In this case, the situation is scaled to a small but important moment, and the game verb is also small. The role, being a mother, shifts the player's perspective and increases the value of that small moment and goal.

8.3 TELLING STORIES

A third approach is to develop the emotional power of storytelling toward a game's empathy goal. The techniques in storytelling for empathy borrow from the rich history of storytelling across a wide range of media, but with one exception. They add the experiential element of choice. Designers in story-driven games aim to tell stories through player action, or inaction, that heighten empathies. This is a combination of both a shift in perspective and a scaled emotion. The aforementioned games rely on a narrative setup (e.g., you are a mother trying to hush your baby so that you can remain hidden) but not a full narrative. Telling stories through or with games creates new affordances for how the story is experienced.

In film, viewers are typically not given a choice about where the story continues and where it ends. They are not given a choice about the twists and turns and are typically subject to the same emotional trajectory. In game terms, film is on rails, like a train, with constant guidance about where the story goes next.

In games, the potential for emotional empathy changes because the narrative is not always on rails. The player can choose to do something or not do anything. If a player chooses to break the law of war and kill non-combatants, as was available in *Spec Ops: The Line* (Yager Development, 2012), then the emotional experience of that event was not forced upon them, but chosen by them. In the game, the player can choose to scare unarmed civilians off by shooting in the air or the player can shoot the civilians.

That sense of choice gives both perspective on the din and clamor of war, but also brings the player into the emotional experience. They are no longer bystanders watching the emotions of others, they are contributing to the emotional experience of others and themselves.

This, of course, risks the emotional detachment that play can offer. Players can recuse themselves from the decision by admitting that it's just a game. But there is the personal decision that remains a part of the player experience. When the player is not required to do something, but does it anyway, they are revealing something about themselves to themselves. Remember that players, unlike with movies and other media, position themselves as central to the experience. The key question in every game, for a player is—what do I do in the game?

For this reason, empathy games offer the opportunity for players to tell stories with additional personal meaning. Stories that involve the emotion of others. The player can choose to kill innocent non-combatants and make that part of their story of play or not. Once they have done it, they have learned something about their story. They have learned that they may have had enough emotional detachment to think, it's just a game, kill them all. Or they may have learned that they didn't have such detachment or simply didn't feel right about it. Understanding the origins of those emotions, feeling those emotions and their conflict, is a power of games that can offer the potential for empathy. The scale of the choice has real meaning by analogy. A player could choose to kill innocent non-combatants because it's part of the game, just as a real soldier could choose to kill innocent non-combatants because it's part of war.

The power is that the analogy of the story supports the power of emotional scale. Even the small moment when a player hesitates gives the player a peek into the emotion of real soldiers in real war. It is such moments, moments that give players pause, that help build an understanding of empathy.

Developing story for empathy is so complex that it could be the subject of an entire book. To start, it's useful to think about the procedural rhetoric that appears in your game's design (see Chapter 7 for a refresher). What affordances does your game provide and how can they be used to develop player empathies? Sometimes, providing role play in the smallest of moments provides as much impact as the complexities of large-scale stories. But complexity often allows for nuance and offers opportunities for emotional investment that short experiences may not.

Stories in games don't always need to be computer moderated or articulated. Role play, of course, is often a non-digital experience. How analog designers use stories varies widely, but the opportunity for choice remains one of the key elements for inspiring empathy. Will the player do something differently because they are playing the role?

Designers must consider the experiences that might drive players to associate and empathize or disassociate and perhaps lose empathy. One particularly effective way to integrate the power of play with the story in the analog game space is through alternate reality games. Alternate reality games allow players to take on the roles of characters in an alternate reality and play through the construct of a story. Other allied play, such as live action role play (LARP), can offer similar opportunities. These are particularly effective when players are given the opportunity to reflect on the choices they made while playing and how their sense of empathy changed through play. The book *Nordic Larp* (Stenros and Montola, 2010) provides a wonderful overview of many such games and hints at the ways in which designers of these experiences designed fictions that affected player empathies.

8.4 COOPERATING EMPATHY

This notion of cooperating between player and designer or player and player is less researched but clearly offers an opportunity in empathy design. The game *Journey* (Thatgamecompany, 2012), for example, has two players working across a network together in ways that have them sharing emotional highs and lows. Players are cooperating toward the same goals, shifting their perspective from the individual to the group. The player moves from asking what do *I* need to asking what do *we* need. This is a clear opportunity for effectively shifting player's understanding of a problem.

In practice, this is most easily achieved by designing role play that encourages cooperation. This may come in the form of a common goal shared among multiple players with different roles, as is the case for games like Pandemic (Z-Man Games, 2008). Games that seek to provide empathy for competing interests in land use, for example, can position players as real estate developers, conservationists, tourism industry professionals, and residents. The players would be responsible for meeting each of the different player types needs, ideally inspiring an empathetic glance into the needs of each. Since the land is a shared resource, such play brings competing interests into a single focused territory.

8.5 THE PROBLEMS WITH EMPATHY DESIGN

This book has largely framed game design as oriented toward providing a player with a goal, an obstacle, and a means to overcoming that obstacle. In short, games are about problems. This is the gist of much empathy design in games. Players must be presented with a problem and experience, or at least witness the emotion of dealing with that problem.

The problem is the *thing* that brings out the emotion. If you consider the many ways in which emotion comes out in games, it rarely comes from the lack of a problem, save for the satisfaction or ease that is conjured when the problem goes away. This is why so much of empathy design is about positioning the problem.

If a game aims to help you change your empathies from one person to another, it merely needs to position the player goals toward the other person. At least, that's the hope. In reality, a shift in perspective alone does not increase an emotional understanding of that perspective. Creating an emotion in a player offers a glimpse into emotional empathy (i.e., I feel how someone else felt), but not necessarily understanding (i.e., I know why someone else feels a certain way and I can foresee how they will feel). As mentioned, playing hours of a war simulation doesn't make a player more empathetic to the emotional challenges of being a solider. In fact, it may do the opposite, glamorizing it in the same vein as movies or books that champion war without focusing on its darker emotions.

This is the problem with empathy design. Empathy is a complex thing. Of all the things someone might want to do with a game, empathy is one of the higher challenges. Empathy seeks to help people understand something that they may not be able to explain—emotion. Empathy aims to hit the sweet spot between apathy and focus. An aim that is somewhat similar to the flow state described in Chapter 4.

Instead of worrying about keeping the player focused, empathy aims to keep the player emotionally engaged. This may mean developing an understanding of the emotion by providing the ramp-up needed to know why the emotions have developed to the state they have. But it may also mean pushing the player toward a place they personally care about. The psychology of empathy is complex and beyond the scope of this single chapter. Instead, it is perhaps easier to understand by analogy to film and television.

Consider early film and television. Watching the comedians in The Three Stooges struggle with their slapstick problems did not trigger an empathetic response. Instead, the eye pokes and other physical comedy of those moments engaged a detached emotional experience. Viewers of such comedy did not feel bad for the actors, they instead laughed at them.

This is by design. Viewers are not emotionally invested in the performers, because emotional investment could turn much of the comedy into tragedy. In video, there are now a wide variety of camera techniques that aim to affect viewer empathy. Taking a wide-angle view of a painful moment puts it into context (you can see everything around the person) but distances the viewer from the emotional content of the moment. Taking a tight, intimate shot of just the person's face brings the emotional substance of the moment into focus but limits the context. To make comedy work, it's a technique of balancing these camera techniques with the story, actor performance, and a variety of other elements. The same series of events can seem tragic or comedic, depending on how it's shot.

The same is true of a game. Beyond employing the camera techniques of cinema for use in a game, the mechanics of a game can be offered in a way that either distances the player from the emotion of the experience or brings them closer to it. One of the easiest ways to do this is to create mechanics that carry their own emotion and allow for scaling from the everyday experience of the player.

Consider, for example, the monotony of a long road trip. If, in-game, the designer wants to encourage the player to feel the tension of waiting for the theater of war to begin, the designer could include a playable driving experience full of minor, non-dramatic turns. Imagine, for example, that the player begins the game with intense training with weapons and vehicles. After an hour of high intensity training experiences, the player must pilot a vehicle across a vast desert. There is the occasional turn, but much of the time is spent in minor banter between non-player characters and occasional warnings from an officer. The tension in that experience, and the emotion of it, comes from the contrast (high intensity to low intensity) and the familiarity of the experience. Many people have driven hours across dull countryside, but the scale of doing so in the game will heighten their emotional experience to it. This, of course, would be further emphasized by the explosion from a land mine that throws the player character from their seat and precipitates a new set of problems for the player.

Returning to film, fast forward to Quentin Tarantino's *Kill Bill* (Tarantino, 2004), and the violence the heroine unleashes on the world around her. She too pokes people in the eye, but when she does it, they lose an eye and their life. The emotion of that film is centered on the drive and vengeance the viewers want her to fulfill. Each time she is punched or cut with a sword, there is some version of an empathetic response. Those abuses she faces are processed as both physical hurt and emotional pain. The experience of the film is one of a journey full of emotion that plays on portions of empathy. But how?

Like many stories, empathy can be developed with a few common tools. By scaling a situation, from something familiar to something grand, the player can have their emotions similarly scaled. Universal experiences are an easy start. Consider problems that each person in the world has had, and how they might scale to increase the emotional weight of the conflict. As a funny example, perhaps start with needing to go to the bathroom. It's a common challenge, perhaps waiting for a public restroom to be unlocked or a sibling to finish in a shared bathroom. Now scale it. Consider the situation of a politician who might need to speak in front of millions of people but needs to pee before they do so. Consider a game that allows the player to make a choice, start the speech late and go to the bathroom or skip the bathroom and go right into the speech. Each has its cost; each is a problem. Starting the speech late might give an opponent just enough time to rally the crowd against the player. Skipping the bathroom might mean wetting yourself in front of a crowd. The scale and cost of these decisions are large and in so doing, the emotion may be increased. This is one way to scale the emotion and ideally, offer some empathy for an emotional situation for the player.

Shifting perspective is another way to address the challenge of building empathy. Shifting perspective may mean more than merely putting the player in someone else's shoes. It can mean changing the goals for the same general perspective. Consider a game where the player starts as a healthy soldier ready to fight evil. Loaded in their transport, they are about to descend into the fog of war. Unfortunately, their transport is bombed, and instead of firing a gun as a hero, the player must spend the rest of the game trying to crawl to safety. The emotional rise and fall of this game can present an opportunity to explain, experientially, the emotion of war. Not everyone charges into the middle and destroys the forces of evil. Some soldiers never get a chance to fight, because that's war. This is the premise of a small indie game by James Earl Cox III of Seemingly Pointless, called [US]SR (2013) (Figure 8.1).

It should be clear that each of these elements can be used in combination to encourage empathy within the player. The previous examples for both shifting perspective and scale are actually rather dependent on story. Likewise, it's easy to imagine that cooperative elements, where the player

FIGURE 8.1 *[US]SR* is a game that provides a different perspective on war, potentially inspiring empathy. (Courtesy of James Earl Cox III.)

is not only aiming to meet their own goal, but must work with others to complete the goal, could be added.

8.6 CONTINUITY, ABUSE, AND PLAYER TRUST

It's important to recognize that much of the cultural and contemporary understanding of story are required to make an effective emotional journey for the player. If a card game breaks continuity or its own fiction, it risks dissociating the player from the experience. If a digital game hammers the player with problems, especially ones that can't be resolved, it may feel less like a playful experience and more like abuse. Just like film, there are many genres and game types. Some types of games are abusive on purpose, to make a point or to attract players to the experience of that abuse. Massocore is a term applied to games that aim to be extremely hard. That extreme affords an opportunity for some types of empathy. Consider, for example, a masoacore game with a social impact focus. A game that aims to demonstrate the everyday struggles of refugees, teachers, or of anyone that the designer wants people to feel more empathetic toward.

Another abusive game of note is the art installation known as *PainStation* (Tilman and Morawe, 2001). This game features a variant of

Pong where the game feedback includes real-world heat impulses, electric shocks, and a miniature wire whip. Players receive real-world physical lacerations and stings. While designed for entertainment, the opportunity to create empathy for other design contexts seems apparent.

However, when not designing an abusive game, it's important to maintain an appropriate relationship with the player. Morally, the ethics behind empathy games are very important. Toying with emotions is not to be taken lightly, especially when designing. It's also important to remember that players engage freely and expect that the experience is designed well. If a game upends the player by breaking its original social contract with the player, it runs the risk of dissociating them from the experience and obliterating any empathy it may have fostered. This can be done by failing to adhere to the fiction, such as randomly introducing spaceships to a game about 15th century Italy. It can be done by giving players a barrage of problems and never letting them solve any of them. It can be done by poorly constructing the relationship between game events, by obscuring possible game verbs, or by making promises in play that are not delivered.

Regardless of the kind of empathy focused game you design, it's essential to note the for every rule there is an exception. There are movies about cowboys and aliens, and there are ways to upend the player's social contract to make a rhetorical and empathy inspired point. Giving the player false information on which to act is a way to make both a rhetorical point and inspire empathy for people who may be operating in such environments. A game about disinformation, for example, might be designed to give the player disinformation as a way to help them empathize with people who operate in disinformation environments. A barrage of problems may be exactly the situation the designer wants the player to empathize with. But, remember that games are played. Destroying the social contract between players or between designer and player can be a mistake as much as an opportunity.

8.7 VIRTUAL REALITY AS AN EMPATHY MACHINE

Drawing from the idea that shifts in perspective and role play are valuable to empathy, many people believe that virtual reality can serve as a kind of empathy machine. The assumption is that the potential for hyperrealism or for immersion can aid the goal of creating empathy. In concept, virtual reality means a new take on concepts that are a staple in cinematic storytelling. Much like games, virtual reality experiences cede control from the director to the player. Instead of choosing the camera's distance for an emotional moment, the player is allowed to go where they want. This is a very big change, as it means new challenges and opportunities in storytelling.

It also means new opportunities to make mistakes. Just as the history of film involved people learning the language of film, virtual reality will develop its own language. That language may be similar to the ludo-literacy discussed in other chapters, or it may emerge as something more distinct.

The concept of an empathy machine comes from film critic Roger Ebert, who claimed that "movies are the most powerful empathy machine in all the arts" in his Walk of Fame speech (2005). Roger Ebert also famously wrote that "video games can never be art" (2010). Therein is the problem. If virtual reality is somewhat like games, and employed somewhat like film by filmmakers, is it also an empathy machine? Can it be an empathy machine?

Recent debates have emerged over the reality or fiction of virtual reality as an empathy machine. Some debate if the promises were part of the hype cycle that supported the rapid growth of the industry. Others focus on the technical distinctions, noting that much work claimed to be virtual reality is instead merely 360-degree camera-based film.

Given what this chapter has worked to outline, it should be evident the potential is there, but not promised. Role play is effective for creating empathy. Games and toys can offer more potential for empathy. Virtual reality can be playful, and it cannot. The debate around the potential of virtual reality to be an empathy machine may be too focused on implementation details than the design. It's a bit like asking if a card game, digital toy, or role-playing activity can be empathy machines. The answer is clearly yes, but the efficacy of those experiences relies heavily on the designed experience.

8.8 PRACTICE WHAT YOU'VE LEARNED

- Undertake an Internet search for empathy games. What games have succeeded and which ones have failed? What are some lessons learned? Did you find some games that inspired empathy but did not intend to do so? Do many commercial games inspire empathy?

- Choose a contemporary issue or group for which you'd like to inspire empathy. Write three different concept statements focusing on a large-scale, medium-scale, and small-scale problem that inspires empathy. What game verbs seem to offer the most potential for supporting a means that inspires empathy?

- Choose an empathy focus and consider how different implementations will affect the player's ability to empathize. How will playing a live action role play differ from interacting with a digital toy? What is the appropriate distance between player action and outcome for these implementations? Should the "camera" distance be far or close? How do you manage the emotional distance to make it a tragedy, comedy, or something in between?

REFERENCES

11 bit studios. This War of Mine. 11 bit studios, 2014.

Antonisse, Jamie, and Devon Johnson. *Hush*. Jamie Antonisse and Devon Johnson, 2007.

Brice, Mattie. "Postpartum: Mainichi—how personal experience became a game." *Mattie Brice–Alternate Ending* (2012). http://www.mattiebrice.com/postpartum-mainichi-how-personal-experience-became-a-game/

Cox III, James Earl. *[US]SR*. Seemingly Pointless, 2013.

DMA Design. *Grand Theft Auto*. BMG Interactive, 1997.

Ebert, Roger. "Video games can never be art." https://www.rogerebert.com/rogers-journal/video-games-can-never-be-art.

Ebert, Roger. Walk of Fame Remarks. 2005. https://www.rogerebert.com/rogers-journal/eberts-walk-of-fame-remarks.

Greitemeyer, Tobias, Silvia Osswald, and Markus Brauer. "Playing prosocial video games increases empathy and decreases schadenfreude." *Emotion* 10, no. 6 (2010): 796.

MECC. *Oregon Trail*. MECC, 1985.

Namco. *Pac-Man*. Namco, 1980.

Pandemic. Mahopac, NY: Z-Man Games. 2008.

Reiff, Tilman, and Volker Morawe. Painstation. 2001.

Ruiz, Susana, Ashley York, Mike Stein, Noah Keating, and Kellee Santiago. *Darfur is Dying*. 2006. http://www.darfurisdying. com.

Stenros, Jaakko, and Markus Montola. Nordic LARP. 2010. http://tampub.uta.fi/handle/10024/95123.

Square. *Final Fantasy*. Square, 1987.

Tarantino, Quentin. *Kill Bill: Vol. I & II*. TF1 Vidéo, 2004.

Thatgamecompany. *Journey*. Sony Computer Entertainment, 2012

Yager Development. *Spec Ops: The Line*. 2K Games, 2012.

CHAPTER 9

Designing for Communities of Play

M UCH OF THIS BOOK has focused on creating games at the scale of
a few players. When most people think of games, they think of
board games around a table, card games, or the experience of staring into
a screen playing a digital game. While these are clearly common ways to
play, they are not the only kinds of games you can design. This chapter
focuses on game design at a larger scale—the scale of communities.

In the parlance of design, there are many different terms that people
use to describe such games. Unlike other chapters in this book that focus
narrowly on a topic, this chapter will provide a wider view of the many
ways in which communities of play can be designed. It's an odd thing to
think of designing for communities and one that you will become more
comfortable with.

The concept is fairly simple. Instead of focusing on the designed experience of a few players around a single game, there are ways to think about
designing for many players around a much larger space. That space might
be the scale of a sports field, a city, or the world. Sometimes, it's a technology that facilitates such design, other times, it's merely a single concept or
prompt.

To understand the potential scale of such play, consider the chants and
group activities at a sporting event. When the crowd at a football game
starts a wave, there's some version of large-scale group play occurring. The
moment that the first person starts the wave by standing up, the people

around them begin to engage in a simultaneous, vicarious play activity. They stand, then sit down, and the people next to them to do the same. Before long, thousands of people are standing and sitting in a rhythm that is amazing to watch at a distance. This is not work, this is play.

Consider that wave from a play design perspective. It starts with a tiny gesture, simply sitting and standing. But that is the cue, the thing that initiates the play state. It's a risk for that first person, as the wave might not catch on. The person takes that chance and does it anyway. The people around them respond in kind, or not.

This is one of the unique features of designing for a large scale. The cue for the play state must not only be initiated, it must be received quickly by a large number of people. It is one of the reasons that simplicity can often facilitate games at this scale. If the wave required a complex hand gesture or other signal to start and follow, it would be much harder to make happen. Instead, it's a single, simple gesture—a stand and a sit.

Think about other ways that large groups of people play together. Dancing is another model of simultaneous community play. People might simply engage in vicarious individual dances or they may do any range of synchronized dancing. They may dance together with the same basic moves, such as the rhythms of salsa. Or they may all do the exact same dance, such as the Electric Slide or the Cha-Cha Slide.

In each of these examples, the wave or the dance, there is a place for the game designer. The game designer is typically both the initiator of the experience and the DJ. The game designer creates the rules that start the experience and paces the participants by leading the rhythms that move them. In a large-scale game, this might be the product of pacing the story of a live action game or it might be in the scale of the objects created for the game itself.

To understand how to do things at this scale, it's useful to understand some of the common models for designing such games. The following is a general introduction to the many common ways that large-scale play is designed. This is not an exhaustive list but should function to help frame the realm of possibility for any project that you are considering.

9.1 BIG GAMES

Big games, or field games, are games designed to be played by large numbers of people in a large-scale environment. They are often focused on players moving through physical spaces like sports fields, public parks, or cities. Games might be adaptations of common digital games like a real-life version of *Pac-Man* played on city streets. Multiple such games have been created, where people dressed as ghosts, or golf carts decorated like ghosts, chase a person dressed as Pac-Man. In some ways, this game might sound similar to tag, and in some ways, it is. But unlike tag, it incorporates a series of rules from a much more complicated version of *Pac-Man*. It also changes the scale of the game, and unlike the digital version, it also changes the audience. Hundreds of people can watch a live-action, big game version of *Pac-Man* in the middle of the night (Figure 9.1).

An important thing to note about such games is that they, like many community games, include a higher level of public performance. Players are inserting their play into a public space. This has a variety of implications both for the design and the politics of the game. As a design constraint, it means that there are many possibilities for unexpected consequences. Playing on city streets with golf carts means that the rules of the road apply. Stop lights, stop signs, one-way streets, and pedestrians all influence the game experience. Other elements that affect play include unexpected potholes and the odd or encouraging looks of passersby. These are part of the reality of the game, that come with mixing the play state with real spaces.

The other reality is that there are and will likely always be, space politics. Playing such a game in a designed play space, such as a roped off parking lot, fits with most people's understanding of play space.

FIGURE 9.1   A photograph of a real world, glowing blue ghost mounted to a golf cart at the 2018 Art Basel, in Miami, Florida.

Doing so means that the territory of play (recalling our five elements of play) is clearly demarcated. The field of play, like a sport, is easy to understand.

However, when play space is a mental space inserted into an everyday space, the politics shift. Imagine, for example, seeing four people run down a street in New York City. They are each wearing a colored chest around them, one blue, one red, one yellow, and one is wearing something that looks like a wheel of cheese. They are darting between pedestrians on the sidewalk. If you've read this book, you might recognize immediately that they are engaged in some kind of big game or field game. But what if you didn't? Would you worry that there's a bullying situation occurring or that someone is getting robbed? Would you be annoyed that they are playing too close to a serious place, like a courthouse or bank? Would you feel excluded from their play? Would you be concerned about the danger of playing so close to the street?

These are all normal reactions and a reflection of the design challenge of such play inserted into spaces that aren't typically considered playful, which can be a kind of political challenge. The politics of space, the notion of public and private space or personal space are part of the human dynamic. The territory of play is often so roped off from ordinary life that when it inserts itself, it is sometimes a source of anxiety or even anger for others.

Worries of safety, for example, are legitimate. We know that the play state is supposed to be a safe space, but the many variables of ordinary life are hard to control. Running between people on a sidewalk can quickly result in spilled coffee, jostling a person with a walker, or worse. This fear or discomfort with playing in ordinary, serious spaces is not new. Ask any skateboarder or rollerblader, as the lure of long rails and odd shaped stairways are often spoiled by no skateboarding and no rollerblading signs.

If you understand this tension, you can design around it. Consider, for example, that even for ordinary, non-play spaces, there are commonly held assumptions about use and time. Watching people playful on the street or sidewalk at midnight, for example, is much more comfortable than 9:00 am a Monday morning. That is, of course, a product of a nine-to-five work culture and the notion that play, whether it's alcohol or party induced, occurs later in the day. Playing in a park, which is typically designed for other playing activities (e.g., fishing, flying a kite, throwing Frisbees), immediately makes those who do not understand the game more commonly comfortable with the notion that it is play.

The politics of space, an understanding, and sometimes a set of laws about where play can and can't happen is essential to the design of such play. Some designers aim to explicitly counter those laws as a political statement, and they assert that by playing in a public space, or playing in private spaces. Such play and its design assert a kind of civil disobedience. The designers and players are not recognizing the dominant rules about what can and can't happen in the space. Instead, they are disobeying through play. The play then becomes political, in much the same way a sit in might be used to draw attention to a political matter.

This is one of the many ways that a designer can do things with big games. Big games provide the power of spectacle, like a flash mob, people will notice it. They also offer the opportunity to engage an audience of players who may not have technical training or access to play. Of course, such games also don't need technology, although technology can aid such play.

Big games are in some ways like recess games in public. Recess games have their benefits. They are usually easy to play. They are available to a wide set of players. They don't cost much to support. They are repeatable.

But like recess games, it's not always easy to impart meaning in the games. While the spectacle of play may be interesting to watch, getting people to understand the meaning of your play may not be as easy to communicate. Sometimes, onlookers don't even know what is being played. This is why big games offer potential, but not a lot of evidence for their effect.

It is perfectly reasonable to create a big game for social impact or a big game for advertising purposes. Red Bull, for example, has created a large-scale flying machine contest that encourages participants to make the wildest, oddly entertaining flying machines. They run this Flugtag in a variety of cities and encourage an audience. The event supports their brand by aligning it with the fun, creative, energetic, and whimsical creations participants make. In some ways, this large-scale event turns itself into a kind of sport, branded by Red Bull.

Such play raises several important design questions too. How do you encourage onlookers to feel like they are a part of the play experience or at least prevent them from feeling alienated from the play? How do you create a pervasive environment for the players when the environment perpetually reminds them that they are in a non-play space? How do you unify the experience to make it feel like a game instead of something else? What do you do to make a location playful?

9.2 LOCATION-BASED PLAY

Location-based play formalizes the experience of a big game by tying play to a distinct location. Location-based play often employs some mix of the physical characteristics of specific locations with technology. The core concept is really very simple. To play a location-based game, all of the players must be in a specific location to play. One of the easiest examples of location-based play is geocaching.

Geocaching is a kind of treasure hunt where players hide items in locations marked by coordinates. Players then attempt to find the cache or stored hidden items. When they find them, they can take the hidden object, but they also generally leave a new item for the next player to find. There are software-based solutions to support this play, although such play can be done without it.

More commonly now, location-based play is centered around player coordinate tracking. A global positing system (GPS) device, or simply a player's phone, is tracked and the location of the player is one of the key feedback items for the game system. Other games use near field technologies, like Bluetooth, to locate players between each other or within proximity of specific beacons.

One of the clear opportunities in such play is the way in which it encourages players to travel to and within specific spaces. If someone wanted to increase tourism to a specific area, a location-based game might be an appropriate solution. If a designer wanted to get players to explore a space, location-based play seems appropriate too.

Consider, for example, a college campus orientation. The college wants new students to know where specific locations and services are. These might include the cafeterias, the health center, the financial aid office, libraries, and their individual department's office. Asking students to tour all of these places may seem awkward. If the average person was told, "here's a map, now go and visit these places," many would not. They would instead wait until they needed to do so. However, a location-based game could use incentives appropriately. It could be wrapped around the fiction of a treasure hunt, where each visit unlocks a new treasure. It could be built around a riddle, where each visit provides a new clue the riddle. It could even involve a narrative that in itself, by visiting the locations, provides valuable information to new students. Or it could simply end with a $5 coupon for the campus store.

Location-based play is simply an easy way to make the territory of the game the focus of the play experience. Analog location-based games deposit hints, clues, or physical items that players collect. In the campus example, players might have to read plaques on the buildings and decipher clues or prompts, like the third word of sentence two on a plaque. Digital versions clearly evaluate the player's location and respond accordingly.

The focus of such play is simply getting people in or around a space. What happens once they are in the situation depends entirely on the goals of the game. If the designer wants them to appreciate the architecture, it may reward the player for counting the number of columns or for describing the painting on the ceiling.

Typically, the scale and accuracy of a location-based game can be limited by its technology. There was a time, for example, when mobile phone GPS was not reliable enough to locate the player within several meters of a location. This is why some location-based games use their own check-in technologies, such as QR codes to be scanned by players or key fobs that register a visit.

While it's easy to get bogged down by the technology of location-based games, it's important to remember that the focus should be on creating an experience that is engaging to a large group of individuals. Unlike big games, which are often played synchronously with all players engaged in play at the same time, location-based games need not be. Location-based games can be played asynchronously, with each player engaging at their own start time and pace. This means that unlike some other types of play, a location-based game can be created and left for players to engage. Once it's set up, and if it's durable, it can persist for months with just a few players or hundreds of players.

The persistence of such games is one of the reasons they are often categorized as pervasive games. The true notion of a pervasive game is that such games pervade the space. A player can engage in a location-based game while others around them are not playing at all. The game persists or pervades into the real world. It, like all play, is a voluntary experience where someone wants to participate in a pervasive game to simply make the ordinary world a bit more interesting.

9.3 ALTERNATE REALITY GAMES

One of the most interesting kinds of pervasive games is an alternate reality game. Alternate reality games are a kind of subscription fiction. The general structure of such games is that players are given an inciting event. This event is an invitation down the rabbit hole, as it's commonly referred. Players are then lured into a world of fiction that seems oddly realistic.

The events of the game mesh into the events of the real world in a way that blends the two almost imperceptibly.

An inciting event for an alternate reality game might be a seemingly realistic free conference about a great new invention. Attendees are greeted by an environment that feels like any traditional business-oriented conference. There are free water and bagels for everyone. When the conference begins, someone takes the stage and begins the conference. After a few minutes, they are interrupted abruptly. The person at the podium looks flustered. They are nervous. A group of people hurriedly take the bagels and water away. Cautiously and awkwardly, the person at the podium announces that the food has been poisoned. Players have 24 hours to find the cure. The perpetrator had planned to poison the inventor but failed to do so.

This kind of inciting event presents the player with a problem. A problem that they may be invested in, especially if they had any of the free food. The players then go out into the real world seeking clues. They talk among themselves. A game master or the game's designer in the background has laid out carefully deposited clues. There may be an envelope under a chair on the stage. There might be a scarf elsewhere. Each answer typically reveals a new problem or question. They follow what in narrative design is known as the mystery structure. Every time a new answer is discovered, it creates a new question. Whose scarf is this? Whose address is on the envelope? Where is the person who announced the poisoning?

If this sounds familiar, it may be because you've engaged in a live-action murder mystery. These are a kind of interactive theater where attendees participate in the drama, often trying to solve a *who done it* styled murder mystery. In some ways, alternate reality games are simply large versions of such play. If you've ever participated in one, you will quickly recognize that it can do a great job of creating a play space. The community of players do not only witness the drama, they propel it.

One of the more interesting, real-world examples of this was a game called the Art of the H3ist (2005). The game was designed to promote the release of the Audi A3. The game was played worldwide and was based on a single inciting event. The first A3 in the world was stolen. Instead of showing the car at auto shows, they displayed signs advertising a reward for the stolen vehicle. There were vehicles advertising the reward and a television advert that announced it was missing. The game employed elements common to art heist films and created a complex web of evidence that supported its reality. There were adverts for the game's fake investigators in real magazines. There were websites that logged the activity of the game. Successful players were invited to exclusive events. In one of the more interesting design elements, a primary character in the game was a fake game designer. The actor who played the designer in the game gave a real-world television interview in character.

Such large-scale and complex alternate reality games to advertise a product or create social impact are not common. Typically, such games require a host of confederates or actors who help move the game's narrative forward. They also often require real-time game design, as the designers aim to keep players engaged by making adjustments that respond to the behavior of players.

The game I Love Bees (42 Entertainment, 2004) was designed as an alternate reality game to promote the release of the game *Halo 2*. It involved a complex set of interactions that thousands of people around the world played. Notably, the game won awards for its efforts and is credited with supporting the community of *Halo 2* players who rallied around its experience.

Another notable pervasive game is Cruel 2 B Kind (McGonigal and Bogost, 2006). The game describes itself as a kind of benevolent assassin. In the game, players must make "kill" other teams in the game. A kill is achieved by one of three specific compliments that are unique to each live game. A kill might be to praise a target's shoes or tell them that they look very nice today. The trick is that players never know who is playing or who is not. The result is a charming set of random people commenting to other people in the hope that they are playing the game. The final winning team is the one that accomplishes the final kill. Since teams grow through kills, there's a kind of momentum to the game, with an army of compliment-ready teammates moving through space. Other than tracking performance by sending text messages to the game organizers, there is no real dependence on technology.

If you've noticed a trend in these last two games, it may be because they come from the same person. Jane McGonigal was behind both Cruel 2 B Kind and I Love Bees. Cruel 2 B Kind was a collaboration between Jane McGonigal and Ian Bogost, who you may remember from Chapter 7 on persuasive games.

This is important because Cruel 2 B Kind in particular is meant to be more than a feel-good game. McGonigal admits that the game is also about the use of public space. At the time the game was launched, players were getting negative press for playing pervasive games in the street. At the same time, real estate developers were turning what used to be public space into private space. This left fewer places to play and exacerbated the dichotomy of wealth and homelessness in many cities. The game aims to assert the benevolence of such play and the right of players to use the space for such play. The game blends the power of McGonigal's large scape community games with Bogost's games and rhetoric work. It's also a good example of a game that targets the politics of space. A rather well-suited aim for both location-based games and alternate reality games.

Designing alternate reality games is not without its risks. In 2001, Electronic Arts (EA) made a rather substantial alternate reality game called Majestic. Majestic was astoundingly novel in its approach. The game was a science fiction thriller with the promotion tagline—it plays you. It employed lots of novel tricks, such as a rabbit hole event that announced that the game you had purchased had been stopped. But there was a conspiracy behind the stoppage, which was, of course, all part of the game. The game itself would call, email, and fax players. It was designed to feel realistic. So much so, that when the events of September 11th occurred, EA stopped the game. Within a year, they stopped the game entirely, citing too few players.

There are, of course, design lessons to be learned here. There is the risk of an alternate reality game being too close to home or too realistic. There is also the risk of attraction. Alternate reality games are partly dependent on a substantial community of players. Too few players and the experience is less compelling. It's a bit like the difference between an empty dancefloor and a crowded one. Or starting a wave and realizing no one else is willing. The play is subject to, and somewhat dependent on, the participation of others.

Successful alternate reality games are supported by community. More players help people feel confident about their play. Too few players and they may feel silly, awkward, or worse. Attracting a sizeable audience is often a key to the success or failure of such design.

9.4 AUGMENTED REALITY

One way to encourage larger communities of play in real-world spaces is through augmented reality. Augmented reality and mixed reality aim to blend the real world and a digital world to make a more engaging play experience. This is typically done through a combination of real-time computing and a blended projection of the environment around players and a digital representation.

The most successful augmented reality game to date is *Pokémon Go* (Niantic, 2016). The game is estimated to have attracted 5 million players and earned $1.8 Billion in the 2 years since its release (Tassi, 2018). Very simply, players were encouraged to explore space and collect Pokémon. The Pokémon could be anywhere in the world, and when they appeared, players quickly shuffled to the space to collect them.

It was, of course, not the first time that the company who made the game, Niantic, had offered augmented reality. Their prior game, *Ingress*, was a relative success for augmented reality but never developed the massive player community that *Pokémon Go* did. The reasons for this are varied, with some analysis claiming that *Ingress* lacked the strength of the Pokémon brand and following, that the *Ingress* mechanics were complicated, or that its fiction was simply less appealing.

The key to understanding the opportunities in augmented reality is really in one simple concept. It allows people to perceive ordinary space differently. Players can turn their bedrooms into intergalactic space war zones or change the face of a building.

While often conflated with virtual reality, the key difference for a designer is that mixed and augmented reality are aimed at bringing players into the real world. Games like *Pokémon Go* don't work well on a couch or a living room. They work best when players go out into the world and move about it. Since players are often also readily identifiable (because of their actions with the mobile device), it's also easy for such play to occur in a public space.

Such games have the potential to change people's behavior, which is one of the most compelling reasons to consider them when doing things with games. Although relatively new, the game has been the subject of research, indicating it may help youths with severe social withdrawal (Tateneo et al, 2016), increasing conservation behavior (Dorward et al, 2017), restaurant review behavior (Kondamudi et al., 2017), and luring players to small businesses (Frith, 2017).

9.5 INTERSTITIAL GAMES

Interstitial games are designed to turn ordinary, mundane spaces into playful experiences. These kinds of games are found most commonly in airports, malls, and other high traffic areas. They typically use basic computer vision to track player movements and large digital signage to display activity. The earliest such play experiences were really just simple interactions with digital interactive displays.

In more recent years, the cost of physical computing, custom computing, and durable displays have created new opportunities to create more interesting, custom interstitial games. One of the most notable is *StreetPong* (ActiWait, 2014). The game is a two-player version of ping-pong placed on pedestrian walk signals in Germany. Two players on opposite sides of the street can play pong with each other on the displays while they wait for the walk signal. Each time pedestrians wait to cross a busy intersection, players can play a version of virtual ping-pong with each other. Once the "do not cross" signal is over, the game ends and the players can cross the street (Figure 9.2).

The game was originally designed as a proof of concept video for improving the experience at pedestrian walk signals. The design, which was originally created by ActiWait, accumulated so much interest that their proof of concept video turned into a crowd-funded game. It's a simple and smart solution for improving public safety through entertainment. Players ideally no longer feel that they are waiting unproductively for the opportunity to cross. Instead, they can play while they wait.

Conceptually interstitial games are not only about physical spaces. They can also serve to fill time spaces, such as waiting rooms. Theme parks often employ line games for long queues at attractions. Players can engage with these playful experiences while they wait to get on the main attraction. While the advent of mobile phones has changed the practical necessity for these games, it hasn't changed their opportunity to engage the community of players waiting in line. It's also common to create

FIGURE 9.2 ActiWait's *StreetPong* is a game integrated into walk signs. (With permission from Urban Invention [http://urban-invention.com/].)

mobile app-based line games that encourage players to keep themselves busy and entertained while waiting for a main attraction. These apps may even keep local scoreboards, comparing performance between other players in the line.

A core characteristic of such games is that they tend to be very short. Unlike alternate reality games, which may take a while to understand and pervade a player's ordinary world for years, interstitial games and play are often focused on merely entertaining the player for a few minutes. As a result, their mechanics tend to be designed around short, shallow experiences. Players often do what they know how to do, such as balancing virtual objects, catching items, collecting items, or matching items. They apply common game mechanics so that players know very quickly what they are supposed to do.

Such games are also often short on story and tend to rely heavily on the novelty. For a game that is trying to grab player attention in a mall, the audience may be willing to accept a distraction. In an airport, that may not be as true, as flight layovers may be short. In lines, the audience is quite captive.

For interstitial games, the challenges vary by environment. The psychographic dimensions often mean that players are not interested in complex or cognitively difficult challenges. They also expect a tight feedback loop where their actions are immediately shown in the game. Otherwise, players fear that the toy or game is broken or that they have not played it correctly.

It's also important to remember that for many interstitial games, they're a bit of performance by the player. Touching a 72" digital display in an airport requires a bit of confidence and curiosity. Some people are nervous, fearing they are trying to interact with something that doesn't actually interact with them. Other times, they are very aware that their play is being watched by others who are curious but potentially critical.

The resulting design constraints mean that designing interstitial games has a lot in common with designing early 1980s arcade games. The design is competing for the attention of the player in an environment where there's a lot of other stimuli. It's also seeking to draw the player away from something else, such as the food court, the conversation they might have with a neighbor, or their own mobile devices. Creating attractive modes that lure players to play can be effective.

However, unlike arcade games, interstitial games are not always placed where people look to play. That means that the business traveler at the airport or the hurried shopper in the mall may be reluctant or even annoyed to see play in the way of their very directed work effort. That means that much like many other community facing games, the interstitial game may collide with the politics of space.

9.6 CROWD GAMES

The design of games for crowds has collected off and on attention over the years. Most recently, the hope was to create games that allowed players to control a single game cooperatively. Such games used computer vision or individual voting to allow people in a movie theater or other large area to control a single game. Players could raise their hands and lean right or left to collectively control a car or make an onscreen selection.

These games tend to share some attributes with interstitial games, as they are typically short experiences designed to advertise a product before a movie begins or otherwise enhance another experience like a large concert. These games aren't particularly popular or common, but they do offer an opportunity for design that others in these chapters haven't. Typically, these games are democratic in nature. They tend to be based on some algorithms related to polling player reactions or choice. The most popular or most evident choice of the group guides the game.

In relation to the politics of space, this provides an interesting opportunity to do a new thing in games. The opportunity to have lots of people in a single room, allowing them to cooperatively or competitively guide a playful experience means that their relationship to each other is different than other types of play. They are sharing the experience, instead of getting their own individual view of shared space. Where the typical multiplayer online game might require players to work collectively through their individual sessions, this type of play is about everyone sharing the same basic session. This collectivist, shared experience may prove useful for certain types of social impact in the future.

9.7 DESIGNING FOR COMMUNITIES OF PLAY

So far, much of this chapter has been about providing an orientation to games about large-scale interactions, public play, and multiple players. It's important to also recognize that sometimes designing for communities of play is not merely about creating mechanics or interaction schemes that encourage larger-scale play. Instead, sometimes, designing for communities of play is about encouraging people to form communities around the play itself.

With the rise of live streaming games, more and more design teams recognize the opportunity to foster community through these environments. A game that is entertaining to watch live streamed may be just as effective at drawing an audience as one that is appealing to play. The rise of games like *Fortnite* are credited in part to their success in live-stream environments.

While partly a function of marketing and promotion, having a game that draws an audience of live streamers can do wonders for the visibility of the game you have designed. The distinct character of such appeal will change, but generally designing a game that affords high variability in play encourages people to stream such content. Likewise, the novelty of the experience or design, the comedy of its play, or the aesthetics may also help.

But understanding the value of streaming games is not merely worthwhile for digital game designers. It's important to remember that fan bases and audiences, especially audiences that want to rebroadcast your game, are extraordinarily useful in creating a community around the play you've designed.

Easily modifiable play environments are particularly good at this. *Garry's Mod* (Facepunch Studios, 2004), based on *Half Life 2*, is a good example. A quick video search for *Garry's Mod* reveals many videos produced using it. It's simply a sandbox physics environment with the objects from *Half Life 2* available for play. The novelty and appeal for people who make the videos is not in the narrative that once carried the original game, but instead in the fun that can be had by making interesting interactions with the object sets. It, like *Minecraft* (Mojang, 2009) or *Roblox* (Roblox Corporation, 2005), functions as a construction set. Once people create, they want to share. It's this sharing that compels a community of play to form around such games.

As a designer, designing such opportunities may make a lot of sense. It means that people engage not only with your game, but with each other. It means that if you want them to talk about a social issue, to consider their own health, or to address issues in their own communities, the game can be the thing that promotes such interactions.

While the discussion of identity is much larger than this short chapter allows, it's important to recognize that some portion of play involves identity. Players rally around the teams they identify with and players sometimes bond over the characters they play in digital games. Identity as it relates to game design is an opportunity to help players develop community. People not only create identity around the games they play, but the types of games they play and even the way they play them. The things designers do with those identities offer an opportunity for players to develop a community.

This is really not much different than the way games have worked in some communities for years. The parks where people meet to play dominoes, chess, or bocce function not only as ways to be entertained, but they form a meeting point for members of the community. Those people might be talking about their day, they might complain about rising fuel prices, or they might chat about the needs of their communities.

Designing for this opportunity varies. It may mean using verbs that encourage individuals to convene in groups to begin or complete play. It may mean encouraging people to share their solutions, creations, or other in-game content. It may mean creating the physical space that supports such interactions.

Recalling that one of the five essentials of games is territory, it should be evident that how territory is defined may help encourage communities of play. Who is in the territory and who is out of the territory will really shape the community. As mentioned earlier, the tensions and politics of space can elicit very strong emotional and cognitive responses in both players and non-players witnessing the play. If you want to encourage players to reach out and interact with the community among which they are playing, then one easy solution is to allow players to expand the territory of the game. Perhaps each player is allowed to bring one or more people into the game, an invitation that can be accepted to the benefit of the player but for which rejection costs them nothing. Such a game offers the opportunity to go viral—to spread quickly and easily. It also invites those who are on the outside in, bringing them into the experience of the game instead of reminding them that they weren't invited.

This pattern of a constantly expanding conceptual territory of play is one of many models that will afford healthy interaction between players and non-players. There are countless more that require practice. This is why we describe game design as a practice, not a system. Every time you solve a problem, you will also create new problems. Each new idea, once practiced, becomes a little less new. That doesn't mean there isn't plenty more to do with it, but it does mean that the practice of game design is ever-evolving. So too are the communities that play them. Your goal is to find ways to keep them engaged, at whatever scale you practice, as a way to enhance their lives, their ability to solve problems, or their motivations.

9.8 PRACTICE WHAT YOU'VE LEARNED

- Visit a public space for players, such as a ball court, practice field, arcade, convention, or similar and examine the kinds of interactions that occur. How are people talking? How does the game influence their interactions and how are non-players involved? How is community fostered in these environments? What design lessons can you learn?

- Review a design you are considering as it relates to scale and community interaction. Are there opportunities to encourage more in-game or out-of-game interactions between players? Does one of the aforementioned game types offer an opportunity you had not considered?

- Do some quick research to learn about the most popular uses of mixed and augmented reality. What has caught the attention of the press and players? What is receiving the most praise and why? Who are the companies supporting the technology and implementing the most exciting solutions? Look and listen.

- Identify your ideal player community in terms of the key demographics, technographics, and psychographics. How do they normally meet and converse? What are their tendencies and how can your game design accentuate or support those interactions? Does one or more of the game types examined provide an opportunity to meet their needs? How will you handle the spectacle of play, the politics of space, and the experience of non-players?

- Design the minimally viable product (MVP) for testing or prototyping a single experience around an alternate reality game you are considering. What are the required timelines? How many people are required to participate to make it interesting? How well is your rabbit hole event working?

REFERENCES

ActiWait. *Streetpong*. AcitWait, 2014. http://www.streetpong.info/.
Art of the H3ist. McKinney. 2005. https://mckinney.com/campaigns/art-of-the-h3ist/.
Dorward, Leejiah J., John C. Mittermeier, Chris Sandbrook, and Fiona Spooner. "*Pokémon Go*: Benefits, costs, and lessons for the conservation movement." *Conservation Letters* 10, no. 1 (2017): 160–165.
Facepunch Studios. *Garry's Mod*. Valve Corporation, 2004.

Frith, Jordan. "The digital 'lure': Small businesses and *Pokémon GO*." *Mobile Media & Communication* 5, no. 1 (2017): 51–54.

I love Bees. 42 Entertainment. 2004. http://www.42entertainment.com/work/ilovebees.

Kondamudi, Pavan Ravikanth, Bradley Protano, and Hamed Alhoori. "Pokémon Go: Impact on Yelp restaurant reviews." In *Proceedings of the 2017 ACM on Web Science Conference*, 393–394. New York: ACM, 2017.

McGonigal, Jane, and Ian Bogost. Cruel 2 B Kind. 2006. http://www.cruelgame.com/games/.

Mojang. *Minecraft*. Mojang, 2009.

Niantic. *Pokémon Go*. Niantic, 2016.

Roblox Corporation. *Roblox*. Roblox Corporation, 2005.

Tassi, Paul. "*Pokémon GO* has made $1.8 billion as it turns two years old." *Forbes*, https://www.forbes.com/sites/insertcoin/2018/07/09/pokemon-go-has-made-1-8-billion-as-it-turns-two-years-old/#77d3a0ac4655.

Tateno, Masaru, Norbert Skokauskas, Takahiro A. Kato, Alan R. Teo, and Anthony P. S. Guerrero. "New game software (*Pokémon Go*) may help youth with severe social withdrawal, hikikomori." *Psychiatry Research* 246 (2016): 848.

CHAPTER 10

Human Computation, Community Action, and Other Social Impacts

T HERE ARE MANY OTHER ways to do things with games than previous chapters have described. This chapter explains in brief some of the emerging and miscellaneous game uses to remind you of other ways to employ games toward your goal. Consider this chapter as a glimpse into the design future. As such, it takes on a different structure, with more sharing of possibility than practical how to. It also provides first-hand reports from the individuals involved in these projects as a glimpse into the process.

10.1 HUMAN COMPUTATION GAMES

By now it should be evident that play is a very powerful tool. Not only is it an effective strategy for engaging audiences, it's also a psychological state that encourages focus, experimentation, and practice. The core concept in employing human computation games is to try to harness that power plus a few others to solve really complex problems.

The earliest, successful human computations game are credited to a professor at the University of Washington. Von Ahn and his colleagues and students have been very active in a field they called games with a purpose (GWAP) (Hacker & Ahn, 2009). One of the first of these games was the *ESP Game* (ESP Game, 2008), created by Luis von Ahn. In the *ESP*

Game, players compete to describe images on a screen. As an example, both players may be given the image of a birthday cake. One player might describe it as a festive cake, the other player describes it as a birthday cake. The system collects both of their responses and rates them against other responses provided by other players. The winner of each round is the person whose most descriptive label matches those most commonly used by others (e.g., in this case, birthday cake is the likely win). The power of this contest is not in the design of the experience, but instead on its result. Using this basic game-like contest, the researchers were able to collect lots of information about images. They were able to get people to play through a very simple task—labeling images. Now imagine this experience scaled to millions of plays.

As you can likely tell, the power of such is not in the design, but in the ability to get lots of people to do a task for which computers aren't particularly well suited. When the *ESP Game* was used in 2006, it was a really clever way to improve image labels. Those images' labels are some of the many tools that make something like Google image search or other search tools work better.

That's because they involve human computation. There are still many things that humans are much better at than software systems. This is, in part, because the average human being has had many years to learn. We call that learning heuristics. From years of seeing many different cakes, for example, the average 20-year-old player can distinguish an image of a cheesecake from a wedding cake, from a birthday cake, and even from an ice cream cake. This is because in 20 years of learning, people learn a lot about cakes (and many other things). An observant person might detect the texture of the frosting or the types of decorations and note specifics that make it very hard for computers to do. Couple this with culturally specific elements, and the need for human observation is obvious.

Human computation games add a person's ability to make observations, act as critical problem solvers, or creative solution finders to typically complex problems. In concept, it's a bit like turning some boring task that must be done into something that isn't boring and where labor is still useful. Think of any chore, for example, and the ways in which people might naturally try to make it more playful and interesting. Making a game out of any task that needs to be done is sort of the first layer of creating a human computation game. The work has to be done, and we know it's going to be more interesting if it's done playfully. These scenarios are common and commonly employed by parents. Parents might encourage children to race to get something done, like putting away toys competitively to win the race. Adults might play a game at work, racing to be the top salesperson for example.

Of course, those examples are contests, not necessarily games. That's because one of the tricks to successful human computation games is turning the work into something that's much more of a game. This is called an isomorph. An isomorph turns one task into another in a way that doesn't change the nature of what players are doing, it simply changes their framing of it. An easy isomorph would be applying imagination to turn one thing into another. While cleaning that dirty room, dirty socks become hot coals worth ten points and dirty pants become fireballs when getting launched into the hamper. The imagined task still accomplishes the goal—put things in the hamper—but the fiction around them (moving hot things from the floor to the target) makes the tasks a little more interesting (and perhaps faster).

For a typical human computation game, the isomorph is a bit more complicated. If you build a game around tagging content like images or music, it's a bit harder to convert the real task (an accurate description) into another fiction that is compelling. This is why many first-generation human computation games were largely contests. Players typically understand contests, and for those players that prefer contests in their play profile, it is a competitive solution.

One of the most successful human computation games was actually a game about protein folding. The game looked a lot like casual games at the time. The objective, however, was much grander in its aims. Players folded structures of certain proteins as perfectly as possible within the game's constraints. The highest scoring solutions were stored in a database and analyzed by researchers, who determined whether or not there was a configuration created by players that could be applied to relevant proteins in the real world. Scientists then used these solutions to create biological innovations (Figure 10.1).

The game was produced by David Salesin and Zoran Popović, then professors of computer science at the University of Washington. The project combined the needs of biochemistry with the computation power of play. Since the game tapped people's creative ability, it resulted in solutions that were better than computer modeled solutions. In 2011, *Scientific American* ran a story about the game—"*Foldit* Gamers Solve Riddle of HIV Enzyme within 3 Weeks" (Coren, 2011)

How could a game be so effective? Not only was it a very clever design and isomorph, it was also played by more than 50,000 people. That means

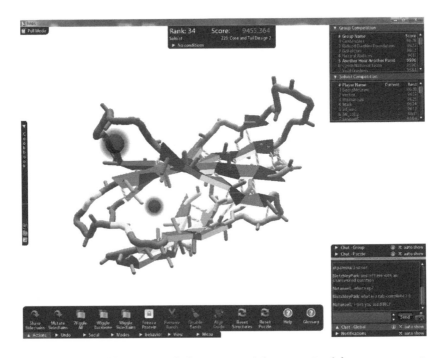

FIGURE 10.1 *Foldit* is one of the most widely recognized human computation games. (Courtesy of Foldit [https://uk.wikipedia.org/wiki/Foldit] through Creative Commons.)

that they crowdsourced an optimal solution by engaging lots of people for lots of little solutions. This is the final element that makes human computation games so effective. Many times, the answers or observation of one person aren't going to paint an appropriate picture. However, if you can collect thousands of those observations, the picture becomes more accurate.

This analogy is most clearly played out in the game Photocity. For players of Photocity, the goal is to play a capture the flag style game in which players take photos of certain areas. In reality, this research game is collecting those photos and creating 3D models of space using image stitching. In short, the people become sensors, doing the work of collecting data while they play.

Imagine if every bird you had flung across the screen while playing *Angry Birds*, or every pellet eaten in *Pac-Man*, was actually for a dual-purpose of entertainment and computation. If a game designer can master the art of the isomorph, this is a possible future. If you consider the evolution of work and play, you can see moments where they diverge and converge.

Where once people got all the exercise they needed by the work of daily living (walking, tilling a field) people now go to gyms for treadmills. Those treadmills, after some time, developed to take the energy of running on them and return it to the device, turning the work of fitness into electrical energy to be used by the treadmill or even by others. The same is true of modern automotive brakes, which now take the energy produced by the friction of braking to create energy the car can use. Isomorphs have the potential to turn the energy and computation of play into something that can benefit everyone.

10.2 DESIGNING HUMAN COMPUTATION GAMES

With my colleague, Dr. Peter Jaimeson, we have written in the past about the many opportunities for human computations games (Grace and Jamieson, 2014). These include not only improving data quality and integrity, but a variety of social impact needs. Consider the combination of big or field games with the low-cost sensors we already carry in performance trackers and mobile phones. Players could be part of a variety of studies around everything from climate change analysis to crowd behavior at festivals. All while they play games like *Pokémon Go* (LeBlanc and Jean-Philippe, 2017) or run from imagined zombies in an alternate reality game. The challenge is that while the history of other types of play is full of decades of examples, human computation games, especially as crowdsourced play, are relatively new.

To get at the specific challenges of designing such experiences, it's often easiest to start with a simpler version of the full game (again iterating on an idea). This is why to help students practice optimal solutions in a specific program language, we created a game that allows players to use real-world code to avoid virtual car crashes. The game, *Verilogtown*, uses the analogy of traffic lights to help students learning the language of Verilog practice its concepts and syntax (Figure 10.2).

While *Verilogtown* has only had players in the hundreds, it's not specifically tied to crowds to come to a specific optimal solution. In this way, the isomorph (programming gates to programming traffic lights), is designed to aid the learner. It's foreseeable that a version of the game would be designed to allow players to design very specific gate/traffic light problems and for other players to problem solve to reach an optimal solution.

Another example of such work in the social impact domain is the game *Factitious*. Our team, when I directed American University's games program and the Journalism Leadership Transformation initiative (Jolt for

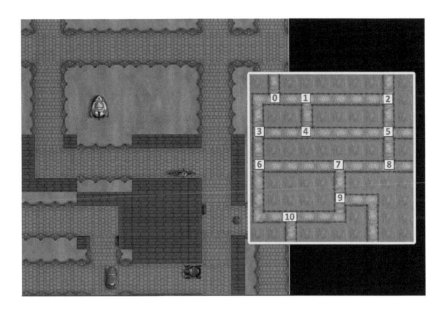

FIGURE 10.2 *Verilogtown*, a game to allow players to practice the hardware description language Verilog. Each numbered gate has code behind it to manage when gates, or stoplights by analogy, are opened and closed. (Original art by John-rhys Garcia. Used with permission.)

short) designed the game around the learning goal of helping players understand the characteristics of fake news. This kind of news literacy, knowing real news from fake news, was a core research concern for the team. What wasn't as immediately obvious, but became so later, was that in digital form, the game could be used as a light human computation game in two ways (Figure 10.3).

First, the game could function as a polling system, collecting the perceptions of a wide audience quickly. This allowed for large-scale data collection on player perceptions of news content. The game could feed players 30 different articles quickly and learn whether or not they thought it was real news or fake news. This a great opportunity to gauge how the public feels about news content. Doing so via traditional online polls or interviews, asking each player to read an article and tell the researchers if it is real or fake, would be extremely time-consuming. Instead, we offered the game, and even asked for players to provide information about themselves (age, education, etc.). While the game is subject to the research limitations of self-reported data (a player could lie) and an uncontrolled environment (people were not playing in a lab under the watchful eye of a researcher),

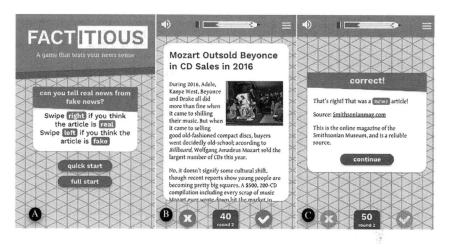

FIGURE 10.3   The *Factitious* game works as a kind of polling system as a well as an educational tool.

it still allowed interesting findings. The data collected from the more 1 million plays of the game helps paint a picture about news perception that would take far longer to collect through traditional means.

This is why the tool's second strength is as a kind of A/B tester. Similar to the ways in which an optometrist might ask a patient if lens one or two is better for their needs (i.e., better one, better two), the game can function to inform news organizations about the perception of their content. It is entirely reasonable to consider a scenario where the game is released to a group with the explicit intent of testing headlines to emphasize, lead copy, or images to make sure that people perceive the content appropriately. Instead of bringing people in for focus groups on a magazine article, the magazine article can be tested with players. Inviting people to play a game is often easier than inviting people to read a few different copies of an article.

To help you understand the process and framing, Maggie Farley, who came up with the original concept for *Factitious*, had some comments (Box 10.1):

BOX 10.1

Real or fake? In today's stream of information, readers are confused by the blurring of boundaries between what is verified news and what is not. To increase news consumers' sense of agency in detecting false news, we designed a game called *Factitious*. The game, designed first as a paper prototype and then developed as an online and mobile game, presents players with stories culled from Internet sites. The player decides whether it is an actual news story or something else: satire, spin, or disinformation disguised as news. The players receive immediate feedback, and see which elements of the story should have tipped them off to its veracity or category.

The more they play, the more familiar players become with common news conventions versus the signifiers of non-news. Game verbs: The design process started with putting the user in the center of the game and asking what we wanted them to do. Unlike traditional journalism, which is designed to broadcast information to readers and listeners, game design is centered around active verbs: to play, to learn, to detect, to share. Good games empower the player to act, and action—in games and news—is engagement.

In *Factitious*, the players must judge. In a playful nod to the dating app Tinder, they swipe right for news, and swipe left for not news. They get immediate feedback. As they level up, the categories get more specific and challenging. To afford agency, *Factitious* equips players with a set of criteria to quickly measure whether a story is believable, sensationalized or made up: what is the source, who is quoted, what is the story's intention, is it verifiable? Players interested in learning more can find quick tutorials on how to check out a story, or to understand as a news creator what the hallmarks of veracity are. By analyzing their reactions, we can also understand which elements of a story might cause distrust or skepticism, and how to better signal veracity.

We launched the mobile version of *Factitious* in June of 2016. About half the games are played during school hours, suggesting widespread classroom use. In November 2018, *Factitious* surpassed 10 million plays.

What we learned:

In the process of designing and playtesting the game, we learned:

- Players were intimidated by large blocks of text. So, we broke the story into small chunks.
- Game players hate asking for hints. They feel like it's cheating. We had put a key piece of information, the source of the article, in as a hint. We wanted people to investigate a little. But no one ever wanted to click on the hint box.
- We made a mobile version because that's where most people get their news.
- Players got better at detecting fake news. As in any game, it takes a bit of play to figure out the rules and what to look for. But they also said they used what they learned about red flags for false news in the real world after playing the game.
- They can use those tips and skills in the real world. They learn that the key to discerning fact from spin is to ask Who says? Why are they saying this? That makes them better news consumers, creators and sharers. Takeaways:

- Decide what do you want the participant to DO?
- Design in feedback for guidance or positive reinforcement.
- Make it playful and interactive.
- Test it out, welcome feedback, and iterate.

Maggie Farley

Factitious is a great case study in turning a real-world need and educational goal into something that orbits the world of human computation games. While many examples of human computation games exist in the science world, it's useful to see how non-scientific problems can be solved by such play.

It's also important to note that not all solutions have to be traditional digital games to work. The game *Urgent Evoke* was originally designed by Jane McGonigal in 2010, as a "crash course in changing the world." Available at urgentevoke.com, the game combines graphic novel content, websites, and mission orientation to engage students in real-world, community-focused problems. The experience is designed around inspiring conversation and ideation. The game aims to evoke new ideas on how to address a myriad of problems in the communities for which it is designed. It was originally created for Africa, but the World Bank has since used it in other regions as a way to get people, particularly young people, to not only think, but act on addressing challenges in their community.

One of the really important elements of the *Urgent Evoke* game is that it's designed to be played by a wide technographic. Since community members may have very different technology to access the play experience, the game's standard is written around very basic equipment requirements. This is a good case study in adapting a game design to the realistic barriers of entry that a community-centered game would want to avoid.

A game that claims to invite the entire community to participate, but then prevents some members because they don't have the technology, won't be as effective as it needs to be. This is true not only of community-centered gameplay, but also of data collection. Consider, for example, the biases that result from collecting human computation data from an expensive technographic. Eventually, the majority of data collected is provided by people who can or choose to have high-end equipment. If the game aims to collect or archive data from a wide audience, the data is already biased toward a narrower one.

10.3 SOCIAL IMPACT PLAY ART

The notion of games and play as art is clearly not new. At the least, its contemporary incarnation can be traced back to Fluxus art in the 20th century. However, games and art in a social impact context have changed, and they continue to evolve. Most notably, the potential for play and social impact is aided by the growth of well-respected art galleries showcasing games and playable experiences, the increase in creative showcases, and the interest in esports and spectator game playing.

For years prior to writing this book, I have championed the opportunity that showcasing playable games can offer to the community of social impact designers. I believe that if the people won't come to your game, it's important to bring your game to the people (Grace, Games for Change, 2015). Showcasing the type of work described in this book is essential to its continued proliferation.

Beyond increasing the audience and encouraging people to play that which they might not have known or sought, there's something more important. Showing social impact play provides social capital. It affords such work the opportunity to sit among its peers in ways it had not previously.

All the way through the mid-1990s, for example, there are quotes of game festivals being described as the "Sundance of games" (even events that are now defunct). This label is a problem for the practice of games. It implies that games need to aspire to a filmic standard. It also implies that games and play must be translated into such forms. That is, playable experiences not only need the status of a Sundance, they need their own Sundance. Imagine if someone described the Pulitzer Prize as the Emmy of Journalism, or the Golden Globe Awards as the NASCAR Daytona 500 of film. These things are very different, and such comparison is often awkward.

There are now many annual selections of best games in social impact. These include the Games for Change Festival Awards (http://www.games forchange.org/festival/awards/), the Serious Play Awards (http://seri-ousplayconf.com/awards/), and the Serious Games Challenge (http://sgschallenge.com/). There are also generally games competitions like the Independent Games Festival (http://www.igf.com/) and others that reward social impact and purpose-driven game design.

The future challenges for games in these domains are not in the recognition of good work now, it's in the archiving, preservation, and durability. Likely as a product of game design's history as a commercial art in the

20th century, the 21st century is still littered with fragments of game history. Games still suffer the social capital dilemma of being consumables. Games and playable experiences are created, played, and often discarded. Unlike a painting or a work of art, which once viewed is deemed worthy of repeated viewing, a game once played is often not worth a second viewing. While this may be a product of a designer failure to make a durable, long-lasting work in the race to produce it, it's also a product of the social capital and status of game-making.

If playable experiences are going to be "serious games," they need to be taken seriously. In the early chapters of this book, there are clear references to the tension of play and seriousness. Remember that the opposite of play is not work, but depression. Play is not the opposite of seriousness, but a compliment to it. It is not only the counterbalance to work, it is a way of seeing and understanding the world. This means that saving that way of seeing is extremely useful in understanding society then and now.

For many years, there have been different approaches to both designing and interpreting playable designs. People have discussed games as performance (Klausen, 1999), games as art (Jenkins, 2005), and I myself have framed it as poetry (Grace, 2011). While such work is valuable in helping move the practice of design forward, it also falls prey to the same trap as a "Sundance of games." It relies heavily on the notion that alignment with other, culturally respected practices (i.e., poet, playwright, or actor) is positive, or at least, useful momentum.

Now consider that in recent years there has been a marked growth in games as a spectator sport. Commercial games, not social impact games, have live spectating and competitions across the world. These esports are not merely about the sportsmanship of teams competing to win *League of Legends*, they are about much more. They are about the identities that people attach to the games, the teams, and their players. They are about the meaning of the game to a sense of community. They are also about the beauty of seeing play, at such scale, pacing, and intensity. They are, in short, beautiful performances of playing.

This is an opportunity for the world of social impact games. Where early theater or poetry may have been formulaic (e.g., following the Greek chorus and Aristotelian structure), and its performance equally so, there was much more to be done.

So too, it feels, there is much more to be done in games. While modern performance play is often framed from 1990s LAN parties of FPSs to the scale and festivity of esports, it's a bit of a shortsighted view. Dramatic readings and reading aloud in the living room also fit this world. Just as playing dominoes or chess in the park do.

The point is that social impact play designers need to think about two things. They need to think about the long-term future of their play. How durable is it? How can it be played for sustained social impact, over decades, not years?

Second, to remain contemporary, they must consider what can be done to make sure the playable experience is audience worthy. Watching a player engage with social impact play via YouTube or a live stream means an audience. It means an audience that may still get the message. Those who invested in in-game advertising, get this. They know that 5 years from now, when someone's watching a video about the first in a sequel of successful games—their brand will still be in that video.

Now the specifics of designing for live-stream audiences or turning a social impact play experience into an esports spectacle are not only beyond the scope of this book, they haven't been determined. Instead, it is useful to think toward the future of this type of design so that it meets its goals for as long as those goals need to be met.

For designers who are considering doing things with games that focus on long-lasting challenges in society, like discrimination, poverty, mental health, and so on—there's a need to focus on the long-game. How will the game design last, technically and thematically? What makes the game durable for audiences?

This is the difference, often, between what is saved in a medium and what is not. Curators of culture and art are routinely selecting those things that that they deem most worthy of saving. While there are only a few games in the permanent collection at the Smithsonian American Art Museum, the hope is there will be more.

The hypocrisy of both highlighting the trap of describing games relative to other media and at the same time aspiring to those markers of success is not lost here. Instead, it's used to remind designers that the need to think about games for the long term is a practical one. Just as some types of books were built to last and remain relevant and usable, others were designed with their own disposability (e.g., catalogs, TV guides, dime store novels). If games are to continue doing serious work, they must be aware of their own need to be archived and understood as cultural artifacts worth preserving.

One such case study in game preservation is the work of Stephen Jacobs and his colleagues at the Rochester Institution of Technology and the National Museum of Play. To end this chapter, consider this case study in Jacob's own words (Box 10.2).

FIGURE 10.4 Screenshots from "The Original Mobile Games," a collection of historical analog games made playable as digital versions.

If you have read every chapter of this book thus far, then you have received a rather large tour of the many way games are used to do things. To some people that can be rather overwhelming. The myriad of choices in approach are vast, but that's what this book is supposed to remind you. It's supposed to help you see the possibility of space and recognize the many ways that games can and do have meaning. It's supposed to help you understand how the designs succeed and fail and what's the best way to proceed given a specific set of aims.

It seems reasonable to share some thoughts from a colleague, Andrew Phelps, who founded one of the most successful game design programs, centers, and studios in the world, the MAGIC Center. He is the founder of the RIT School of Interactive Games and Media, the founder of the RIT Center for Media, Arts, Games, Interaction and Creativity (MAGIC), and the founder of MAGIC Spell Studios at RIT, the last of which is a $25M public-private partnership between RIT and the State of New York. As a games professor and trained artist, he provides some tips for getting ready for that first project (Box 10.3).

BOX 10.2

"The Original Mobile Games" is an app with playable reproductions of historic "dexterity games/puzzles." Often thought of as just "ball-in-maze" games there has been a wide range of types of games, puzzle, and play involved in them. The app is a co-production of The Strong National Museum of Play, RIT's School of Interactive Games and Media and it's MAGIC Center and educational game studio Second Avenue Learning.

Shipping with six playable games, the app also provides its players with the history of each of the games and photographs of the actual games in the museum's collections. Five packs of DLC (downloadable content) allow motivated players to have a mini-museum of 27 playable games in their pockets. The iOS version was released at the end of 2018, on Google Play at the end of August, and as of this writing, the Nintendo Switch version is being readied for initial submission.

Dexterity Games/Puzzles

While in some forms, these types of games go back to antiquity, the first widely successful industrial release of these, "Pigs in Clover" dates back to 1869. It was so popular that over 8,000 a day were manufactured during the heyday of the game. A competition between senators in Congress for the fastest time made it the subject of political cartoons and other media treatments; even a satirical "moral panic" article in the Chicago Tribune that suggested that American daily life had been brought to a screeching halt by the arrival of the game. Recently HBO gave a "tip of the hat" to the game at the end of the first season of "Westworld," where "The Maze" the characters were searching for was found to be a round "ball-in-maze" game packaged in a box with reimagined "Pigs-in-Clover" cover art.

Soon a large number of these games appeared from multiple manufacturers, with a wide "equipment." Ring toss variants, enclosed jigsaw puzzles, dice, dominoes and more were all enclosed in plastic or metal boxes with clear faces and challenging the player to complete them singly or in competition. They were often themed around current events like the launch of the Queen Mary, the international competition to reach the North Pole, Lindbergh's flight from New York to Paris, and the birth of the Dionne Quintuplets. British company R. Journet & Co., the most prolific manufacturer of these puzzles and games for decades even brought them to special service during World War Two. Some units of their "Niagara Puzzle" and "Radio Puzzle" were shipped to British POWs in German camps with small silk maps, files, and compasses hidden in the bottom layer.

Exploring Digital Versions

Jon-Paul Dyson, vice-president of exhibits at The Strong National Museum of Play, had wanted to see digital replicas of these games for some time. The historic games are played by tilting, tapping or shaking the cases, mechanics that he believed could be replicated on today's smartphones. In the Spring of 2017, Dyson, Steve Dubnik, president and CEO of the Strong, and Stephen Jacobs, professor in the School of Interactive Games and Media at the Rochester Institute of Technology, agreed to try to replicate a set of the games from the museum's collection of over 100 of them on mobile phones. Jacobs has held a visiting scholar appointment at the Strong for over 10 years and RIT provides funds for full-time student Co-Ops (paid internships) to work on projects at and/or related to the museum.

In the summer of 2017, the first team of three students did research in the collections with curator Nicolas Ricketts and conservator Hillary Ellis, worked with Professor Jacobs to catalog formal elements of the games, and built rough prototypes of six of the games that demonstrated the range of possibilities. When the administrative team at the Strong couldn't stop playing the alpha versions of the games during the student's final presentation it became clear that the prototyping effort would be expanded. A new team was brought on in the summer semester of 2018 to polish the first set of six demo games and make rough prototypes of another 30–40 more, as the Museum wanted to explore the idea of additional packs of games as DLC in addition to an initial free release of six.

As a second validation effort, the beta version was part of RIT's annual playtesting session at the Game Developers Conference. The digital antiquities were a hit and the decision was made to engage a local studio to support the students' efforts and ship a commercial strength product by the end of the summer.

RIT and the Strong chose to partner with Second Avenue Learning, an award-winning educational game studio in Rochester. The student developers, some supported by RIT's Neurodiverse Hiring Initiative, were embedded in the studio, as was Jacobs.

Production Challenges

Thankfully these were mostly technical, and mostly surmountable.

On the human and enterprise interaction side things went smoothly. Jacobs had worked with Second Ave on several projects over the years and all three entities had a history of cooperation as well. This history of collaboration, and shipping product on iOS and Android, resulted in Nintendo granting each of the three entities developer credentials and dev kits to move the project to the Switch. Even the addition of student developers on the autism spectrum into the studio went well and it was these students who led a well-reviewed end of project presentation to the entire company at the end of the summer.

Technically there were several significant challenges.

Physics and the Unity Game Engine

The biggest challenge here was in replicating "jumping beans." These are plastic, oblong capsules reminiscent of pharmaceutical capsules with a small ball bearing inside. The ball bearing rolling inside the capsule will cause it to flip end over end. Though the team tried several different approaches to replicating this action, none of them were ever flawless and in the end. we had to eliminate the games or puzzles we'd wanted to use with this "equipment" because the "feel" of the gameplay wasn't right.

Cross-Platform Compatibility

Several of the historic games use drops of mercury instead of ball bearings. After a long series of attempts, the team got the qualities of motion and deformation required applied to a digital ball of "mercury" on Android. Once ported to iOS, the "balls of mercury" transformed into flattened disks. Several attempts to fix the problem all failed. As we wanted identical sets of games across Android and iOS, we had to abandon the "mercury" games.

Nintendo Switch Joycon "Drift:"

This is an issue for both developers and players on the system. It seems that the hardware used in the controllers is less accurate than the hardware in smartphones. The only way to reliably compensate for this is to recalibrate the joycons from time to time.

A Success!

Despite these minor issues above, everyone involved with the project and its players have been extremely pleased with the product. By the time this book is published, we hope there'll be an approved, released version on the Switch as well.

STEPHEN JACOBS

BOX 10.3

I think one of the things about social impact games that strikes me is that at this moment in the field we (i.e., academia, game designers, developers, etc.) are being asked to do a lot with very little. And when I say "very little" I mean that in a couple of contexts. The first is the obvious notion that games are, in fact, expensive to make: relative to other forms of media they incur more costs due to the interactive nature of the medium, the current technical challenges of developing and delivering content, etc. A simple essay such as this one is infinitely easier to author, and could have just as much impact based on readership, timeliness, content, etc. There is a dangerous thing with games where people outside the field want to conflate the form of a game with its impact, which is to say that something will have impact simply because it is a game. The truth is that many games will not, and this is neither a fault of the medium nor a failure of the designer. In academia right now, there seems to be some kind of collective amnesia where we've forgotten that games are hard to make, that good art is not a guaranteed outcome of a solid process in every instance, and that research is exactly what it implies: a quest for knowledge and a process of discovery. All of those things tend to be iterative, and that means costly, time-consuming, detailed, and somewhat exhausting. I can't for the life of me figure out why we then turn around and say "but games should be easy because the product is supposed to be fun to engage with"—it is a nonsensical statement. But over and over again in higher education, we're asked to make games to change the world with a bit of string and maybe a bottle cap.

The second way I mean that we are working with very little is that our understanding of games and their effects is still very much in its infancy. Games in higher education really kicked off maybe as early as 2000–2001, and as I'm writing this it's 2018. We certainly didn't claim to know everything about the ways and means of impact regarding film or television or literature or anything else in that timeframe. But once again games scholars are being asked to not only create games for impact, but to then measure that impact not as a game, but comparatively against some other intervention. Is a game a good preparation vs. a lecture? Is a game an effective tool vs. an interactive slide show? How will we know a game is working unless it helps the player perform better on an assessment mechanism designed for a different context such as a standardized test? The traditions, funding apparatus, and culture of higher education in this instance has trapped the study and exploration of games for impact and held it tight against that which is not games. The ivory tower has to some extent sought to hold at length the study of games as games, the study of their impact as potentially unique.

Thus, I would say to any aspiring designer, to dream big and start small. It is my continued belief and desire that games change their players and thus the world. But as a first step, a first game, a first effort (or fifth, or twentieth) start small—what can you make with the resources available to you? What one thing can your game try to change? Instead of "solving education" what is one direct, concrete, changeable thing that your game can address? And how can it do so in a way that is engaging? Creating games for impact means focusing not just on the impact, but also on the fact that it is a game, on exploring what that means, on remembering the reasons people play games in the first place, and examining and exploring that context freely and without bias. Only then can we really understand what impact games have, and design accordingly. Good luck!

ANDREW PHELPS

10.4 CONCLUSION

When these choices seem overwhelming, it's always useful to remember that game design is a practice. This chapter touched on a few of the ways of practicing that are emerging, but there are many, many more to consider. Instead of worrying about the optimal solution, it is often better to accept that your individual practice is going to be different. No two concert violinists practice the same way, nor do two doctors. They may practice the same thing, but they do it in the way that is best for them, given their limitations and propensities, their interests, and their passions. As you proceed, think in those terms. And don't forget that as the old proverb goes, every journey starts with a first step. That's not a leap into an abyss. That's a step toward a goal, knowing there will be some obstructions, but you'll find the means to achieve what you started.

REFERENCES

Coren, Michael J. "Foldit gamers solve riddle of HIV enzyme within 3 weeks." *Scientific American* (2011). https://www.scientificamerican.com/article/foldit-gamers-solve-riddle/

ESP Game. 2008. http://www.gwap.com/gwap/gamesPreview/espgame/.

Grace, Lindsay D. "Heuristics from curating and exhibiting game art in the 21st century." In *Proceedings of the 8th International Conference on Digital Arts*, 101–108. ACM, 2017.

Grace, Lindsay. *Social Impact through Exhibition*. Games for Change 2015. Video at https://youtu.be/ygSD__45Etc.

Grace, Lindsay D. "The poetics of game design, rhetoric and the independent game." In Digital Games Research Association (DiGRA) Conference, Utrecht, Netherlands, 2011.

Grace, Lindsay D., and Peter Jamieson. "Gaming with purpose: Heuristic understanding of ubiquitous game development and design for human computation." In Marios C. Angelides and Harry Agius, eds., *Handbook of Digital Games*, 2014, 645–666.

Hacker, Severin, and Luis von Ahn. Matchin: Eliciting user preferences with an online game. In *International Conference on Human Factors in Computing Systems*, Boston, 1207–1216. 2009.

Jenkins, Henry. "Games, the new lively art." In Joost Raessens and Jeffrey Goldstein, eds., *Handbook of Computer Game Studies*. Cambridge, MA: MIT Press, 2005, 175–189.

Klausen, Arne Martin, ed. *Olympic Games as Performance and Public Event: The Case of the XVII Winter Olympic Games in Norway*. New York: Berghahn Books, 1999.

LeBlanc, Allana G., and Jean-Philippe Chaput. "Pokémon Go: A game changer for the physical inactivity crisis?" *Preventive Medicine* 101 (2017): 235–237.

III

Implementation

CHAPTER 11

Prototyping, Ethics, and Testing

T HROUGHOUT THIS BOOK, MUCH of the focus has been on design inten- tion and expected result. However, what a designer intends and what actually happens can be very different. This chapter is aimed at provid- ing a brief introduction to the core concerns around both doing things with games and the results of the things you do. In more formal terms, it focuses on the design intentions and their consequences.

While consequences may be intended, it's important to be able to notice and correct unintended consequences. It's also important to make sure that the design is being evaluated the right way. Often when games are designed, it is much easier to ask the people closest to the project if it works. That's a bit like asking your parents if they like the job you did. If they are supportive, they're going to say they loved it regardless of its quality.

It's also tempting to ask people who have a vested interest in the proj- ect's success. While the people at your job or school may not necessar- ily have an investment in the project, they may be worried about your opinion. Faculty who poll students about their impressions of a game the faculty member made may be forgetting that students are just as worried about giving the faculty member a favorable impression of them as they are about providing honest feedback.

This is undeniably why the best feedback is collected from impartial audiences that can give unbiased feedback. This is, of course, an ideal. Inviting research participants for an unpaid 2-hour session with a game is in itself part of a self-selection bias. If you aren't interested in games, you are unlikely to volunteer for a 2-hour unpaid session. Like all such research, it's more often about getting a reasonable balance of the ideal. Time, money, project scale, and scope will all influence how feedback is collected. A game created in a single weekend is probably not a good candidate for a month-long evaluation, just as a 6-month project should have more than a 1-hour focus group.

Likewise, part of game design is learning the who, what, where, and when for those tougher questions. It's about learning to know what to do when the answers weren't what you hoped or learning how to get better answers than you expected. This chapter is designed to help you on that part of the game design journey. Every project is going to be different, so there is no one-size-fits-all solution.

11.1 PROTOTYPES: HOW AND WHEN TO TEST YOUR IDEAS

If you've read this book to this point, then you probably understand that testing your design early and often is the best plan. That typically means you should adopt a prototyping mindset. As soon as you have an idea, you should start to design and implement something that can be quickly evaluated. Often that's something on paper, but for those that are comfortable with it, software prototypes can be just as valuable.

The important thing to remember with prototypes is that they are most useful to the design process when they are low cost. Cost is a product of time and money. Building a prototype using $100 worth of software over months can be much more expensive than building one from $1000 software over a week. It all depends on what you are testing and how valuable your time is. If, during those months with the $100 tool, you, as a designer, are learning something you are likely to use again, then it may be a high-value proposition. If, on the other hand, the $1000 tool helps the designer or design team collect feedback on a future design sooner without the need to learn something they won't use again—the $1000 option is clearly worth it.

There are a variety of economic models that can outline when and how much you should spend on a project. The idea here is not to help you understand those formal structures but instead to encourage you to think critically about prototyping. Prototypes are designed to do one thing—get feedback for future versions. That means that they are generally disposable. The sooner you can get what you need from a prototype, the sooner you can discard it and move on.

The other reason low-cost prototypes are useful to design is that the less you spend on something, the more you can accept its criticisms. When a game prototype that took 3 months to build isn't received well, it's harder to take the feedback than if it took a few hours to create it. The trick with prototypes is to have the appropriate distance from it. The more time, money, heart, and soul a designer puts into the prototype, the harder any negative feedback will be to process. Likewise, it's quite wonderful to build something quickly and see that it works. It means that the core of the experience has plenty of potential.

One of the most debilitating experiences for a project is when the designer can't see the strengths or weaknesses of a design. It's a bit like a captain who keeps steering a ship into an iceberg. Each prototype is an opportunity to make a course correction, to steer toward success and away from failure.

In short, the answer to when to test your ideas is typically as soon as you can. If you're making a game in a single weekend, then it's in the first hours of your design process. If you're making a game over 3 months, then it's in the first weeks of the project. The scale and scope of the prototype are going to depend entirely on the complexity of your design goals.

Borrowing from the previous ship and iceberg analogy, when and what to prototype is largely a product of how much you are doing as a designer which is new. There are existing maps for all sorts of game designs. FPSs and the mechanics therein are so common that many tools offer out of the box solutions that provide much of what most games using those mechanics need. If your design is simply an FPS with a new type of gun, then you need only build prototypes to understand the lure of that gun. The same is true of platformer mechanics and many card game mechanics. If your game is a derivation of Apples to Apples, for example, you're more likely to need to test the content of your game in that context, not the mechanics (unless you are doing something new with the mechanics).

The idea with any prototype is really to just start by understanding what you don't know. Anything you build should help fill in the blank. If a sailor is traveling to uncharted territory, they can easily begin with the maps of the places around that uncharted territory. After that, it's time to explore. Prototypes are simply your exploration tool.

In the days of prospecting, if you were looking for gold, you didn't start by digging as deep as you could in one place. Instead, you dig a little, hope for a vein of gold, and then follow it. You might have to dig 10 times before you hit one, but once you do, you follow it. Your prototypes should be structured similarly. You will make several, and some will come up empty. Sometimes, you'll emphasize the wrong elements and get further from your goal. Other times, you'll hit it just right, and that's what you need to follow in subsequent iterations.

The trick is knowing what questions to ask and how to ask them. When prospectors dug for gold, they panned, looking for tiny nuggets. Designing and evaluating prototypes works the same way. The designer needs to know the signs and shapes of design gold. Something that will really work for its intention. This is often developed by experience but reading about it and talking to people who have done it before will get you there faster than the generation before you. They will help you refine your map, so you know where you are and where you want to go next.

One of the easiest ways to determine how much of a prototype you need for testing is to think in terms of the minimally viable product, or MVP. An MVP is the smallest, simplest solution you can create to test a specific design question. MVPs can be digital or analog. As an example, if you are testing a currency system in your board game, you have lots of ways to make an MVP. You can use low value coins (e.g., pennies and dimes) as play tokens, you can borrow them from another game like Monopoly, or you can simply write monetary values on index cards and distribute them. If you are testing the system, not the look and feel of the money itself, any of those solutions will work. They are part of the MVP for testing the currency system in your game.

The point with an MVP is to focus on what you need to test. If the system is good, you may want to expand the test to different types of representation of money (e.g., paper, coins, scorecards). If the system is bad, you can keep testing it, or after a few runs, you may simply realize there is no need for a currency system at all in your game. When you use an MVP, you are allowing your prototype the best opportunity to succeed. As you refine the prototype, you'll move from the structural elements (i.e., game verbs and interactions) toward the aesthetic experiences (i.e., look and feel) and more nuance. In the beginning, your MVP will be cobbled together, at the end, it will be the model of your game.

Prototype thinking is really about iteration. It's about pulling together the least amount of playable experience you can and learning from it. The idea is build lots of small experiences with the intention to learn something specific about each. Designing a small experience, with ready-made elements, makes the entire process simpler. It also allows you, as a designer, to process feedback with less emotional investment. The more you design, the more you will develop the thick skin that allows you to learn when something works and when it doesn't without being saddled with the emotional anxiety that comes from sharing your work with others.

It's also important to recognize that collecting feedback on simple prototypes is an expense. It costs time, energy, and sometimes real money. It takes time for your testers and can be taxing for them. Conducting too many prototype evaluations can burn through the pool of people to whom you have access.

For this reason, it's common to prototype and test in a kind of concentric circle. The first versions of the prototype are tested with people nearer to the project. As the project scales, so too does the audience that will evaluate it. The first version of a playable experience might be tested by a significant other or co-worker, the second by a few friends, and the third by complete strangers (Figure 11.1).

For independent developers and those who do not have the support of a full-time game studio, this pattern is common. It often means that a prototype of the game may be tested at a public conference, summit, or convention. These venues offer a great opportunity for a well-developed prototype to get fresh feedback from individuals who are not invested in its success. It also means showing a game publicly, which can be a challenge emotionally and logistically. Conventions and conferences often have submission criteria, sometimes submission fees, and very often some curation. Not every prototype submitted gets accepted, so it's important to plan accordingly.

Some types of playable experiences are much harder to prototype than others. Getting feedback on a draft of a multi-day alternate reality game is not as easy as a 5-minute digital toy. Emailing a link is easier than packing

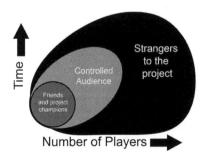

FIGURE 11.1   The testing audience circle grows in the time your game develops, as will the number of players that engage with your work.

and shipping a board game. All of these should factor into your prototyping plan.

11.2 METHODS FOR PROTOTYPING

There are many, many ways to prototype a playable experience. It's common to prototype in a completely different environment than the planned release. A 3D digital game may start as a board game prototype. An analog card game may start as a digital toy. Typically, the rule of thumb is to design and implement something that will get the appropriate feedback as quickly as possible.

The following are a few ways people typically meet this need.

- *Wizard of Oz*: The game is provided for feedback with some of the intended elements faked. If the game involves artificial intelligence (AI), the Wizard of Oz version might have a person acting as the AI. If the game involves an algorithm not yet written, the algorithm is faked. This works particularly well for paper versions of soon to be digital games or for digital games that involve complex new systems.

- *Paper prototypes*: For both digital and analog games, paper prototypes are a common way to collect feedback quickly. Since paper is so easy to discard, it's a low investment implementation plan. Some people prefer to do paper prototypes with game interface elements and other scale items to get information about the interface. Others think more abstractly and use the paper prototype to understand elements of player interaction (with each other or the Wizard of Oz system that has not been implemented yet).

- *Digital drafts*: More typically for digital games, it's often easy to draft elements of the planned game in digital tools. Simple game engines like YoYo Games GameMaker (http://www.yoyogames.com/gamemaker), GameSalad (https://gamesalad.com/), and Twine (http://Twinery.org) are particularly useful for building drafts. Doing so allows some people to build their game iteratively, potentially allowing their final version of the game to be in the same environment they had originally built prototypes. It's also a good way to test some of the dynamic elements of a game that may perform differently based on the tools used to build it. Digital drafts are often required for technical solutions to test their viability.

- *Digital and analog drafts*: Sometimes, the prototype may be about environmental factors or attributes that need to be envisioned by the player. This might be true of a large-scale analog game involving a distinct physical environment or the virtual reality game with a unique virtual world. Tools like Google Sketchup, for example, offer an easy way to draft environments for both digital and analog experiences. People render 3D scenes and offer them as static on-screen images, print outs on a page, or videos. Depending on skill sets, it's sometimes easy to render several scenes and allow the players an opportunity to click a website to navigate between Sketchup rendered scenes.

There are many more ways to implement a prototype. It's common to blend these approaches depending on what's being tested. Again, there is no one-size-fits-all solution. Instead, it's smart to design a prototype with the same level of intention as designing the game itself. Think critically about the feedback you are trying to collect and design accordingly. Always design a prototype with at least one key question the prototype can help answer.

Common questions include:

- Is the core concept engaging and playful?

- Are the challenges balanced?

- Is the message clearly delivered or is it being obscured?

- Do players understand how to play?

- Is it easy to break the game system?

While questions help aim the prototype, there are often surprises that arise while people play the prototype. It's important to be receptive to these as people play your prototype, as they may actually aid in your design.

In this way, prototypes can function as a kind of participatory design task. Formal participatory design encourages the active involvement of all stakeholders. It is, for example, important to share prototypes and their feedback with subject matter experts or clients of the project. This not only helps collect feedback, it allows them to understand the design's journey. To return to the boat-steering analogy, stakeholders who participate in the design via prototypes understand why the design traveled the way it did.

It doesn't black-box the design decisions but instead exposes them. When the project is complete, it allows for a much more transparent process and prevents the challenge of defending designs decisions late in the production process. It's like sharing blueprints before the house is built. Except the feedback shapes those blueprints, so that the designer can say, from experiential feedback, why the final design looks and feels the way it does.

11.3 ETHICS: WHERE (NOT TO GO)

It's important to keep in mind the many potential spaces where ethics can be breached in a game design. While in academic circles many universities employ institutional review boards (also known as IRBs) to evaluate research protocols and make sure that people are acting ethically, it's easy to lose sight of that when fully engaged in a game design. Generally, the number one rule of any such works applies to games too—first, do no harm.

In an ideal world, designers are always aware of the way their game design may be affecting an audience. They know what their game intends to do and know that it is doing nothing more. In reality, doing harm is an easy oversight. As an example, in classrooms, it is common to provide a trigger warning. This warning prefaces the exposition of some image or portrayal of a situation that can be unnerving to others. In the most basic, it's a warning about violent or sexual content, but the kinds of content that unnerve or upset someone can vary. The victim of a violent crime may be triggered by the portrayal of a scene in a movie that is uncomfortably close to their own experience.

In games, it is rare to provide such warnings. But the repercussions for the experience that players have fully engaged themselves can be high. The bulk of this book is focused on the power of play and games to affect people. This is something that is wonderful about games, but employed in unethical ways, it could be a detriment that scars the entire practice and community.

This is more than the small-print disclaimer to the power of play. This is a real reasonability for designers. Designing playful experiences involves a kind of social contract between the player and designer. When a designer does something unethical, they are breaking that contract. Sometimes, they are breaking that contract intentionally, sometimes, they are breaking it without intent. The better you become at designing, the more controlled your efforts will be. The more refined your craft as a designer, the more you control intent and result.

Providing examples of unethical design is a bit antithetical to promoting ethical design. It's a bit like giving directions on how to create a bomb, and then telling people not to make one. Instead, it's a bit more useful to explain ways in which a design might lose sight of its intent and border on unethical behavior. Some examples include:

- Embedding lies, calumny, or other false reports to sway a player's perspective

- Hiding content that may be regarded as audience inappropriate as a way to increase interest in the game (e.g., sexual content to minors or illegal content disguised as appropriate content)

- Making claims about the effectiveness of a game without appropriate proof

- Designing experiences intentionally meant to do physical or mental harm, especially without disclosing to players and allowing players the option to opt-in or out of the experience

This list could be much longer. The thread that binds these is that they are the same tricks used by unethical creators in other domains. They are the activities of swindlers, scam artists, and those that seek to exploit others for their personal gain. They are, at heart, aimed not at supporting the people who engage with them, but instead in turning a quick profit for those who created them. Historically, those who engaged in such work are discovered, embarrassed, ridiculed, reviled, and sometimes worse.

This is exceptionally important for people who produce work that extends beyond their own country's borders. Governments around the world have explicit restrictions on the kind of content and activities that are explicitly prohibited. Many of these laws are designed to protect citizens and prevent them from being exposed to detrimental content. While it is also true that in some countries such restrictions are also designed to control the population to an unhealthy amount, it is a tough ethical line when any creator seeks to exploit people in a call against a governing body. Acting badly among those who are acting worse, doesn't make you a good person.

There are no hard and fast ethical rules around game design and doing things with games. There are playful design decisions that are completely ethical for some contexts and unethical in others. Often, for example, games presented in an arts experimentation context can be considered less ethically bound than those provided for an educational context. This is a combination of both modern contemporary views of art and the audience expectations of educational content. It's also part of the core definition of play—that it is voluntarily engaged.

There's an old saying about pornography that applies here. You may not be able to define unethical game design, but you know it when you see it. At the very least, one of the easiest ways to avoid questions of ethics in game design is to fully disclose the content and reveal any elements that may border ethical lines. If you think you're doing harm, then you're likely on the wrong side of the ethical meter.

If you would like more depth on ethics and its relationship to game design, consider reading Miguel Sicart's *The Ethics of Computer Games* (2011).

11.4 TESTING

Examining a game design is a combination of many disciplines. It is one of the many reasons that game design is a kind of 21st-century liberal art. Thorough game testing incorporates statistics, interviews, visual critique, user experience analysis, copyediting, effect analysis, and a variety of other activities. While the very first test of your game may not involve everything, it's important to recognize the elements that a formal evaluation of your game undergoes.

11.5 PLAYTESTING

The first and most common evaluation of your game is an obvious part of the design process. Every game needs to be playtested. Playtesting is the activity of evaluating the elements of the game when they are presented as one unit. It's the moment, by analogy, when the band gets together to see how they sound together. It's when the entire ensemble plays as one. It's also the moment you realize who has been practicing, and who needs more work.

Playtesting is best accomplished early and often, like prototyping. Most games are made by teams of people. That means that individual elements of the game are made at different times by different people. This is even true of the solo developer, who might spend time as an artist and then switches to be a programmer. That means that when all the parts come together to make the full game, they aren't going to fit perfectly together the first time. In the analog world, that might mean physical mishaps like cards being too big to hold or too easy to see by other players. It might mean round times are too long or too short. For digital games, it can be everything from assets being too big or too small, to code mishaps, or anomalies the team had never foreseen. Ideally, you may have tested for this in a prototype, but prototype oversights appear in playtests.

That's what the playtest is for. Players test, just like every other quality product gets tested by its users. It's highly likely the first boat ever built sank. If they tested it correctly, they would have learned from that failure and kept moving forward.

What's most important from a design perspective in a playtest is to have a playtest mindset. A playtest mindset is an open mind. It's a mindset that is not as emotionally attached to the designed experience as it is critically open to what each playtest teaches you about the game.

Far too often we use the analogy that the thing designed is the designer's baby. It's not your baby yet. It's an idea. An idea that has been implemented and is likely to go through several iterations before it is done. The baby shouldn't be discarded. Prototypes and game elements can and often should be. An open mind reads the playtest for this information and moves from there.

The best way to go into a playtest is with an open mind that is objective. The objectivity lets you notice things that you might not see because of emotional attachment. Players never care if it took 2 hours or 2 days to create an art asset, they only care if it makes the experience engaging. As the person behind the artifact, you know the labor, and that labor may steer you toward the wrong decision. It may have you keep things you shouldn't and discard things you should keep.

While there are several books and resources that cover playtesting in more depth, there are a few key tips to a successful playtesting experience.

1. *Prepare to take notes.* Lots of notes. Where did players get stuck? What didn't they understand? What engaged them? What annoyed them? The simplest way to learn what the player is thinking is to ask them to think out loud. Tell them to communicate their thinking while they play the game or immediately after if you don't want it to affect other players.

2. *Don't try to explain anymore of the game than you must.* Most games won't have the benefit of having the designer present when it is played. So you shouldn't rely on that for your playtesting. Understand what

the players need to get going quickly and then let them play. Their natural tendencies and misunderstandings are worth noting and will help you understand how the game will be played when it's not under your direct control. In a prototype, you may explain lots, in a playtest, there should be little explanation and lots of play.

3. *Control the environment.* Playtests should be conducted in an environment that allows you to hear the players, take effective notes, and allows the player natural interaction. The more advanced your prototypes and games toward their final product, the less you'll want to control the environment. In early prototypes, players mishearing the directions or missing an audio cue could negatively affect your design, but as your design evolves, these elements are a part of the real world and may need to be part of the playtesting environment. Testing in an artificial environment is fine early on (i.e., for prototypes), but unrealistic in a playtest, since it's close to the end of a game's design cycle.

4. *Change players often, but make sure your players fit your target audience.* If you use the same playtesters for each revision of your game, they are affected by previous versions of the game. If you use players who aren't part of your intended audience, then you may be getting feedback that isn't very useful. Depending on your game, playtesters who haven't seen your prototypes might be the best.

5. *Look not to prove, look to learn.* Instead of conducting a playtest to demonstrate why your game is great, you should design the playtest simply to learn about the game. Some of the most effective playtests push the team in a fresh direction. It's easy to start a playtest pitching the merits of your game, but instead, try to remain objective and simply explain your intention and the game. If your game relies on a late reveal, then you can hide your intention but should remain ethical in the execution.

It's important to recognize that not every playtest is going to happen where it should. If your analog game is designed for parties or the living room, it's not going to be practical to visit 20 people's parties or living rooms for the final playtest. But do your best. If your game is planned for web release in social media, playtesting might reveal that the game's dimensions make it look like an advert or that the social media website's Chrome changes might make a part of your game unplayable. Both of these have happened to projects on which I've worked, but because of limited playtesting, we didn't discover them until release.

For more tips and tricks to playtesting, consider reading "Playtesting with a Purpose" (Oden et al. 2016). This short read provides details on playtesting for novice designers, focusing on encouraging testers to be thoughtful about intention.

11.6 USER TESTING

Playtesting can be formal or informal, but generally follows the informality of play. User testing, on the other hand, tends to be more specific. It aims to test the functionality of a game and its elements and how they are perceived in the game. User testing is particularly useful for games that have distinct user interfaces or are designed for very specific audiences. The practice of user testing is more mature than playtesting and has many resources online and in print to guide you through the appropriate structure of a formal user test.

11.7 EFFECT AND AFFECT ANALYSIS

Often, when you want to know whether or not a game has done the thing it was intended to do, you want to ask questions about effect and affect.

In the great comedy of English language rules, these two words are often confused. In the context of doing things with games, effect focuses on the documented change a game may create. These changes are often in the form of a change in interests, activities, or opinions, but could also involve an increase in propensity, educational mastery, or anything else the designer aims to achieve.

Affect, on the other hand, references the players mood, demeanor, or general feelings. This is the definition often used by psychology to describe feelings and emotion. It is common to see academic writing and analysis of a game's efficacy analysis and its affect analysis. The efficacy analysis describes the effects of the game in general terms, while affect analysis examines the way it affected player emotion or feelings. An affect analysis might ask how people felt during the game for example.

If you designed a game to strengthen the perception of a brand or to demonstrate the merits of a certain health practice, you'll want to analyze the game's effect. This is commonly done through a pre-post test or an A/B test. These are simply shorthand ways to describe a process of examining what the game does to players as an effect or change in affect.

A pre-post test involves collecting information about the player before the game experience (i.e., pre), and at the least after (i.e., post). Some people run a mid-game test as well. The core concept is simple. Did the player change their interests, opinions, or activities as a result of playing the game? If so, what changed, how much did it change, and what factors seem to amplify the effect. Typically, good study design is tracking the same characteristics before and after the game has been played.

An A/B test is a way of comparing two solutions. If a game is supposed to be more effective than a short film or book, the effect for the game can be compared with a population that engages with the alternative medium. One or both populations are measured for a change based on their exposure to the game, varied version of the game, or to alternative media. In a formal controlled study, it's also reasonable to track a population of study participants who are not at all engaged in either activity. This group serves as a control, so that if there are changes in effect you can differentiate them from the experience and normal fluctuations.

The art and science of writing good surveys, polling players appropriately, and designing effective studies is also beyond the scope of a single chapter. However, there are many resources that can help with this process. It doesn't hurt to get the help of a subject matter expert in such areas. There are user experience (UX) professionals, game user experience (GUR) professionals, psychometricians, and a variety of professionals who are well trained in designing means to test the efficacy of an interactive experience. Designers don't need to become specialists in these areas to work well, but working with such people will greatly increase the effectiveness of your work.

Instead, what's important for the designer is understanding that these are available and how they may be used to inform the design. Conducting interviews, ethnographies, and other qualitative measurements are very useful in understanding how a design is working if at all. This kind of research works well to augment the large-scale statistical or quantitative research that a game may require. Just as there is no one-size-fits-all solution for prototyping, there is not one-size solution for understanding the effects of a game.

It's typically best to select methods that are appropriate to the scale and scope of the project. There's no benefit to over analyzing and there's an opportunity for mistakes in under analyzing. Projects that are looking for wide-scale effect may require more substantial analysis, where mere playful gestures may require none.

In the end, players will always provide some kind of feedback. That feedback may come in the form of downloads and sales (or lack of sales), and it may come in the form of kudos from reviewers or criticisms in public. Understanding that pre-emptive feedback from playtests and formal large-scale analysis provides a map that at least allows the project to avoid hitting any unforeseen obstacles (or icebergs).

11.8 DESIGNING FOR EFFECT AND AFFECT ANALYSIS

It may be strange to consider testing as part of the game design process, but it's actually essential. Beyond designing through playtesting, and conducting tests, some designers incorporate data analysis tools into their game designs. While this is clearly more easily done when implementing digital games, it's a real benefit to the formal process of game assessment. Consider, for example, a game in which players are learning a new language. If the words players are exposed to vary between each play session, it's useful for those analyzing efficacy to know which players received exposure to which words at which time.

This is why many games, particularly in academic environments, include session trackers. A session tracker merely gives each player or play session a unique ID, and then logs the activities of that session. A researcher who follows up with an evaluation of the game can look at the game and understand what each player's experience was both from a general lens to the very specific events of a given second-by-second window. The resolution of this data varies greatly depending on the game and the researcher's needs. In some games, a second-by-second log of what each player did makes sense. In others, it may be minute-by-minute or even a mere time stamp when a player takes action. The higher the resolution or frequency of the data, the more data there will be to evaluate. If the resolution is too high, the amount of data can be overwhelming. If it's too low, then there may not be enough to make proper conclusions.

The other reason creating data tracking in games is useful is that it can provide a means for doing large-scale analysis of a game. Conducting playtests and taking notes on a few players at a time is reasonable, but when games are tested by hundreds of players, it makes more sense to automate much of that note taking. This is why when games move toward large-scale release, the process of redesign starts to move toward more statistical models. On a large-scale game, designers will know that 13.5% of the players will quit in the first 5 minutes. Their task as a designer may simply be to move that number down to 5%. Likewise, such logs reveal bugs, sticking points for players, and points of tension in the game's design. They become the report, of the game's performance.

Designing with this kind of data tracking in mind offers real potential for large-scale improvement of the game. Good designers and developer are able to implement games that even allow teams of researchers to adjust the game itself to adapt to the needs of the study. This is a practice derived from game mods, where the end user of a game has the ability to modify the game to their specific needs. As an example, for some game designers, A/B tests can be conducted with the same game, simply by adjusting the game for test version A or B.

Allowing researchers to do this affords many benefits. First and foremost, it helps isolate the designer from the evaluation. Keeping in mind a good analysis is objective, if the designer or implementation team must participate in the analysis of a game, they are likely to skew the data's perception at the least. Once you've worked on a game, it's hard to remain objective about it. However, when a design team can simply hand the game to an independent team to do evaluation, allowing them to make the tweaks they need to conduct an effective study—it's a win for both designer and evaluator. It affords for the separation of tasks and more objective findings.

As the old adage goes, with great power comes great responsibility. Logging player activity, sharing it with others, and potentially failing to disclose that you are doing so borders on ethical considerations. Laws in specific regions actively limit the legality of collecting data without disclosing it, so it's important to know what you can and can't do legally. Additionally, it's important to know what your team is comfortable with ethically. Often, to avoid some of the liability of being able to connect individual performance with play session data, teams use permanent identifiers, or PIDS, to give each user an anonymous ID. This is particularly important when reporting data, as anonymity of player performance in academic publications is an important part of objective reporting and maintaining privacy. It's one of many ways to first do no harm.PRACTICE WHAT YOU'VE LEARNED

- Go make some prototypes of game concepts you've drafted in earlier chapters. Begin by identifying what unique items need to be tested and move toward building simple prototypes of those elements. Don't forget that a prototype can consist of elements of an existing game, such as Scrabble letters or digital templates for common game mechanics.

- Design a playtest. What is the structure of the playtest for your project? How long will players interact with the game? Write a script for a playtest including the language used to introduce the game, the time it would take to play the game, and the kinds of things a person conducting the playtest should say.

- Do some research on the legal limitations of game content and user log tracking for your project's planned community. If it's to be tested in a school, check the school's IRB requirements. If it is to be used on a corporate Intranet, check to see what limitations are mandated for that environment.

REFERENCES

Choi, Judeth Oden, Jodi Forlizzi, Michael Christel, Rachel Moeller, MacKenzie Bates, and Jessica Hammer. "Playtesting with a purpose." In *Proceedings of the 2016 Annual Symposium on Computer-Human Interaction in Play*, 254–265. New York: ACM, 2016.

Sicart, Miguel. *The Ethics of Computer Games*. Cambridge, MA: MIT Press, 2011.

CHAPTER **12**

Thinking about Implementation

T HERE ARE, OF COURSE, a variety of ways to go about making your game. One of the most important things to know about game-making is that players generally don't care about how you made the game, simply that it works.

In technical circles, it is common to ask what you used to create the game. There is an old tendency to see merit in the technical complexity of the software or tools you used to make the game. It's a bit like asking a traveler what kind of transportation they used to get to a specific location. It may be more interesting to travel by train, or fastest by jet, or a really great story to travel by horse. In the end, the only thing that matters is what solution is best for the problem. It generally doesn't make sense to fly 20 miles when a car or train can get you there faster, more easily, and with less fuss. Likewise, the right implementation strategy is entirely dependent on the aims of your project, the tools available, the skill set of the team members, and the amount of time available.

There's a reason one of the last chapters of this book is the one that tells you what to use to implement your project. It's because the design dictates the right implementation. If, after playtesting, you discover that there really isn't a need for a 3D environment, you may as well discard any 3D toolset. If, after a few prototypes, your card game becomes a board game, or perhaps a digital game, it's better that you commit to the tools you are going to use later in the project. You don't pack for a trip until you know where you are going. Until you build a few disposable prototypes and finalize your game's design, you typically don't know what you're going to need.

It's important to understand that every tool offers affordances and limitations. Your design is the specification that helps you determine which affordances you need and which you can live without. It's really important to recognize that every tool comes with benefits and costs. This chapter helps you understand some of these benefits and limitations as they stand now. Keep in mind that particularly in the software world, changes happen faster than books are printed. It's always best to check websites for latest versions and to browse your options for new tools that may not be listed here.

It's also important to note that when considering the cost of production, cost is not merely the amount of money. It's also time. As discussed in prior chapters, it's important to recognize the balance of cost. Time is an asset just as important, if not more important than, money.

12.1 ANALOG OR DIGITAL?

It's really easy to decide early in your project whether or not you are going to be creating a digital or analog prototype. As you no doubt realize, this may actually change in the middle of a project. Generally, there are a few common benefits and drawbacks to each. These vary by project, but generally, the following paragraphs outline some considerations for production.

12.2 ANALOG VS DIGITAL

Analog games can typically be cheaper to create in low quantities but become more expensive to produce in larger quantities until scaled into the hundreds. For analog games, the initial costs of printing small sets are relatively low, when compared with software costs. Using low-cost materials like paper and purchasing common sets of player tokens, markers, and so on, is low cost in comparison with purchasing software distribution licenses and paying digital game artists and programmers.

Your primary initial implementation costs for any game are production costs (e.g., labor and printing), shipping, storage, and packaging. Some costs can be amortized over the entire production, such as the cost of a graphic designer for art assets in your game. Other costs don't really change when the game scales to larger distribution. Shipping, for example, is relatively stable until scaled, so the difference between making five copies and 50 copies of your game doesn't mean the cost of each game is reduced by much. However, when an analog game is scaled to the thousands, some of those costs go down significantly because of economies of scale. Shipping a box with 25 of your games to a retail outlet will generally be cheaper per game unit than shipping individual boxes direct to consumer.

Now consider the cost of producing a digital game. Generally, digital games cost more upfront to produce, as some software licenses alone can set production costs at several thousand dollars minimum. However, digital production scales much more easily with almost every cost easily amortized over all sales. Distribution, packaging, and storage remain about the same regardless of the number of units sold (or given away for free). While most outlets like Google Play, the Apple App Store, and Steam take a portion of sales costs, the percentage is relatively small (10–25%) for the scale of the network (millions of potential players).

Generally, if the intention is to produce a game for a small community of non-distributed players, it may make sense to make an analog game. On the other hand, if the goal is thousands of distributed players, it may make sense to go digital based on cost.

12.2.1 Distribution

Distribution is rarely an initial consideration for game makers, but it should be. As the adage goes—if a game is never played, is it still a game? Getting to players should be part of your strategy for doing things with games. Distribution depends largely on audience, whether a continent away or in the next office. As previously discussed, demographics, technographics, and psychographics really matter. Will your players be more receptive or averse to a digital or analog game? Will they have the right kind of hardware and software to run a digital copy of your game? Will they have access to a group of players for your board game? Where and how do your intended players typically interact with other games? If your intent is serious, are they more likely to understand it as serious in analog or digital versions? If it's internationally distributed, does a digital version lend itself more easily to translation than an analog version? Some of these answers come from design analysis, others from prototypes and playtesting.

All of these questions and more influence your distribution strategy. If your goal is merely to complete a class project, then distribution may seem too large a concern. But even then, students fail to recognize the challenge of carrying a 1 × 1 meter, non-folding game board into class.

People often make distribution mistakes. They fail to remember that a game intended for the dinner table must fit on the dinner table (which may be smaller than average for urban players), or that the intricate 3D model they printed as tokens won't make it through the rough and tumble process of shipping internationally.

On the digital distribution end, file size, packaged installers, and hardware requirements all factor into your final implementation strategy. It's common for junior designers and developers to forget that the state-of-the-art computers on which they developed the game are far more capable than the ones their target audience of low-income middle-schoolers will have. Thinking about distribution is merely a design constraint related to audience. What does your audience need for a playable experience?

For this, and many other reasons, it's important to outline a plan for distribution early in the implementation cycle. Even if your plan is simply to submit the game for consideration at festivals and competitions, knowing what is needed to get it in front of them is essential. Your custom controller digital game may not get a second look by your favorite game festival simply because they have no way of distributing it to their judges. I know, because this happened to me with my game *Big Huggin'*. The game required a player to hug a giant teddy bear to control a platformer (Figure 12.1).

Your best bet is to think strategically about who will be playing your game. Outline their demographics, technographics, and psychographics generally. At least, do a little bit of research to understand how you will

FIGURE 12.1 The game *Big Huggin'* being played in the street. The game's giant teddy bear controller made it hard to submit to festivals.

get your game into the hands of the people who will play it. You may even want to produce personas or model profiles of individuals you think are going to want to play your game. Are they going to order it on Amazon or buy it on a whim? Are you really looking for libraries to acquire it? Do you prefer to ship each copy of the game from your home or office? Each of these is a legitimate question to ask when embarking on the implementation of your game.

12.3 COMPUTATION NECESSITY

One thing that digital games can do exceptionally well is compute. Some game designs simply avail themselves to digital production because they require the kinds of computation and networking that computers do best. A game that requires input from thousands of people may need the power of the Internet. A game that requires management of lots of different scores, complex simulation, or other computational tasks typically needs to be digital, at least in part.

When deciding on implementation strategy, it's important to understand why a strategy is being adopted. Digital play supports computation well, but it doesn't always support socialization. The improvisational moments that come from a game of charades are not easily supported in a digital environment, especially when the player is working with or against the computer. If there is a high computation necessity to your game, then it often makes sense to assume it's going to be digital. It is better to have a computer grind through calculations, something computers do well, than to ask your players to grind through the same calculations. That is, of course, unless grinding through calculations is part of the learning experience of your game.

Also, remember that a computer offers a kind of objectivity to the game design. This may be useful to certain types of games and a detriment to others. Games that require judging are sometimes more engaging when the judge is a person present to share their opinions. Other times, it's nice to know that the evaluation is the same every time because it is mandated by a computer algorithm. Without the aid of a well-conceived artificial intelligence or digital bot, games involving argumentation may be a bit disappointing in the digital space.

12.4 DURABILITY

Designers don't always think about the shelf-life of their game, but they should. Durable games last, in part because of the design of the game, and in part because of their materiality. In concept, digital games should be the most durable, as they typically have no physical elements to degrade. In reality, digital games degrade as much if not faster than many physical games. This is because software and hardware durability are subject to a kind of atrophy. A game designed to be played on an Apple II computer from 1985 is not easily played today. However, that copy of Monopoly sitting in someone's attic from 1975 is still playable (Figure 12.2).

Some software tools produce more durable games than others. In the history of game engines and toolsets, for example, those engines that have persisted the longest tend to make the most durable games. As you review options for game engines, if durability is your concern, consider larger stable toolsets and technologies that are likely to be around 10–15 years from now. Tools with large user communities, standards, and distribution networks are more likely to produce stable, long-standing games.

With analog games, durability is largely a product of the materials. Higher bond paper may mean fewer tears and longer durability. High polish materials, with high-quality printing processes, can mean that players handle the artifacts of your game with less risk of destroying them. It also means higher production costs. Custom plastics are highly durable, but relatively expensive to produce in low quantities. They are also bad for the environment. Wood is great, until it gets wet, which is a problem not only by the pool, but in damp climates.

FIGURE 12.2 Games on 5¼-inch floppy disks are hard to play now because the technology is outdated. It's important to choose technology that will last and to move your game to new platforms to assure it can be played in the future.

If you're building a game for a specific event, then durability may not be a factor at all. Print on demand and similar solutions allow some of the durability concerns to diminish. With print on demand, the copies of an analog game are generated when they are requested. But, since print on demand is subject to the changes of a printer, durability moves from a material durability concern to a process or manufacturer durability concern.

It's also easy to forget that durability is also a product of reusability. A game that is packaged with expendable, non-reusable artifacts is only usable until those artifacts are gone. This means that if you build a game with invisible markers, the game is only as durable as the markers. When they run out of ink, your game may be a whole lot less appealing. While paper pads, pencils, and even timers can be substituted, sometimes games depend on items that are not easily replaced. Keep this in mind when deciding on your implementation strategy. It may make more sense to implement an invisible ink experience digitally, where the ink never runs out, than to depend on low cost, analog equivalents.

12.5 MAINTENANCE

Maintenance is not always the first thought when you are about to build a game. Like buying a house or a new car, you're interested, and the focus is on the here and now. Yet, the difference between a successful game and an unsuccessful game is sometimes in its ability to be maintained. For most analog games, maintenance isn't much of a concern. With analog designs, as long as the items in your game are durable, maintenance shouldn't be much of a concern.

However, digital games require far more maintenance than many people recognize. This is particularly true when dealing with mobile games and web games, which are subject to the perpetual changes of the Internet and mobile device manufacturers. While initially it seems really convenient to have a mobile app-based game, if your aim is to affect players over more than a few months, you can expect to maintain that app. Screen resolutions change and bugs develop from software changes outside your game (e.g., operating systems upgrades and revisions to web standards). Remember that players don't care how you made your game, just that it works. When it fails to work, it won't take long for those players to become critical. It doesn't matter that it worked well yesterday, only that it doesn't work well today.

When proposing a budget for a game, it's easy to forget maintenance costs, but they will always be there. By analogy, many people who buy a luxury car are surprised by their luxury maintenance costs. Those who leave enough space in their budget, perhaps buying a little less luxury, are often able to handle the costs. Also keep in mind that the more exotic your implementation, the more likely you will have unexpected, exotic maintenance issues.

If you are using a third party to develop your game, it's easy to forget to draft maintenance as part of the contract. However, this is essential for a healthy game release. If you've hired someone else to make the game, make sure you understand the choices they are making to implement the game. Sometimes it's easy for them to make exotic implementation choices that will cause large-scale problems when it comes time to maintain and revise your game. These decisions can vary from depending on rare pieces of software to using rarely used or outdated programming languages and game engines.

12.6 COST AND AUDIENCE

Remembering that cost is not only money but also time, it's important to think about the audience when understanding the final cost of a game. Obviously, your costs of production are going to depend on many factors, and it's not unreasonable that some game projects are designed to take a loss. A public service game, aimed at providing social benefit, may be distributed for free even though it costs many thousands to create.

The audience for your game, your player community, is going to pay something for playing your game. If they aren't paying money, they are spending time. The implementation of your game can affect the final cost substantially. A complex board game, one that requires 30 minutes of direction reading and another 20 of setup, might be too high a cost for a 1-hour class session. They would only have 10 minutes to play the class, or a teacher would need to add the 30-minute setup to their schedule. A 2-minute play experience that requires a virtual reality (VR) headset may not be worth the effort of unpacking the equipment. Like all things in game design, this is about balance. Remember to respect your player community's costs when balancing your own.

There are ways to design opportunities for efficiency. Multiple versions of a game, with quick play instructions or low or high computation versions helps. It's reasonable to do things like offer a quick play version and a more complete version that allows the player to provide more information and to get a benefit. This is what we did for the game *Factitious* (Figure 12.3).

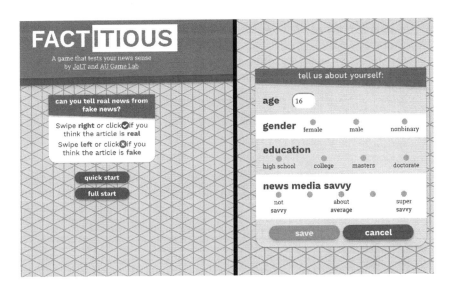

FIGURE 12.3   The *Factitious* game offered a quick start or a full start. Full start allowed players to have a play profile persist over each play. It also allowed the team to collect demographic information.

Offering a simpler version as teasers for more complete sets can also help by influencing the cost in both time and money. Terms like "freemium" are often used to describe such implementations. The player may get a limited version of the game, with the opportunity to pay for more content. This is the same basic strategy employed for older shareware games, where Level 1 might be free but the additional nine levels cost the player. This can be done for both digital and analog games, as both can be provided as free versions with available, paid expansion packs.

The key is to understand what the marker of success for the game will be. It's easier to get more players if the cost of playing is low. That's true both of money and time. However, some objectives can't be met by bringing the cost of both to zero. Zero time would mean the game was never played, and completely free games are sometimes perceived as less valuable than paid games (i.e., if you're giving it away for free it must not be worth much or good). The challenges of price marketing are complex, but knowing more about your audience will help substantially.

The dynamics of game marketplaces have changed greatly as they have evolved. Many free web games were ported to mobile device app stores, creating a flood of low production cost games in those markets. When the first games were offered on app stores, it was easier to sell a game for a dollar than it is now. In the past few years, developers across the range of foci (including educational game developers) have started selling game bundles: $2 can purchase five games that used to be sold for $1 individually.

Other ways to manage costs include embedding ads, gaining independent support through grants, and all the other ways that media offered to the public for little or no cost have found support. IndieGogo.com, Kickstarter.com, and other crowdfunding websites are full of people seeking money to support their game implementations. Many of those developers are looking to do something with games, like you.

12.7 HYBRID: ANALOG AND DIGITAL

The reality is that a game doesn't have to be one or the other, it could be a hybrid. There are great games that combine digital and analog experiences. Such games use the Internet as a party-game resource, combining the latest technology with a board game or offering augmented reality experiences. The dichotomies presented in this chapter were designed to help you, as a designer, think about two ends of a spectrum. The challenges and opportunities of hybrid game design can mean that you are likely to encounter the benefit and challenges of each approach.

12.7.1 Implementation

In the average game, implementation is often perceived as the largest part of the process. While it does vary by project, implementation can be quicker than the design process. That's because, for some types of games, the prototyping process is the implementation. Consider, for example, a field game. The implementation occurs when people get together to play the game. The same is true for some types of alternate reality games. Lastly, depending on how you implemented prototypes, the prototypes may translate directly into reusable pieces of code or artifacts for your game.

12.7.2 Analog Game Considerations

Typically, high-quality analog games combine some craft with aesthetic design. Board game pieces, cards, and other artifacts are designed with aesthetic intention. The colors, images, and other aesthetic characteristics of the final implementation provide much to support (or hurt) a game.

Analog game pieces can be purchased online or printed. Printing can be done at a variety of specialty print services, of which TheGameCrafter.com is most popular. This service can print games using a variety of specific, common formats for board and card games. It also sells board game elements for prototypes and final implementations. The service includes a print on demand service that supports people in the distribution of their games. As a one-stop solution for creating artifacts for a game and selling a boxed game, it is one the best options. Production times are often too long for small projects or for last-minute students in a class.

For short notice, commercial printing services are often useful. Printing at an office mega store can be expensive for multiple copies of a game, but it is a good option for playtesting or for high fidelity prototypes. If you've never done this kind of work, it can be a bit overwhelming to understand different paper weights, costs for cutting, and ways to use products like spray adhesive to glue thin prints to cardstock or foam cores.

An exceptionally cheap way to make color prints is to use photo printing solutions. With costs below $0.10 per photo print, some game elements can be produced for little cost. Cutting photos and attaching them to foam core or other elements will take time.

As this chapter emphasizes, it's important to remember that cost is a function of time and money. It's often tempting to go with low-cost solutions, but they often look like low-cost solutions. There's no point in spending a long time designing your game, only to implement it with a shoddy, makeshift aesthetic. It's also important to remember the benefit of economies of scale and that your labor is a cost, even if you're not getting paid to do it; $1 a sheet for professional cuts may seem like a lot, but the time it will take you to do the same cuts hundreds of times for a card game may help put the cost in perspective.

These implementation strategies are centered on the first version of your game. That version will likely not be the one that is distributed by a major game company. It serves instead as the proof of concept for later production. For some games, final distribution may come from mass production by an established game company. The costs and benefits of such agreements depend entirely on your project goals and expectations of royalties. As with much of the world of designing playful experiences, one size does not fit all.

12.8 DIGITAL IMPLEMENTATION

Most digital games are produced through some version of a game engine or implementation platform. The specific platforms are outlined in Chapter 13, but it's useful to understand how the process works before determining which software package to use.

Generally, implementing a digital game comes down to matching a design to the software available. The typical design constraints that influence which software is used depends on a few key decisions.

12.8.1 Play Perspective

Is the game going to be 2D, 3D, isometric, or something else? Some game-making environments only support one type of play perspective. While some 2D games are made in 3D environments (e.g., by locking the player's perspective and aligning all content on a 2D plane), it's typically more work than it's worth. Sometimes, if the game only needs the impression of 3D, 2D environments can fit the need.

12.8.2 Play Hardware and Software

Is the game only going to work with specific hardware or software? Does it have a unique controller of its own or does it need to be controlled using a common piece of hardware (e.g., an Xbox controller, an eye tracker, a specific VR headset)? Some software platforms do not support certain types of hardware. You can't really implement a full VR experience in a 2D game engine like GameSalad. But for some 3D games, the requirement of using a web plug-in to play the game limits the audience. This additional software, or the need to install the game on a computer, may prevent players who have corporate firewall restrictions (common on institutional machines), the inability to install a game on their computer (e.g., shared computer labs with install restrictions), or concerns about the safety of doing so (e.g., anti-virus software warnings). Installations also take time, which may add to the cost of playing the game.

12.8.3 Design Requirements

Are there specific design requirements that necessitate a specific software or hardware solution? Does the game need access to a device's microphone and will the chosen platform support that access? Does the game require artificial intelligence, data logging, access to a database, the Internet, and so on? Taking an inventory of the specific requirements of the design will help outline which implementation technology is best for the game. Many games may require very standard game activities, so the design requirements may not affect which technology is used.

12.8.4 Distribution

How the game will be distributed is heavily influenced by the technology. Games for mobile devices may need to be compiled into their native formats. Sometimes, a web-only implementation makes sense, and occasionally, the game's complexity is beyond what the average HTML5 browser will support. While many game engines export to a variety of formats, some do so more easily than others. Sometimes, game engines only export to a limited set or the cost to export to other formats is higher than a project's budget.

12.8.5 Complexity

Game engines and technology range from the extremely simple to the extraordinarily complex. Often, the more complex can offer more potential, but that potential only matters if the design requires it. By analogy, a Ferrari is a great car for its purpose, but a pretty lousy choice if you want to travel with five people. Complex game-making systems are not right for all projects, nor are simple ones. Try to match the game's implementation technology to the complexity of the game itself. It's often easier to stretch the limits of a simple tool as a design constraint than to wrestle with making simple things happen in a complex environment.

It's also worth noting that with these choices, there's always the option of building from scratch. For some solutions, coding the game without the aid of a game engine or development tool is a reasonable solution. Some of the games I've made for clients were coded directly with scripting and programming languages like JavaScript or PhP. When dealing with more complex languages like C++, the overhead of doing what a game engine would automate is often not worthwhile, but it all depends on the game's design.

12.9 PRACTICE WHAT YOU'VE LEARNED

- Develop a persona of the ideal player for your game project. What are their wants and needs? How much time to do they have to play? What are their demographics, technographics, and psychographics? How will they receive your game when you distribute it?

- Take a technology inventory. Survey the game design and development community for the tools they most favor. List the software and toolsets with which you are most familiar. If you are working on a team, list the team's skills and match them to specific implementation strategies. This inventory will help you understand what's already available to you.

- Outline an implementation strategy for a game you've designed. What are the characteristics of the game that indicate specific needs in the implementation? Is it analog or digital? What technical requirements exist? How long does it take to play the game to completion and how much time does it take to set the game up?

CHAPTER 13

Implementation Tools

THIS CHAPTER IS WRITTEN with the expectation that you have absolutely no experience making games. That may be fair for some readers and an absolute offense to others. That's why it's an easy chapter to skip around with lots of white space.

The sections of this chapter are designed to artificially segment tools into single categories. In reality, some art tools can be used to build prototypes of a game. Some of the user interface (UI) tools (particularly Adobe XD) are also capable of making functional, interactive prototypes. As with anything new, you should expect to spend some time learning the tool, even if you've used products like it in the past.

Generally, digital games require visual, logical, and audio content. Analog games typically have some visual content and logical content. While the logical content may simply be a set of rules or a social contract among players, sometimes, wireframing and UI tools help with these tasks in analog game design. It's not common to think of UI as part of analog design, but figuring out what's the most ergonomic and easily understood experience for the play experience is a UI and user experience (UX) focus. Save for the digital production and prototyping tools, each of these tools has some relationship to both analog and digital game implementation. Even prototyping the qualities of an in-game buzzer can be aided by the use of an audio editing tool.

For effective prototyping, it's sometimes more efficient to use a tool you know than to learn a new one. If you already know how to make a website, you might want to do that instead of learning a tool that makes clickable links to images and other content. It's also important to note there are often free options available for these tools, but they don't always offer the same quality as the paid versions. It all depends on your project's needs.

Also keep in mind that game production is often about using multiple tools together. Your artists might produce work in 3D Studio Max to be used in the Unity game environment, while your audio person works in Audacity. The suite of tools used to make the completed playable experience is often described as the content pipeline. The pipeline includes all the different tools and processes that contribute to the final product of your game. Some pipelines are more complex than others, but it's important to note that often tried and true pipelines are more reliable than exotic ones. A pipeline might involve moving between software applications, perhaps playing to the strength of each. That's perfectly appropriate for some projects. Remember, no one cares how you made the game, just that it works.

To that point, don't forget that there are many great content resources. A variety of art and audio asset stores exist that support much of what some basic games need. It's often cheaper to buy a ready-made 3D model than to hire an artist to create something similar. But remember that one size does not fit all. The assets you find on the Internet may be too high resolution or simply not fit the aesthetic of your game.

Likewise, it's important to remember that intellectual property rights should be respected. If you are using assets from an online repository, read the usage rights carefully. Paying $20 to use a font is going to be cheaper than a lawsuit. For students and teachers, fair use may apply, but only if the project doesn't go commercial.

This chapter offers at least three commonly used tools for each focus in game implementation. Generally, at least one industry standard tool and one free tool is offered. Small projects with limited budgets and access to software should obviously consider the free tools. Those looking to develop professional skills should aim at the industry standards.

13.1 GAME UI, UX, AND WIREFRAMING

Some games have distinct interface elements, flow between elements, or other experiences that should be drafted and tested. Wireframing is one way of doing this. It allows the relationships between game elements to be specified. While you can do wireframing and UI work in drafts without software, it's often useful to use a software tool to support such work.

Besides refining the work, the tools can often help you think more critically about the process and the kinds of decisions being made. Simple projects typically don't need wireframes, but some people like doing them even if they are very simple. Many of these tools are designed for large-scale software applications and websites, but they work well for many games designs too. Other applications for these tools include narrative design and outlining game states and gateways, as well as their traditional uses.

- *Adobe XD*: Adobe XD is a vector-based tool developed and published by Adobe Inc. for designing and prototyping UX for a variety of apps, including games. Available for macOS and Windows, and free to try, XD supports vector design, website and interactive wireframing, and creating simple interactive click-through prototypes. For complex projects, the wireframing is useful, but for all projects being able to design and implement a quick interactive prototype is very useful. In 2D games, the tools can help. Adobe interfaces with the cloud, so for projects that require strict security of on-site data retention, this may be a problem.

- *Axure RP*: Axure RP Pro is a wireframing, rapid prototyping, documentation, and specification software tool aimed at a variety of applications. It offers similar benefits to Adobe XD but lacks the Adobe suite relationship. Axure has been around for years and is part of the canon of wireframing tools. Axure communicates design decisions to stakeholders who are less familiar with these technologies.

- *Invision*: Invision is designed to offer an entire product design workflow and offers users the ability for mockups and wireframing in one toolset. It focuses on using a collection of prebuilt assets which can be useful for building quickly, although problematic for the distinct elements of most games.

- *Figma*: Figma shares many aspects with Invision, but adds a more collaboration focused orientation. The similarity to Invision is mentioned by many users and makes the choice between the two a bit more ambiguous.

Wireframing and basic UI drafts can also be produced with tools as basic as Microsoft PowerPoint or Google Slides. Basically, anything that allows you to draw shapes and lines easily. This is especially true for prototypes. There's nothing wrong with drawing by hand, just remember to take photos of those drawings to make it easier to share and archive the work. Whiteboards are great, until they are erased.

13.2 ART TOOLS

The dominant art tools for game-making are dependent on whether your work will be presented in two dimensions or three. Both types differentiate themselves by the way the art is produced. For 2D images, the dominant approaches are vector or raster. For 3D, it's typically a modeling or sculpting pattern.

Two-dimensional digital images can be created on the computer using one of two standard formats. Specific software applications typically focus on using either vector graphics or bitmap graphics. When searching the Internet for stock images, buying art assets, or collecting them from an artist for hire, the distinction is important.

Vector graphics are graphics created by putting many individual shapes together. Vector graphic programs are usually called "drawing" programs. They are based on the idea that one picture can often be broken down into a set of simple shapes.

Vector graphics are sometimes called object-oriented graphics because they use these objects, or shapes, to create an image. Vector graphics can be enlarged and shrunken without losing image quality. Vector graphics file formats include encapsulated postscript (eps) and Adobe format (ai). Vector graphics are often useful in games, as the scaling allows for a variety of display formats both in digital and analog games. One digital art asset can be used for a very small screen or print, and it can be reused for a very large one. Vector images are often simpler than bitmap images, making them common for interface elements, icons, posters, and other places where simplicity and scale matter.

A bitmap, or raster, image is created by mapping pixels to specific locations on the screen. Bitmap graphics programs are usually called painters. Bitmap file formats include tag image file format (tiff), joint Photographic Experts Group format (jpg), and the Graphics Interchange Format (gif). Bitmap files do not scale well because the software that displays the graphic must interpret where individual pixels should be when the image is shrunken or expanded. The result is pixelation, which degrades the image's clarity (Figure 13.1).

As you have no doubt noticed, bitmap graphics are the common format for photos. This is because the format works well for capturing photographic data. With bitmap images, the resolution indicates the amount of pixel data in the file. Higher resolution images will have more data and will be larger in data size (depending on what's in the image) and display

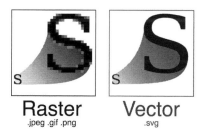

Raster
.jpeg .gif .png

Vector
.svg

FIGURE 13.1 The difference between bitmap and vector images in practice. (Courtesy of Yug [https://commons.wikimedia.org/wiki/User:Yug] through Creative Commons.)

size. File sizes matter to games, as large image files sizes can slow down a game's display.

You'll also notice that for some 2D game projects, vector graphics are easier to manipulate for animation. If you're completely unfamiliar with basic animation, there are many online tutorials that can walk you through the basics of creating a character walk cycle or using built-in motion tweens for specific software. If the words walk cycle or motion tween seem like a bit much, you may want to hold off on animation until you obtain more information on it than this book can provide.

- *Adobe Photoshop*: Adobe Photoshop is the standard industry tool for raster (or bitmap) image production made by Adobe Inc. and available for macOS and Windows. Originally created in 1988, Photoshop is a mature tool that is standard for most image manipulation. It's an appropriate tool for designing certain elements of both digital and analog games. Board backgrounds, especially if they are photorealistic, are likely to be done as raster format in Photoshop. It's also worth noting that some basic manipulations of 3D objects are supported in new versions of Photoshop. This allows 3D objects produced with 3D software to be imported and converted into 2D images. Turning 3D models into images for the back of cards, or backgrounds in digital games, can happen through Photoshop. Also keep in mind that for 3D activities like creating textures, Photoshop is commonly used.

- *Adobe Illustrator*: Adobe Illustrator is a vector graphics editor developed and marketed by Adobe Inc. since 1985. It is available for Windows and macOS. It is the standard industry tool for creating vector-based graphics. For games, Illustrator is useful for doing graphics that need to scale or that have designs that are optimized for vectors. Some artists prefer to start their work by drawing in Illustrator, as opposed to painting in Photoshop. This is particularly useful because rescaling images in Illustrator is trivial and results in no loss of quality. If, for example, a game character was originally designed to be played on a mobile device with only 1024 pixels of width, when the standard increases, rescaling the art doesn't mean redoing it. With Photoshop designed art, it may mean redoing the asset to avoid pixilation.

- *GNU Image Manipulation Program (GIMP)*: The GNU Image Manipulation Program, commonly referred to as GIMP, is a free and open-source image editor. It is offered across macOS, Windows, and Linux. It offers similar tools to Photoshop although with a different layout. For people familiar with Photoshop, there is a version of the tool that mimics the Photoshop environment.

13.3 3D MODELING AND ANIMATION

There are several ways to make a virtual 3D object. They are typically divided into the concept of modeling versus sculpting. Modeling involves adding or splitting 3D geometries into shapes, such as turning a single cube into a house. With modeling, it's typically about building a complex geometry from a simple one, such as turning a rectangle and two circles into a car's basic shape. Modelers might extrude those 2D shapes into 3D shapes to make the rectangle a long cube (i.e., the car body) and the circles into one torus each (i.e., the tires). They might also use subdivisions to slice the simple geometries into more complex shapes, adding windows, a trunk, and a hood.

In the early days of computer game-making, it was common to use polygonal modeling because the resulting models were relatively small (i.e., lightweight or low file size). Nowadays, higher resolution models can be used in games, as the computation capacity of computers and game consoles has increased. Since games render real-time graphics, computing the light, shadows, collisions, and other core elements can slow processing and rendering times. Experience modelers, including those who come from non-game focused backgrounds, will be aware of other non-polygonal modeling techniques like non-uniform rational B-spline (or NURBS for short). If leading a team, it's important to make sure that the kinds of models implemented for the game will work well. Higher resolution 3D models may be good candidates for certain elements of the game, such as cut-scenes, printed posters, attract screen, and more.

The other common way to create 3D models is through sculpting. Sculpting allows the artist to make distinct definitions and give a model much more detail. It's analogous to sculpting clay.

These descriptions are gross simplifications of the process. They also leave out the much more complicated process of animating 3D models. Experienced artists know how to make efficient models that work well within games, blending everything from technical implementation to conventional knowledge about color theory and other art practices. They are provided to help you understand the basic considerations for these technologies. There are many good books on 3D art in games that will introduce these topics in more detail. As you work with 3D models, you will hear terms like rigging, polycount, and more. For the designer, these are technical implementation details that may factor into implementation challenges and influence a design. Clear communication between individual team members should help explain these challenges as they arrive.

Also, keep in mind that creating 3D models isn't limited to digital designs; 3D models can be used to create 3D prints of analog game elements and in supporting art. It's perfectly reasonable to use 3D rendered scenes for analog game elements. Considerations for file size and rendering change, but they do remain. A high-resolution image is important to the print process, so more detailed 3D modeling or sculpting can be useful to analog designers.

- *3ds Max*: Autodesk's 3ds Max (http://www.autodesk.com/products/3ds-max/), commonly known as 3ds or Max, is a professional 3D computer graphics program for making 3D animations, models, games, and images. It is a standard that is used at both independent and professional game studios. It has a long history as a product used for making art for games and offers distinct benefits to game artists. It is not the easiest way to make 3D images, but it offers high quality for its learning curve.

- *Autodesk Maya*: Autodesk Maya (http://www.autodesk.com/products/maya/), commonly referred to simply as Maya, is a 3D computer graphics tool that runs on Windows, macOS, and Linux. It, like 3ds Max, is an industry grade tool. Feelings about whether or not 3ds Studio Max or Maya are better are often based on artist experience.

In many school environments, it's common to teach Maya as it has applications both in games and film.

- *Blender*: Blender (http://www.blender.org/) is a free and open-source 3D computer graphics software toolset used for creating a variety of 3D content including animated films, visual effects, 3D printed models, and video game content. Two of the most distinguishing aspects of Blender are its cost and its support community.

- *ZBrush*: ZBrush is a digital sculpting tool that combines 3D and 2.5D modeling, texturing, and painting. It uses a proprietary "pixol" technology that has historically dominated the space sculpting focused tools. ZBrush is relatively expensive and more appropriate for large scale, high budget projects.

There are a variety of other 3D tools, but these are the ones that tend to dominate the practice. You may find utility in using older pieces of software for prototypes. Bryce, for example, is an extremely easy to use software tool for rendering simple 3D environments (http://www.daz3d.com/bryce-7-pro). Google's Sketchup (http://www.sketchup.com/) is a simple tool for creating basic 3D models, particularly of environments. Their motto for the tool is "3D modeling for everyone."

The landscape for 3D modeling tools changes as does the content. You may find that marketplaces for 3D models, such as the Unity Asset Store (http://www.assetstore.unity3d.com/) and TurboSquid (http://www.turbosquid.com/) have what your project needs. Often, game assets are unique to a game, but the cost of getting professional 3D models is sometimes too expensive for small projects.

13.4 AUDIO TOOLS

It's a common mistake to think about audio after much of a game has been implemented. The pitch, loudness, and timbre of audio in a game can strongly influence the mood of the game. Trying to drop in sounds to a project that are clearly recorded in different environments might create a very disjointed experience, detracting from the impression of a cohesive fiction in a game. Likewise, audio content with the wrong mood, perhaps eerie sounds and music for your comedic game will clearly affect how it is received.

The two key elements of audio for a digital game are the sound effects and music. Some tools are more useful for creating songs than editing individual sound effects. Others offer all the right elements to add echo, shorten, adjust pitch, and other common tasks. In thorough game implementations, audio design is applied not only to in-game elements, but to interface elements from start menus to pause screens. While the topic of good sound design and engineering is beyond the focus of this book, it's useful to at least know some of the tools that will allow effective editing of audio content to meet a project's needs.

- *Audacity*: For independent game makers, the completely free open-source tool, Audacity, has been a staple. It's easy to use and allows both sound editing and recording. Anyone familiar with basic concepts in sound editing should be able to use this relatively long-standing tool for the quality of their game. Audacity works in Windows, macOS, and Linux.

- *FMOD*: FMOD is a proprietary sound effects engine and authoring tool for video games developed by Firelight Technologies. It supports playing and mixing sounds and audio tracks of varied formats. It supports a wide array of platforms.

- *Miles Sound System*: Miles describes itself as featuring "a no-compromise toolset that integrates high-level sound authoring with 2D and 3D digital audio." It's a piece of middleware that is useful for game audio work that involves both programmers and sound designers. So, for example, doing any kind of algorithmic audio or context sensitive audio cues.

There are a host of other tools for audio. Audio, especially for games, is a very specialized field. Common tools like Adobe Audition are certainly worth considering if you are already working with the Adobe Creative Cloud Suite.

13.5 PROTOTYPING TOOLS

The following tools are great for generating a functional prototype that's more than a clickable set of images. These tools come with basic physics engines and some other useful plug-and-play functions that make building something playable very easy. They work well for doing everything from designing levels to designing a final game. Some notable social impact games have been created and released with these or similar tools. Many also have marketplaces or online repositories of templates, allowing new game developers/designers to implement elements of their game very quickly. This is why they are so handy for prototyping.

- *GameMaker Studio*: GameMaker Studio is a cross-platform game engine developed by YoYo Games. GameMaker Studio, commonly just called GameMaker, and its predecessors have been a standard for indie game makers for years. The tool has a large community of users, so many solutions are a search away. GameMaker 8 and earlier produced extraordinarily durable games, and some still function on Windows 10 years later. While most people create 2D games with GameMaker Studio, it is possible for an advanced user to do some 3D work. GameMaker Studio uses a visual programming language (VPL), so understanding computer programming concepts is not essential to using it. Users simply click and drag to build playable experiences.

  GameMaker accommodates the creation games for desktop, web, mobile, and console games. The capacity to make games for certain platforms greatly affects the price of this tool, so make sure your project has the appropriate budget for the planned platform.

- *Gamesalad Creator*: GameSalad Creator, or commonly referred to simply as GameSalad, is an authoring tool used by educators and non-programmers. It uses a kind of visual programming language that allows people who have never programmed to click and drag. The drawback is that unlike GameMaker Studio, it's not really easy to see the code behind these actions. However, GameSalad has a very low barrier to entry. I have given workshops teaching people who have never created a game. With GameSalad, it takes about an hour before they are playing comfortably. That's exceptionally fast for a game-making tool. Gamesalad Creator has both macOS, Windows, and cloud/Internet-based versions. In the years that GameSalad has been available, the macOS version has been the most stable and reliable. The tool is a bit harder to use on Windows.

  GameSalad supports a variety of platforms, so resulting games can be played as native apps for Android and iOS, as well as macOS and HTML5. All games are 2D.

A few other solutions are available for making basic games with little investment in time or code. The Game Creators have offered products for years that allow people to make games very quickly and simple. Their FPS Creator was a very simple click and drag first-person shooter creator that is now open source (http://www.thegamecreators.com/product/fps-cre ator-classic-open-source). Their newer products are more advanced, but similarly simple.

If prototyping a basic interactive narrative or experimenting with some story focused experience, Twine (https://www.Twinery.org) is also a common tool. Twine exports HTML and uses elements from CSS and HTML5. People with web design or development experience should find twine very easy to use. Since it's free, it's also an attractive option for low budget projects.

Other notable tools include Scirra's Construct 3 tool (http://www.con struct.net/) for cloud-based 2D game making, and Stencyl (http://www.stencyl.com/). The focus of all of these is to avoid coding through some click and drag interface. Such environments allow designers to create games without learning how to program. Of course, there are tradeoffs to more advanced tools that do require programming, but for some types of projects, these are all easy, low-cost ways to make a playable experience.

13.6 PRODUCTION DEVELOPMENT TOOLS

It's important to note that it's completely reasonable to use some proto- typing engines to release final implementations. GameSalad, GameMaker, and others listed in the prototyping tool section have award-winning games in their portfolio. The benefit of producing final versions in these game-making tools is that prototypes can reuse code from them. They are also easy to use, allowing inexperienced game developers to implement functional games quickly.

However, the simplicity of these tools comes at a cost. They are not always industrial grade. This means they may not stand the test of time or support the level of polish required of the game. They also may not sup- port some of the specific requirements of an industrial grade team. Items like version control and code optimization aren't available to the degree that the more advanced tools support.

If the goal of your game is to offer a very high level of polish, perhaps on par with popular commercial games, these are the environments that will help you get there.

- *Unity*: Unity is a cross-platform game engine developed by Unity Technologies. It supports 27 distinct platforms, making it an uncommonly versatile tool for making 3D and 2D games. Games made in unity will have a polish that is hard to accomplish with lesser tools. They will also typically require much more technical savvy than the simpler prototyping tools listed previously. When a making a game in Unity, there is typically some programming involved. A few tools, like Fungus (a free Unity plug-in) minimize the need to know how to program, but when it comes time to release the game, it will be useful to edit some code. While some people choose to prototype in Unity, it's often easier to work elsewhere (especially if you are not a developer). Unity offers a free version for personal use, but limits this by project budget and resources.

- *Unreal Engine*: The Unreal Engine is a game engine developed by Epic Games. Its foundations are in the 1998 first-person shooter game, *Unreal*, so it is not a surprise that many people build games with FPS characteristics in the environment. The quality of graphics, potential complexity of play, and the portability of its code make it a good candidate for experienced developers.

There are other tools that are available to create very high-quality experiences for final game production. Amazon's Lumberyard (https://aws. amazon.com/lumberyard/), although not as widely used as hoped, offers high-quality interactions that mimic elements of AAA commercial releases. Lumberyard is free to use.

It's important to remember that if the goal of your project is to develop game-making skills, it's useful to practice with industry standard tools. But not every project needs this level of polish to meet its goals.

13.7 ANALOG GAME IMPLEMENTATION

Implementing a high-quality analog game is often more involved than printing at home or using the local print shop. Sometimes, you need a full package, box, and even help with distribution. There are several services that specialize in producing initial prototypes or that handle the print on demand service of producing your non-digital game for buyers. These services can greatly improve the polish of your final project. They aren't always the cheapest solution, but the durability and professional presentation of your game are often greatly improved. Some of these services even offer ready-made items like player tokens.

It's important to remember that with some of these services, the template-based implementation of a game will affect the novelty of the design. Creating custom packaging shapes or distinct patterns of cards is sometimes not an option. It's also not surprising to find out that the template your game was designed against has been discontinued by the company that offered it. But compared with the way board games were produced, even as prototypes, 30 years ago, this is a big leap forward in accessibility, time, and production quality.

- *The Game Crafter*: The Game Crafter (http://www.thegamecrafter.com/) is a one-stop shop for buying, selling, and creating an analog game. It's an easy to use resource that provides many of the typical elements of a game and includes consulting services to help with some of the more custom elements of your game's design. Since you can both buy and sell games from the site, it helps to handle distribution of a game you've designed.

- *Ad Magic Print and Play*: Print and Play (http://www.printplaygames.com/) is a similar service for creating non-digital prototypes. The site provides ways to buy and sell games and tends to focus on the print-to-play game space. There are resources to find artists and other support as well.

Other services offer varying degrees of support. At the time of the printing of this book, Print Ninja (http://www.printninja.com) offers board game printing services in addition to self-publishing services for a variety of books. Such a service would be useful to a game involving a graphic novel, games master guide, or other books that are more substantive than the typical instruction set.

Using the aforementioned tools is not the only way to implement a quality game. Like much of the themes in this book, there is always more than one way to do a great job. The task of a designer, any designer, is to understand constraints and work toward goals within them. A game project isn't always just about a game. Sometimes, it's about exploring and learning a new tool. Sometimes, it's about experimentation, and other times, it's about making sure the project gets done on time and under budget. The more experience you develop in making these decisions, deriving appropriate production pipelines, and reading the needs of a project, the simpler the task of selecting the right implementation strategy will become.

Regardless of the chosen implementation strategy, it's important to remain true to the design. Recall, as you learned in reading this book, the elements of playful experiences, the way playful experiences engage players, and how to optimize those experiences. The implementation is the realization of your final play. It's a way to turn ideas into action. Playful actions that help you do the thing you aimed to do. This is the goal of doing things with games.

Index

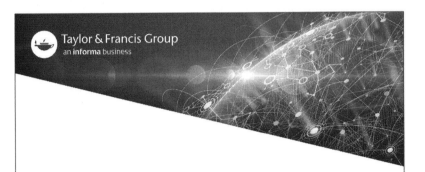

Printed and bound by CPI Group (UK) Ltd, Croydon, CR0 4YY

25/10/2024

01779548-0001